BUSINESS ETHICS

BUSINESS ETHICS

David Stewart
Department of Philosophy
Ohio University

Boston, Massachusetts   Burr Ridge, Illinois
Dubuque, Iowa   Madison, Wisconsin   New York, New York
San Francisco, California   St. Louis, Missouri

McGraw-Hill

A Division of The **McGraw·Hill** Companies

This book was set in Sabon by The Clarinda Company.
The editors were Bill McLane and Eleanor Castellano;
the production supervisor was Louise Karam.
The cover was designed by Top Desk Publisher's Group;
the cover illustration was done by David Flaherty.

BUSINESS ETHICS

3 4 5 6 7 8 9   BKM BKM   9 0 9 8 7 6 5 4 3 2 1 0

ISBN 0-07-061544-6

Library of Congress Cataloging-in-Publication Data

Stewart, David (date).
    Business ethics / David Stewart.
      p.   cm.
    Includes index.
    ISBN 0-07-061544-6
    1. Business ethics.   2. Business ethics—Case studies.   I. Title.
HF5387.S727   1996
174'.4—dc20 ·   95-40756

About the Author

DAVID STEWART has taught philosophy at Ohio University since 1970. He received his Ph.D. from Rice University (Houston, Texas) and is the author or editor of nine books. Other works in ethics are *Exploring Ethics* (co-author; Macmillan, 1986), and *Medical Ethics: A Reader* (co-author; Prentice Hall, 1992). At Ohio University he received the University Professor award for teaching and is a Fellow of the Charles J. Ping Institute for the Teaching of the Humanities. Among his other textbooks are an introductory text entitled *Fundamentals of Philosophy* now entering its fourth edition (co-author; Prentice Hall) and *Exploring the Philosophy of Religion* (Prentice Hall), now in its third edition.

This one is for Audrey.

Contents

Preface

I had been teaching business ethics for several years when a student came up to me after class and asked, "Why don't we ever talk about cases of ethical business behavior?" The question surprised me. Not only did I realize that the text I was using featured only bad examples of corporate conduct, I had to admit to myself that I could not ever remember bringing into the class discussion a case of ethical business behavior. I can't recall exactly what I said to the student—it was something to the effect that we can learn best from mistakes, that the literature was dominated by examples of ignoble business behavior, and, besides, I could find some good examples of ethical business behavior if I wanted to.

The latter task proved more difficult than I had imagined. Most of the business texts contained the usual litany of corporate misconduct; few even mentioned companies committed to socially responsible behavior that also had solid bottom lines. My best source for examples of ethical corporate behavior came from books on management, especially those by such business gurus as Tom Peters and Lester Thurow. These discussions did not focus primarily on the philosophical underpinning for ethical behavior but rather on the long-term business success accruing to companies with a strong corporate culture that valued the product they made, treated their employees with respect, and dealt with their customers in an ethically enlightened way. These are some of the reasons for my writing this book.

I agree with Kant that one cannot build an ethical view from examples alone. As Plato pointed out centuries ago, one cannot recognize a definition (or an example) as an instance of the quality being sought unless one first has an understanding of that quality. But as Aristotle also knew—and here is where the recurrence of an emphasis on virtue ethics is important—moral exemplars are important in the process of moral development. Of course, in any discussion of business ethics, philosophy is vital. What does it mean to treat employees with respect? How can we understand the development of a corporate culture with ethical foundations? What are the limits of cost-benefits analysis, and when do individual rights take precedence? Alienation, abstraction, bad faith, justice and fairness—all are philosophical concepts that influence how we perceive business behavior.

For the above reasons, chapters one through four are philosophical in nature. However, the selections from philosophical texts included here are brief, not only because of space restrictions but also because each user of this book must decide which philosophers provide the most useful pedagogical platform. I usually supplement a business ethics text with either Mill's *Utilitarianism* or Kant's *Foundations,* both of which are available in inexpensive paperback editions and give students good exposure to sustained philosophical discussion.

This book is not filled only with examples of ethical corporate conduct because we can sometimes learn from the mistakes of others. The primary emphasis, however, is on good examples of business behavior that benefit the companies that observe good ethical practices even in poor economic times. Woven throughout the book are brief cases ("A Case in Point . . ."), moreover, for those who desire longer cases, each chapter ends with a case study of greater complexity. There is a reason for this approach: if we only provide students with a discussion of unethical business practices, we reinforce the fallacious notion, that business ethics is an oxymoron and that good business behavior is the exception rather than the rule.

There are many persons to be thanked for their assistance with this project: my colleagues in the philosophy department for their help and support; my students whose research and interests generated many of the examples included here; my colleagues at Ohio University such as Stephen Fuller, Frances Fuller, and Bill Day, former dean of the College of Business Administration, and Jim Bruning, the provost to whom I reported primarily when writing this book for allowing me the time to do it. I would also like to thank McGraw-Hill's philosophy editors: Cynthia Ward, who was the book's acquiring editor; Judy Cornwell, who also worked on the project; and Eleanor Castellano, who saw the project to completion. I also want to thank my wife Audrey who not only gave encouragement in many ways but also brought her librarianship skills to bear on much of the necessary research for the project's success. Thanks also to David Bruce for his careful proofreading and indexing skills.

Finally, thanks also to those business leaders who contributed statements on business ethics to this text. However, these statements should not necessarily be construed as endorsements of the views expressed in this book.

It is also important that I acknowledge the help of the many reviewers who provided valuable insights during various stages of the book's preparation. They include Richard Bond, Ramapo College of New Jersey; Jeanne

Calderon, NYU Stern School of Business; David Flagel, University of New Brunswick; Paul Gallagher, Assumption College; Hal McMullen, Lord Fairfax Community College; Marshall Osman, University of Laverne; Dinah Payne, University of New Orleans; James Smith, East Carolina University; John Stevenson, Columbia College; and Richard Toenjes, East Carolina University.

David Stewart

List of Abbreviations
Used in Notes

BW	*Business Week*
CD	*The Columbus Dispatch*
FORB	*Forbes*
FORT	*Fortune*
HBR	*Harvard Business Review*
JAMA	*Journal of the American Medical Association*
NEWS	*Newsweek*
NYT	*The New York Times*
TIME	*Time Magazine*
USA	*USA Today*
WSJ	*The Wall Street Journal*

BUSINESS ETHICS

PART ONE

ETHICS AND BUSINESS

"Of course, honesty is one of the better policies."

Why Business Needs Ethics

Ralph Schey
Chairman of the Board
Scott Fetzer Company

"As nations race toward a global marketplace, the need for commonly accepted ethical standards has taken on new dimensions of even greater importance. Economic development—and the political forces trying to accelerate it—requires that ethical standards substitute for the use of force. Since trade, technology, and finance are the primary tools of business, there is a crushing need to make business ethics an integral part of business training."

Before considering the need for ethics in business, let's look at what you can expect from an ethics course. Whenever you sign up for a course, you probably have a pretty good idea of what to expect: An algebra course will teach you algebra, a history course will teach you history, a management course will teach you principles of management. But will an ethics course, a *business* ethics course, teach you to be ethical?

There are some skills that one can learn by reading a book or by taking lessons. Others can only be acquired through a developmental phase during which a person gains the right kinds of habits. The first kind of proficiency is what the ancient Greek philosopher Aristotle calls *intellectual* virtues and includes such things as learning how to build a house or play a musical instrument. The second kind of proficiency, that which requires an extensive developmental phase, is what Aristotle calls the *moral* virtues; learning to be brave in the face of danger or learning how to control one's temper are examples. Aristotle's point is that you cannot learn to be moral except by acquiring a moral disposition and developing moral habits. Developing a moral disposition is not something one does overnight or by reading a book or taking a class. In short, the ethical orientation that you bring to this book is what you have developed over your lifetime, and reading a book on ethics will not quickly change it. However, studying ethics can be part of your moral development, and a course in business ethics can assist you in thinking about how to be moral in the workplace and to analyze cases in business ethics when neither your reputation nor your job is at stake.

ETHICS AND CHOICE

People encounter ethical problems when they are genuinely confused about which moral principle to follow: Should I lie to save a life? Does the mother's right to control her own body take precedence over the rights of the unborn fetus? Is capital punishment an act of murder? Business examples are numerous: Which is better, retrench the work force so that the company can recover and perhaps rehire these people later, or keep full employment with possible dire consequences for the company, including bankruptcy? Should a business allow itself to be the object of a hostile takeover, which could result in the loss of many jobs of those currently employed? Or should it resist the takeover by paying "greenmail" (buying the stock of a corporate raider at higher than market price so the raider will go away)? Or should the company load itself up with debt to decrease its attractiveness to a raider, even though this may reduce the company's profits? How do we assess the raider's promises to make the business more efficient by stripping away waste and strengthening the company's competitiveness, thereby increasing the real value of the company to the stockholders? How would you answer these questions if you were an employee of the company? But what if you were a manager? A stockholder? A member of the community where the business is located? If we cannot clearly see all the ethical ramifications of our actions, we are often unable to isolate all the morally relevant aspects of the situation and choices become difficult.

There are many situations in business where individuals are tempted to do something that violates their ethical standards. So many issues, whether in business or private life, concern the perpetual problems: lying, cheating, stealing. The unethical conduct of some businesspeople, chronicled in the daily newspapers, concerns not uncertainty over ethical choices but fundamental errors in human conduct. As we will discuss in Chapter 8, a continuing puzzle is why otherwise moral persons act immorally in business matters.

Whether you enter the world of business or not, life will present you with ethical dilemmas, and this book will help you think through some of them before they are encountered in a real-life situation where the consequences will be substantial and sometimes irreversible. In this book we will look at the writings of moral philosophers, examine actual cases of both ethical and unethical behavior in the business world, and set up hypothetical cases and become involved in actual decision making. To make effective decisions, you need to be able to identify and articulate the ethical issues at stake and reason your way through the various alternatives presented. In some instances we will be able to identify clearly the best course of action—that is, the one that we as rational individuals are prepared to defend with argument and analysis. In other cases we will not be so successful, for real-world choices are often ambiguous and not easily decided.

WHY ETHICS IS IMPORTANT

Before turning to the question of why business needs ethics, let's look at the more sweeping question of why a framework of ethics is important for society in general.

Imagine a situation where there is no moral structure for one's actions, no legal system, no power greater than the individual's to adjudicate conflict, and where all people are free to pursue their own interests. This is the state of nature that the seventeenth-century English philosopher Thomas Hobbes describes with great clarity. Although the prospect of pursuing our own self-interest, unhampered by bureaucrats, environmental protection laws, taxation policies, restraint of trade legislation, and other limitations on our conduct, might at first seem attractive, Hobbes shows why it is not. In such a state everyone would be at war with everyone else, and all would be constantly at risk of losing property and life. The standards of behavior of civil society would be absent, and violence would be the order of the day. The words *justice* and *injustice* would have no meaning. Hobbes calls this

---

HOBBES ON THE STATE OF NATURE

Nature hath made men so equal, in the faculties of the body and mind; as that, though there be found one man sometimes manifestly stronger in body or of quicker mind than another, yet when all is reckoned together, the difference between man and man is not so considerable, as that one man can thereupon claim to himself any benefit, to which another may not pretend as well as he. For as to the strength of body, the weakest has strength enough to kill the strongest, either by secret machination, or by confederacy with others that are in the same danger with himself. . . .

Whereby it is manifest that during the time men live without a common power to keep them all in awe, they are in that condition which is called war; and such a war as is of every man against every man. . . . In such a condition there is no place for industry, because the fruit thereof is uncertain: and consequently no culture of the earth; no navigation, nor use of the commodities that may be imported by sea; no commodious building; no instruments of moving and removing, such things as require much force; no knowledge of the face of the earth; no account of time; no arts; no letters; no society; and which is worst of all, continual fear and danger of violent death; and the life of man, solitary, poor, nasty, brutish, and short. . . .

To this war of every man against every man, this also is consequent: that *nothing can be unjust.* The notions of right and wrong, justice and injustice, have there no place. Where there is no common power, there is no law; where no law, no injustice. Force and fraud are in war the two cardinal virtues. . . . It is consequent also to the same condition, that there be no propriety, no dominion, no *mine* and *thine* distinct; but only that to be every man's that he can get; and for so long as he can keep it.

Source: Thomas Hobbes, *Leviathan,* Chap. 13.

Bill Watterson's Hobbes shows Calvin just how inconsistent it is to want to act on one's own self-interest while expecting others not to do the same.

Calvin and Hobbes © 1989 Watterson. Reprinted with permission of Universal Press Syndicate. All rights reserved.

condition of war the "state of nature,"[1] and in such a state each person would become the enemy of the other. Unrestrained self-interest might seem attractive, but in the state of hostility that would result, only the interests of the strongest would prevail. In the state of nature human existence would be miserable or, to use Hobbes's famous words, life would be "solitary, poor, nasty, brutish, and short." All rational persons, Hobbes thinks, would want to find a way out of the brutish hostilities of the state of nature.

From the State of Nature to Civil Society

Getting ourselves out of the state of nature, Hobbes argues, is simply a matter of good sense and reason. We will be better off when pursuing our own self-interests if we accept some constraints on our actions in return for restraints being accepted by others. We will be freer, even though we have accepted constraints, because we are no longer in danger from everybody else. Only in an organized and civil society can the forces of business and industry function well. We see this point illustrated all too clearly in countries where there is civil disorder as a result of war or governmental upheaval. Hobbes, however, thinks that most people are not sufficiently enlightened to seek their own best interests, so he advocates the development of a strong sovereign power to force people to follow the laws of nature. Though Hobbes is an important figure in the history of political theory, he is definitely not a defender of democracy.

Being in a civil society means that we accept the responsibility of obeying the law, abide by our private agreements, and submit disputes to impartial judges. How we arrive at such ethical principles, Hobbes argues, is through the use of natural reason (natural here as opposed to supernatural revelation). "The passions that incline men to peace," Hobbes says, "are fear of death, desire of such things as are necessary to commodious living, and a hope by their industry to obtain them. And reason suggesteth convenient articles of peace, upon which men may be drawn to agreement."[2] The following are some of the natural laws drawn from Hobbes's discussion that are most applicable to the practices of business:

- We should claim as much liberty as we are willing to grant to others.

- We should keep promises and perform contracts to which we have agreed.
- We should acknowledge the equality of all.
- We should not demand of others things we are unwilling to do ourselves.
- Judges should be impartial.
- Things that cannot be divided should be shared in common.
- People who disagree should submit their dispute to arbitrators.
- We should not do to others what we don't want them to do to us.

This is an interesting list not only because it seems to reflect the moral precepts that we have learned from many other sources but also because its doctrine of self-restraint starts from the premise that self-interest is the motivating force behind human behavior. But Hobbes tests the limits of self-interest and shows that unrestrained self-interest is not in one's interest at all. We might call Hobbes's view "enlightened" self-interest.[3]

Hobbes's analysis remains important because it argues that social cooperation is necessary for any truly human society. Businesses, no less than individuals, need such standards of cooperative conduct. Unless a majority in a society accepts a standard of moral conduct—tells the truth, doesn't steal, keeps promises, does not harm others—it would be hard to see how any organization could function at all, to say nothing of functioning well. A business needs employees who are honest and loyal. How else could a company trust its employees with proprietary information, money, access to important planning documents, and so on? We can see that at this level ethics, in the sense of rules for getting along together, is inescapable. Without ethics, neither businesses nor individuals could function, and we would be struggling in Hobbes's state of nature.

The Limits of Self-Interest

A word of caution about self-interest. There are cases where several individuals see their self-interest in conflicting terms. The egoism of individuals, no matter how enlightened in their self-interest, prevents resolution of moral conflict unless a standard of evaluating decisions other than self-interest is in place. The contemporary philosopher Kurt Baier argues this point convincingly in his book *The Moral Point of View*. Noting that morality is needed precisely because there are cases when conflicts of self-interest arise, Baier says, "If the point of view of

---

A Case in Point . . .

The government bond market was rocked in 1991 by revelations that Salomon Brothers, a giant securities firm, had illegally dominated auctions of government securities. The sale of government bonds is a loosely regulated market that relies on a law that limits any participant in the market to no more than 35 percent of the total bonds being sold. By exceeding this limit, Salomon Brothers was able to manipulate the price of bonds to its benefit and its customers' detriment. One effect of this kind of manipulation of the market would be higher costs for home mortgages and business loans, which are tied to changes in government interest rates.

One month after the scandal broke, profits at the investment house had fallen 20 percent. The fallout from the scandal affected more than just Salomon Brothers. It generally undercut the public's confidence in government bond markets and caused other Wall Street firms to scrutinize their operations with care to root out any hint of unethical or unlawful behavior. Salomon's CEO resigned along with three other senior executive officers.

Writing under the headline "On Wall St., New Stress on Morality," *New York Times* writer Richard D. Hylton reported, "The Salomon Brothers scandal has sent tremors along Wall Street, as firms rush to clean house and distance themselves from employees who may have violated securities laws." The effect on Salomon Brothers was not only a loss of profits but also a precipitous drop in its stock price and a bevy of civil lawsuits, the costs of which *Business Week* estimated could exceed $1 billion.

Sources: CD, Sept. 9, 1991; NYT, Sept. 11, 1991; BW, Sept. 16, 1991.

---

morality were that of self-interest, then there could *never* be moral solutions of conflicts of interest." He goes on to point out that "when there are conflicts of interest, we always look for a 'higher' point of view, one from which such conflicts can be settled." This point is not only a practical one, it is a logical conclusion as well.

> Consistent egoism makes everyone's private interest the "highest court of appeal." But by "the moral point of view" we *mean* a point of view which furnishes a court of arbitration for conflicts of interest. Hence it cannot (logically) be identical with the point of view of the interest of any particular person or group of persons.[4]

Even if we take Hobbes's approach and begin our consideration of ethics and society with the view that self-interest is the most basic fact about human behavior, his call for what we might term rational or enlightened self-interest is not an adequate basis for ethical decision making. Individuals, or businesses, that base their decisions on self-interest alone, no matter how enlightened, could not be said to be acting ethically.

THE ROLE OF THEORY IN ETHICS

Casuistry and Its Problems

Another alternative to self-interest is to force moral behavior through comprehensive sets of rules that guide not only individual conduct but also provide for the general welfare. Called "casuistry," this approach to ethical decision making leaves much to be desired. First, the rule-governed approach to behavior leaves open the question of what to do when there is no specific rule to apply to a given situation. The obvious answer is to develop more rules; but as these rules prove to be inadequate, the need will appear for still more rules. A casuistic approach to ethics, therefore, will result in a constantly expanding set of increasingly detailed rules.

A second problem with casuistry is that we need another set of rules to help us decide what to do when our rules conflict with each other. There are rules for applying the rules, rules that tell us which rules to use in which situation, and still more rules for telling us when to apply the rules.

A third difficulty is that obeying the rules leads to the sense of having acted ethically, whereas actually one might have done only what is minimally required and not fulfilled the spirit of the rules at all. Closely related to this problem is a fourth difficulty: rule-bound forms of conduct tempt us to look for loopholes, ways of satisfying the technical

---

PROBLEMS WITH CASUISTRY

1 Requires continual growth of rules to cover new situations.
2 Requires rules for applying rules.
3 Creates false sense of morality through meeting minimal requirements.
4 Encourages the search for loopholes.

demands of the rules while still doing things that the rules were intended to prevent. This distinction is important in discussing the difference between doing what is merely legal and doing what is moral. When accused of misconduct, business leaders will frequently claim that they broke no laws, or that the government did not prohibit their behavior, or that the standards in use at the time were fully met. Although such statements are true, the question of the moral acceptability of such actions still remains.

The Advantages of Ethical Theory

The disadvantages of casuistry have led philosophers away from sets of rules for guiding conduct and toward moral theory. Ethical theory searches for principles for guidance, general understandings that help us make moral decisions in a variety of circumstances and assist us in discovering the morally relevant aspects of our decisions. Whereas the casuistic approach to ethics tries to develop rules for each specific situation, the philosophical approach looks for a moral framework within which to assess our actions and for general principles to apply to a variety of individual cases. In many respects this approach is similar to the development of theories of business management. Such theories allow managers to search for general principles by which to run their businesses. Individual case studies may help illuminate these principles, but the goal of business theory is to discover those general approaches that will help managers deal with a wide range of specific cases. For example, a rule such as "treat your customers right if you want your business to succeed" does not give specific guidance in each individual case, but it does provide a general principle that a skillful manager can appeal to in making individual decisions.

As we look in more detail at several specific moral theories, we will see that each contributes important insights to our ethical thinking but that none of them alone seems adequate to address all ethical issues with which we are faced. It is for this reason that we will be looking at several moral theories that can help us think through important issues in business ethics. It will also be apparent that it is a *misuse* of ethical theory to use a "cookbook" approach in which, when faced with a moral decision, one looks up the theory, finds the recipe for action, applies it, and thereby makes a moral decision. Theories in other disciplines do not function like this, and neither do moral theories.

The great advantages of moral theories, such as Kant's ethic of duty, Mill's utilitarianism, and Aristotle's virtue ethics (each discussed in subsequent chapters) are that they help us penetrate the complexities of a real-world situation and isolate the morally relevant aspects of actions. Because each of the moral theories we will discuss helps us understand different aspects of moral choices, and none of them completely captures within its theoretical structure all the relevant moral features of an action, the very existence of multiple moral theories shows the limitations of any single point of view. Mill's utilitarianism, for example, emphasizes the greatest good for the greatest number of persons, thereby increasing the total sum of happiness. This is certainly an admirable goal, but utilitarianism runs the risk of sacrificing the interests of the minority for the greater good of the majority. Utilitarians have attempted to bolster the theory in such a way as to protect the rights of individuals and minority groups,[5] but such protection seems to be better afforded by theories, such as Kant's theory of duty, that emphasize respect for the individual and the importance of fairness as moral criteria.

Multiple ethical theories provide a range of insights for dealing with moral choices, and "having used a particular ethical theory to initiate ethical analysis of a specific moral problem, we can legitimately combine insights from several theories in attempting to identify all the morally relevant features of that problem. When those features are identified, some of them are likely to conflict with each other. We must then make a judgment call in which some morally relevant features of this specific moral problem are deemed to take precedence over other morally relevant features."[6] We are faced with not so much a contradiction among ethical theories as an interplay of theories, each of which partially guides our moral analysis but none of which totally provides a comprehensive view.

We will discuss other contributions of these three ethical theories, but here are two important ones that hold true for all moral theories: they give us a vocabulary for discussing ethical choices, and they help us identify the morally relevant aspects of our actions.

A Vocabulary for Discussing Ethical Choices   No human activity can proceed very well without a shared vocabulary among its participants. This is true in ethics no less than in science, the arts, the building trades, finance, architecture, medicine, law, and so forth. Sometimes such a shared vocabulary takes on the characteristics of jargon, thus impeding discussion for all those unfamiliar with that particular form of discourse. Whatever its disadvantages, however, a shared vocabulary does two things. First, it allows discussion of important issues by ensuring that all participants in the discussion mean the same thing when they use a term or refer to a concept. Second, and this is closely allied to the first, such discussion can only proceed after carefully defining the terms. For this reason moral philosophers spend much effort analyzing and defining terms that are important in the discussion of ethics: rights, responsibility, justice, autonomy, honesty, obligation. Sometimes the effort expended in defining terminology aids the discussion of the issues themselves. For example, given an understanding of the meaning of autonomy, what contributes to it, and its status as an important ethical principle, we are in a better position to judge the moral dimensions of any action that limits autonomy.

Identification of Morally Relevant Features of an Action   Part of the value of theory in any discipline is that it helps us identify and isolate factors relevant to the theory. Newtonian mechanics, for example, tells us that to explain the motion of a body we must consider such factors as force, mass, and acceleration and ignore such irrelevant considerations as the body's color or shape. Similarly, moral theory highlights the morally significant aspects of a specific issue. When we look at a particular situation, a plant closing, say, if we want to raise moral issues we will have to do more than look at the effect of the closing on the balance sheet. We might want to consider such factors as the commitments made by management to the community when the company built the plant.

In a case involving a decision by General Motors to close a manufacturing plant in Flint, Michigan, a judge ruled that the corporation, in return for tax abatements, had promised to provide jobs for an extended period and that closing the plant would violate that promise. Given the fact that the plant was profitable (though not as profitable as others), the judge found no compelling reason why the corporation should not keep its promise.[7] Though the decision was later overturned on appeal, the court's original decision shows that plant closing is a particularly difficult issue in business ethics because the action involves so many conflicting interests. In the case in question, the dispute turned on the nature of the agreements management made with the community. However, if the company does not consistently return a profit, it cannot remain in business for long and therefore will be unable to fulfill its obligations to any of those to whom it has made commitments. How to balance these competing obligations—to stockholders, workers, community, bondholders—is not easy.

This, then, brings us to the question of what is the moral good. What makes an action good or bad? How are we to judge the moral worth of an action or a goal? These are philosophical questions, and to answer them demands that other questions likewise be considered: How can we justify a moral point of view? Is the intention or the consequences of an action the basis for assigning moral worth? How are we to balance the individual's good with the overall social good? And what do we mean by "good" in the first place?

This book is about business ethics, not about philosophy, but one cannot really deal with issues in applied ethics without placing the questions in a philosophical context. Accordingly, the first part of this book deals in some detail with three principal views on ethics. The first is the view that the moral worth of an action is determined by its consequences, and the goal of action should be to bring about the greatest good for the greatest number of persons. Known as *utilitarianism,* this way of thinking about ethics has had a profound effect on Western societies and finds its place in business thinking in the form of cost-benefits analysis. The second view places the primary emphasis on the intention and motives of the individual and centers its concerns on individual rights and duties and is referred throughout this book as the *ethics of duty.* The third approach is seen by many contemporary philosophers as incorporating the insights of the first two moral views and is referred to as *virtue theory.* This approach to ethics focuses on the development of the moral individual and a common cultural tradition that reinforces shared moral values. In business applications something like virtue ethics is frequently embodied in what has come to be known as the corporate culture. This way of thinking about proper corporate behavior is reinforced by stories that underscore the moral values to which the company's culture is dedicated.

We will deal with each of these moral points of view later in the book, but notice that among those listed we did not include the view that says values are relative to the individual or group that agrees to the values, or even the view espoused by Hobbes, enlightened self-interest. The relativist view will be examined in some detail in the last chapter, for we confront its claims squarely when dealing with international business. Hobbes is another matter, however, for the view he presents is essentially that of a jungle in which each is the enemy of all and from which a society can emerge only through mutual cooperation and restraint. How much restraint and how much unbridled competition should be allowed continue to be points of dispute among both philosophers and social theorists.

THE IMPORTANCE OF ETHICS FOR BUSINESS

Throughout this book you will see the case being made that good ethics is good business. This flies in the face of the popular stereotype of big businesses. Even jokes reflect such attitudes: "I hear you are taking a course in business ethics; must have the smallest textbook in the world." Others think the term is an oxymoron, a contradiction in terms, like "luxury budget hotel" or "gourmet diet meals." Part of the problem is in the presentation of business leaders by the entertainment media. When is the last time you can recall that either a film or television program presented a business leader as an example of virtue, a concerned and active citizen, family oriented, an important member of charitable boards, and a generous contributor to worthy causes? The more typical presentation is the business leader as a scheming, untrustworthy, and dishonest manipulator of others. J. R. Ewing is Hollywood's archetypal mover and shaker. We should not be too hard on the entertainment industry, though; after all, its business is fantasy, not reality, and it does not treat other professions much better. Members of the clergy are portrayed as bumbling wimps, librarians as bookish nerds, accountants as timid bean counters, and professors as absent-minded savants. The stereotype of businesspeople presented in the entertainment media may have a gradual effect on attitudes, however. The PBS documentary "Hollywood's Favorite Heavy" claims that "by the age of 18, the average kid has seen businessmen on prime-time TV attempt over 10,000 murders." Perhaps this figure is too high, but even if we halve the figure and reduce it by half again, it is still a large number.

Problems occur when people who take jobs in business cannot distinguish fantasy from reality and think they should act like J. R. Ewing and lie, cheat, even steal to get ahead. As Robert Solomon and Kristine Hanson point out in their book *It's Good Business,* unethical behavior is a sure way to end a business career.

> To err is human, perhaps, but to be caught lying, cheating, stealing, or reneging on contracts is not easily forgotten or forgiven in the business world. And for good reason: Such actions undermine the ethical foundation

on which the business world thrives. Almost everyone can have compassion for someone caught in an ethical dilemma. No one can excuse immorality.[8]

Good ethics is also good business because it allows businesses to avoid outside restrictions. If business is not self-regulated, it will be regulated by others. Unethical conduct brings about those things that businesses least desire: government regulations and restrictions, hostile employee relations resulting in an unproductive work force, and consumer rejection of its products and services. The point is that we cannot have two sets of moral standards, one for businesses and another for the rest of the world. We see increasing pressure from society—expressed through legislation and in the courts—to hold businesses accountable to the same standards of conduct imposed on individuals.[9]

Notice throughout the discussion and in the analysis of Thomas Hobbes's natural laws the repeated use of the term "should." *Should, must, ought:* this is the language of ethics. Philosophers describe this as the *prescriptive* use of language. When we use such terms we are not describing how people behave but are making claims about how they should behave. Ethics, then, is prescriptive, not descriptive. Moral philosophers have developed theories that allow us to give account of such questions as how we can justify moral values, how to determine what our duties and obligations are, and how to evaluate moral pronouncements. A good deal of philosophical thinking over the years about ethics involves not the analysis of specific moral issues but the questioning of the nature of ethical judgments and moral decisions themselves.

CHALLENGES TO BUSINESS ETHICS

One of the challenges to business ethics comes from philosophers who think that ethics cannot be taught. They base their claim on a point of view advanced in the early twentieth century by a group of philosophers who argued that philosophy should be based solely on the analysis of statements of fact. If a statement could not be verified—that is, proved either true or false by methods of scientific analysis—these philosophers rejected it on the grounds that it was not meaningful. Statements that did not pass muster under the scientific criteria could be used to evoke strong emotions, persuade others to follow one's example, or express one's own private point of view; but without the rigors of empirical proof, no statement was to be accorded worth.

Known as "positivism," and sometimes referred as *logical* positivism because it uses logical techniques of formal analysis, this point of view initially attracted a great deal of support because it seemed to be scientific. But further reflection showed that this was not the case.

For one thing, such a limiting attitude toward what counts as worthy eliminates most scientific theories and laws because they cannot stand up to the tests of empirical proof demanded by positivism. Why? Because scientific theories and laws themselves determine what counts as empirical proof and are generally viewed as organizing principles for the analysis of empirical data and not verifiable by the empirical means. Worse for positivism, however, is that it could not even prove the truth of its own assumptions. When a positivist argues that "only statements that can be empirically tested are meaningful," the positivist is making a statement that itself cannot be empirically tested. These and similar difficulties with the positivist approach have pretty much caused it to be abandoned; a few philosophers may be still trying to argue for the theory, but for the most part—to quote the contemporary philosopher John Passmore—"Logical positivism . . . is dead, or as dead as a philosophical movement ever becomes."[10]

Though positivism may be dead as a philosophical theory, it is still alive and well in some business approaches. One of the difficulties in using case studies—and more will be said about case study later—is that they can be used to bolster the view that more and more facts, additional data, and the piling up of information will somehow lead the analyst to the best course of action. There is an approach to business ethics that devotes most of its concerns to the gathering of empirical data and to analyzing the views of people in business regarding their business practices. Even some textbooks on business ethics approach the topic in this way. There is certainly nothing wrong with the gathering of facts, for data collection and analysis of facts can often lead to improved business decisions. But this approach does not capture the important issues raised by values and ethics and really reflects a limited, positivistic view of ethics. Ethics deals with values, and values are not the same as empirical facts.

This brings us back to the distinction made earlier between statements that merely describe and statements that prescribe. Of course, many statements are mixtures of both modes of discourse, but even in such mixed discourse we can separate out the descriptive from the prescriptive elements. To test this claim, examine the following statements and indicate which ones are descriptive, which are prescriptive, and which are mixed.

  1 The sales goals for this year are higher than last year's.

  2 The management principles of this company are similar to those of other companies in our industry.

  3 The management principles of this company are better than those of other companies in our industry.

  4 It is wrong to steal proprietary information from others.

  5 Many people in business believe that stealing proprietary information is wrong.

  6 Although many business leaders treat employees as so many cogs in a machine, I believe such an attitude is wrong and will result in decreased productivity.

  7 Even though bribery is an expected practice in many developing countries, such practices stifle creativity and make industries uncompetitive in a global market.

  8 The prevalent presentation of business executives by the entertainment industry is that of greedy, scheming, and unscrupulous individuals.

  9 Good ethics is good business.

  10 One ought to encourage ethical business practices.

Note that all are descriptive except for statements 3, 4, and 10 (which are prescriptive) and 6 (which is mixed). Even statement number 9 is descriptive, because it is making a claim that is, at bottom, empirical. It uses the value term "good," but it is essentially making a claim about the link between moral practices and business results. It is saying, in effect, that a company practicing good ethics, as measured by an appropriate standard of conduct, will also experience good business results, as measured by the appropriate index, such as increased profits, repeat sales, good cash flow, or whatever standard expresses the company's strategic goals.

Challenges from the Right

Another challenge to business ethics comes from those who argue that the only duty of business is to make a profit. In a completely free marketplace, where people are allowed to seek their own self-interest, the forces of competition will produce the quantity and variety of material goods essential to civil society. This was basically the point of view of the eighteenth-century philosopher and economist Adam Smith (1723–1790). In one of the most famous quotations from his book *An Inquiry into the Nature and Causes of the Wealth of Nations,* Smith claims that "it is not from the benevolence of the butcher, the brewer or the baker that we expect our dinner, but from their regard for their own self-interest." In a free market the forces of supply and demand act as a sort of "invisible hand"—again, to use Smith's salient phrase—that restrains individual greed and stimulates productivity. The term "invisible hand," though used only once by Smith in his book, has come to be a kind of mantra for the unrestrained economy, a laissez-faire approach to the marketplace.[11] A closer reading of Smith, however, shows that he feels that the market should be balanced by social institutions and personal relationships. And, as a contemporary writer in business ethics notes, "Smith's notion of 'self-interest' is not at all the asocial or antisocial sentiment that it is usually made out to be. . . . It is already intrinsically social, and doing good is neither a matter of duty nor compulsion (whether by contract or force) but a genuine source of pleasure for its own sake."[12]

A contemporary advocate of a completely free market after the model of Adam Smith is Milton Friedman, a University of Chicago professor and Nobel laureate (1976).[13] Friedman's view is simple: keep government out of the marketplace. Let business do what it will, and the forces of the marketplace will restrain the greed of unscrupulous entrepreneurs who produce a shabby product at exaggerated prices. How does this work? Consumers will not buy a shoddy product, so its producer will be driven out of business. If a producer places too high a price on products brought to the marketplace, other producers will enter the market, creating an oversupply and driving down prices. Eventually the market will produce a kind of equilibrium where enough producers produce enough products to satisfy consumer demands at a reasonable price.

It is hard to argue against a free market these days, given the fact that much of the world is rushing to embrace the idea. The planned centralized economies of Eastern Europe and the former Soviet Union could not match the economies of the West in levels of productivity and quality, and they all but collapsed under the weight of bureaucratic inefficiency and waste. Friedman seems to be vindicated in another way, too; he argues that individual freedom and economic freedom go hand in hand. One cannot have a truly free society unless the marketplace is free as well. Friedman, however, is nothing if not consistent. He extends his model of economic freedom broadly, including the issuing of licenses to practice a profession (everything from selling real estate to the practice of medicine). Should the government require special licenses and proof of competency before allowing people to enter a profession? Not at all, Friedman says. The market will drive out inferior quality and reward excellence. No need for the heavy hand of government to do these things. Friedman also argues that business has no social responsibility, and that to use the profits of a company for social goods is to make a decision for the stockholders that they should make for themselves. Businesses serve society best, Friedman argues, when they keep to their true mission, which is to make a profit. If by "business ethics" we mean the social responsibilities of business, Friedman counsels business to stick to business and leave social concerns to others.[14]

As convinced as Friedman is about the unfettered free market, he does accept a Hobbes-like view that government's proper task is to be mediator and enforcer of laws and contracts. Its role, he says, is "to provide a means whereby we can modify the rules, mediate differences among us on the meaning of the rules, and to enforce compliance with the rules on the part of those few who would otherwise not play the game."[15] Few people agree completely with Friedman: we want physicians licensed in order to provide at least some assurance of competence, we expect government to set standards of purity for our food and drugs, and we have found through bitter experience that some activities of business, such as insider trading and stock manipulation, need to be curtailed by law and threat of punishment. But notice that we all agree that there must be a framework of rules of conduct if we are to have anything resembling civil society. Notice, too, that the best way to keep government out of the marketplace is for businesses to conform their activities to principles of good ethical behavior. In short, ethics can be thought of as the rules and principles rational human beings use to live together in peace, harmony, and—one hopes—prosperity.

Challenges from the Left

Critics of business activity on the left of the political spectrum often see business as inherently immoral. If one starts with this premise, to speak of business ethics is an oxymoron. One of the most severe antagonists, and certainly one of the most influential, was Karl Marx (1818–1883).

Because his views are known chiefly to the world through the slogan-eering pronouncements of leaders of communist states, Marx's theoretical basis for his antipathy to business is frequently misunderstood. Marx based his analysis of the state of industrialized Europe on what he experienced of the practices of industrialized countries in the nineteenth century, and by any standards the plight of workers was desperate. Long hours, little pay, scant or nonexistent benefits, and a complete lack of job security characterized the situation of workers of mid-nineteenth-century Europe. Marx set about to discover the causes of this misery and to suggest a cure. Much of Marx's analysis is plodding, dull, and academic; yet running through all his writings is a strong humanistic concern and a determination to suggest a more just distribution of the products of an industrialized economy.

The classic model of economics is that there are three factors in economic growth: land, labor, and capital. The workers have no land or capital. All they have is their labor, and the organization of the productive capacity of industrial states conspires to protect the interests not of the workers but of the owners of the means of production—that is, the owners of the mills, factories, shipping lines, railroads, and other productive capacities of the society. Similarly, the government uses its power to protect and extend the control of those who own the means of production and will even use the police or military to enforce the claims of the owners.

Marx expresses these criticisms of industrialized economies in many ways, but three of the claims that are prominent in his critique are the inevitability of the class struggle, the surplus value theory of labor, and the alienation of the workers. We will look briefly at each of these criticisms.

Marx begins his analysis with the claim that the most fundamental facts about any society are the economic arrangements whereby people produce goods and services. He called these arrangements the "economic substructure." From this economic substructure flows the "social superstructure," which includes all the social and cultural arrangements of that society, the educational system, art, and even religion. For example, in feudal society the economic substructure was based on the ownership of land, with power centered in the hands of a few individuals and culminating in the king. These economic realities led to an ideological view that legitimized this state of affairs, and we can see this in the art of the times, the philosophy, even the religion, which defended the divine right of kings to rule. In industrialized cultures, primacy shifted from the ownership of land to the ownership of capital, the means of production. Marx calls these owners the "bourgeoisie," as opposed to those who only had their labor to sell, the "proletariat." The class struggle Marx envisions was between bourgeoisie and proletariat, a struggle that he thought would become so intense that it would inevitably result in revolution, the outcome of which would be the passing of the ownership of the means of production to the workers.

Also included in Marx's analysis of the proletariat was their relation to the labor they sold, the only economic factor under their control. When workers put in a fourteen-hour workday (not uncommon in the nineteenth century) and receive for that work a sum of money, that monetary reward does not represent the full value of the workers' labor. There is the *surplus value* of labor that the owners of the means of production appropriate for their own benefit. For example, let's say a worker produces $20 worth of value and receives only $8 in wages. The $12-dollar difference represents surplus value, which the worker gives up to the owners. For Marx, the seizure of this surplus value by the owners is tantamount to robbery. In a capitalistic society, the owners convert this surplus value of labor into additional wealth that they use to expand their control of capital further in the form of larger factories, bigger production facilities, and even more powerful industrial empires. The lower the wages paid to workers, the greater the surplus value; and the dynamics of capitalist economies, Marx argues, is to force workers into ever longer workdays at ever lower pay.

The economic forces that Marx describes not only lead to the inevitable clash between bourgeoisie and proletariat but also produce an alienated worker. This *alienation of labor* is a somewhat technical point for Marx and can best be understood when contrasted with the work of preindustrial persons. Contrast the relation between work and life of the aboriginal peoples of North America. These individuals took from nature what they needed to survive; they fashioned their tools according to social custom, and the things they made were extensions of their own life and personalities. Even simple artifacts from such societies were decorated with distinct tribal designs, the implements of hunting or agriculture were made according to a cultural norm, and the work of the members of those societies was an extension of their life. All this disappears in the industrial society. Factory workers do not identify with their work; their labor becomes a means to a way of life, which, in the nineteenth century in which Marx lived, was often at a subsistence level. Further, workers in a capitalistic economy are alienated from each other because they compete for the opportunity to sell their labor and are often forced into ever lower wages in order to survive. For Marx, alienation includes three things: workers are separated from the products produced by their labor; the capitalist owner converts the surplus value of labor into more capital, further alienating workers from the fruit of their labor; and workers are alienated from each other when forced to compete for scarce opportunities to sell their labor.

Throughout Marx's writings is the sense that he has discovered scientific laws of social development. He sees revolution in industrial societies as the outcome of the inevitable class struggle between proletariat and bourgeoisie. He does not so much call people to revolution (though he and Engels did write a revolutionary tract, *The Communist Manifesto*) as announce the inevitability of capitalism's collapse. From the vantage point of one hundred and fifty years, we can easily diagnose Marx's many errors. The revolutions he announced did not occur in industrialized countries; rather, Marxist regimes came into power in preindustrial societies (Russia, China, Cuba) and were imposed on the industrialized economics of Eastern Europe by the might of the Red Army. Neither did Marx envision the self-correcting forces that would transform the robber baron capitalism of the nineteenth century. Social policy changes that outlawed child labor, imposed a limited work week, set minimum wages, prevented monopolistic business practices, and brought the power of government into the marketplace to prevent workers being placed in unsafe environments and the destruction of the environment were changes in capitalistic economies that Marx could not imagine. Neither did he catch a glimpse of employee stock ownership plans, profit-sharing arrangements, the emergence of labor unions with their ability to counterbalance the power of industrial empires, the ownership of productive capacity by millions of stockholders and workers through their pension plans, or the often vast social safety net provided by governments to protect workers from the cyclical changes in business activity, such as unemployment compensation, job retraining programs, and government guarantees for worker pension plans.

Though most Marxist regimes around the world have collapsed, and the Marxian critique is now seen as based on only one phase of the development of capitalistic societies, there are still those critics who harbor some sympathies for Marx. For these critics, profit is still viewed as a kind of robbery, and they suspect that Marx may have been correct in his diagnosis of the inherent incompatibility of the interests of workers and owners. To be sure, businesses sometimes do still behave, if given the chance, in the classic nineteenth-century way. Relations between labor unions and owners are sometimes warlike, and not all businesses have the interests of their employees high on their lists of corporate priorities. When businesses violate their public position by illegally restraining trade, polluting the environment, engaging in unfair marketing practices, misrepresenting their products, subjecting their work force to known hazards, or otherwise behaving in a way that violates the social contract within which they function, these behaviors only reinforce the skepticism that many outside observers bring to their analysis of business.

SOME PHILOSOPHICAL DISTINCTIONS

Earlier we addressed the role of ethical theory in approaching questions of business ethics. Along with ethical theory, other methods of philosophical analysis come into play in a discussion of specific ethical issues, and a brief review of some of these will help prepare for the analysis presented in the following chapter. Most of the discussion here addresses techniques derived from logic, that part of philosophy concerned with distinguishing between correct and incorrect reasoning. Today philosophers use symbolic notation based on Boolean algebra to capture many of the fundamental distinctions of logic, but because this book is not principally about logic, we will use discursive rather than symbolic modes of description.

First, however, it is important to note that logic, like philosophy generally, is prescriptive, not descriptive. Logic does not tell us how people think (that is properly the role of psychology) but, rather, how they ought to think. It sets up standards for distinguishing between correct and incorrect reasoning. The following are some of the more important distinctions of logic.

Truth and Validity

One of the important distinctions in logic, one that was probably first formulated in Western philosophy by Aristotle, is that there are two ways our reasoning can go wrong. One is when our reasoning is based on incorrect data. The other is when our reasoning itself is faulty. Philosophers capture this distinction in the terms "truth" and "validity." There are deep waters here, for the standards for truth form a major philosophical discussion in their own right. In general, however, to say that a statement is *true* is to make the claim that it accurately depicts reality or a state of affairs. *Validity,* on the other hand, is concerned only with the structure of reasoning. All of our statements may be false, but the reasoning is correct (which is to say that the outcome of our reasoning would be the case provided the data we use are correct). Such a mode of thinking would be valid, even though based on false data.

To take a simple example, all reports from the company's divisions show that sales are ahead of last month's. Last month we made a profit, so it follows that we will make a profit this month also. Here the reasoning is correct, but if the data are false (not all divisions do exhibit sales increases), the conclusion does not follow. An example of reasoning where data are correct but reasoning is faulty is to say that everyone who has attempted to break into the market with product X has failed; therefore if I do not try to break into this market my business will not fail. This line of reasoning is faulty because there are many other reasons why your business might fail other than your decision not to enter the market with product X. In sum, there are three ways our thinking can go wrong: faulty data and correct reasoning, faulty reasoning and correct data, and faulty data and faulty reasoning. What we seek are conclusions based on correct reasoning and accurate data, which philosophers refer to as "sound" reasoning.

Dilemmas

A *dilemma* occurs when we face two choices, both of which lead to less than desirable consequences. An executive whose business faces a deteriorating bottom line may reason that there are only two choices: either adopt an illegal strategy and risk going to jail, or do nothing and risk going bankrupt. One way out of a dilemma is to search for a third choice (find a new product line, new sources of funding, improved sales techniques), or simply refuse to accept one of the options (come what may, illegal activity is not acceptable). It is not a dilemma to confront choices. The dilemma occurs when each of the two choices leads to unacceptable or unwanted consequences. So unpleasant are dilemmas that we frequently speak of being caught on the "horn" of a dilemma. In an argument, forcing the opponent into a dilemma is a strategy that may result in your opponent's abandoning one of the claims altogether or discovering that there are other alternative actions that will avoid being gored by the dilemma's "horns."

Dialectical Reasoning

Just as dilemmas may force the reconsideration of the choices that lead to the dilemma, another strategy of philosophical analysis is dialectical reasoning. *Dialectical reasoning* is attempting to discover the truth about something by working one's way through a series of partial truths. Start with a claim or a proposal. Submit it to rigorous testing and analysis. Retain what survives but modify the claim in light of the criticisms. Then start the whole process over again. Reiterate the process as much as possible until you reach the insight you seek. This is an ancient method of philosophy, one well known because of its use by the ancient philosopher Plato. Basic to Plato's dialectical method is the conviction that truth emerges through the clash of opposing ideas and that dialogue—philosophical conversation—is the avenue toward understanding. Plato brought the dialectical method to prominence in his philosophical dialogues in which his old teacher, Socrates, plays the principal role of interrogator. Plato positions Socrates prominently in the dialogues as a way of honoring him but also acknowledging Socrates as the originator of the dialectical style of seeking truth. Thus this method of reasoning, often used in law schools, is called the Socratic method. Start with as much of the truth as you know, even if there is a major admixture of confusion. Examine and criticize this partial truth, discover its inadequacies, reformulate the question, and continue the process of examination and criticism.

Dialectical reasoning has had a long and important role in philosophy and even received highly formalized expression in the philosophy of G. W. F. Hegel (1770–1831). However, when referred to in discussions in this book, dialectic is not meant to have Hegelian overtones but, rather, to refer to the general opposition of ideas or points of view. Because it involves the clash of views, sometimes dialectical reasoning begins with the antagonism between opposing ideas. This opposition is referred to as "dialectical tension." Unlike the dilemma, where one faces a forced choice between two equally unattractive options, dialectical tension exists when one is faced with opposing positions but is not forced to choose one or the other. One can recognize the legitimacy of both poles of this tension by refusing to eliminate one of its poles.[16] For example, the claims of stockholders and employees are not always in agreement. The claims of each have some legitimacy, yet to eliminate one pole of this dialectic would be to delegitimize the claims of the other. If the only concern of management is the welfare of employees, the legitimate claims of stockholders will be ignored. But if management concerns itself only with stockholder interest, the reasonable claims of employees will be lost. Further, to attempt to relax this tension would serve neither interest well. To manage only with stockholders' interests in view would destroy employee morale, reduce productivity, and, perhaps, even lower profits. None of these things would be in the interest of stockholders. Yet if management directed its concerns only to employee welfare, stockholders would revolt, stock prices would fall, capital would be hard to find, and workers might find their jobs in jeopardy. One way of responding to this dialectical tension has been through the development of a "stakeholder" approach, a generic term that refers to all those who have a "stake" in the well-being of the company: not only employees and stockholders but also the community, customers, government, even society at large.

As we work through various issues in business ethics, we will find that these and other techniques of philosophical analysis will prove useful in helping to isolate the central ethical questions raised by business choices. At times the outcome of our analysis will be inconclusive, at others we will face a dilemma with no clear sense of a third alternative. We will encounter dialectical tension between rival claims and will explore various ways of responding to this tension. In other issues we will see that the dialectical clash of opposing views leads to revised understanding, which we can again submit to rigorous analysis and criticism. In philosophy generally and in business ethics particularly, not all issues are settled. When dealing with some questions we may have to accept a partial truth, given the present state of our knowledge. Because of the limited facts at our disposal, we may not know how to reach the desired conclusion in our reasoning (here is the truth/validity distinction again).

You may find it puzzling that there are several ethical theories, each of which has a contribution to make to our analysis. Our earlier discussion of the role of theory in ethics offers a partial perspective on this issue, but a final important point needs to be made. However, before we do so, remember that whatever their differences, the various ethical theories agree on the idea that ethical behavior is better than unethical behavior. Transferred to a business context, the point of view of this book is that good ethics is good business. This does not mean that bad business behavior is not profitable or that crime does not pay. Even a casual reading of the daily newspaper provides evidence to dispute that. Furthermore, sometimes businesses that engage in ethical conduct suffer as a result, especially if their competitors are behaving unethically. Nonetheless—and this is our final important point—a convincing case can be made, and this book will attempt to make it, that on balance and in the long term, it is better for businesses to act ethically than unethically. Remember, too, that philosophy, as a prescriptive discipline rather than a descriptive enterprise, should reach beyond the way things are to search for the way things ought to be. But these prescriptions will not be of much use if they speak only of an ideal world rather than the real world in which we live. It will help if we can find real examples of real businesses in the real world doing the right thing and prospering as a result. To do this in business ethics is not as hard as you might think. There are numerous examples of exemplary corporate conduct. The business community has many leaders who bring the same high standards of behavior to their corporate conduct as they apply in their personal lives. Such examples serve to remind us that ethics is not just a theoretical discipline but serves to guide us in our everyday choices.

HOW TO USE THE CASE STUDIES

The primary emphasis of this textbook is on what can be described as the conceptual analysis of important issues in business ethics. These concepts are largely philosophical, and the resources for this analysis are drawn from the writings of philosophers themselves. The purpose of this approach is to help clarify the basic principles of ethical thinking before applying them to problems in the workplace itself.

In addition, throughout the text are scattered short cases (A Case in Point . . .) that allow the reader to think through the principles being discussed as they could apply in a workplace situation. The real world is rarely as neat and tidy as conceptual analysis might imply, so it is important to confront firsthand the ambiguity of moral decision making in the context of conflicting duties and obligations. Several readers of the manuscript have suggested, however, that a lengthier approach to case study is required, and in response to these suggestions, each chapter in the book concludes with a longer account labeled Case Study.

Previously the argument was advanced that there is a fundamental difference between descriptive and prescriptive concerns and that the role of philosophy is the latter. The application of prescriptive distinctions arrived at through conceptual analysis can be served, however, by the analysis of factual material. It would be naive, and incorrect, to think that the more facts one has, the easier it will be to make a moral judgment. As the American philosopher William James noted, the amassing of facts, though important, will not take the place of the often risky enterprise of making a moral judgment. What case studies do offer is a real-world venue for the application of principles arrived at through conceptual analysis. The noted case method advocate C. Roland Christensen cites the philosopher Alfred North Whitehead's comments in just this defense of the case approach: "In the process of learning there should be present, in some sense or other, a subordinate activity of application. In fact, the applications are part of the knowledge. For the very meaning of the things known is wrapped up in their relationships beyond themselves. Thus unapplied knowledge is knowledge shorn of its meaning."[17]

The case method of study has been made famous by the Harvard Business School in its MBA program and is used there as the closest thing possible in a classroom environment to simulating the challenges that will be faced by these managers-in-training. The case studies presented in this book are not nearly as long as are typical Harvard cases (though the last one in the book is; indeed, it is a Harvard case study), and the variety of case studies included here allows for various approaches. Rather than providing a problem-based analysis, some cases are accounts of ethically commendable corporate behavior and others of behavior not so commendable. Such cases allow readers to insert themselves into the narrative and raise "what if" types of questions. Another approach is to ask what events could have occurred that would have altered the outcomes described in the case. In still other cases it is possible, assuming this book is being used in a class, to assign the various roles in the case to different class members and ask them to represent the points of view of their assigned roles even to the extent of going beyond the issues described in the case itself.[18]

Here are some of the questions that can be asked as one works through a case:

1 What are the ethical issues raised by this series of events?

2 How did this situation develop from the manager's point of view? How did the situation develop from your point of view, as an outside observer?

3 What actions could management have taken to bring about a different outcome than the one described here?

4 How would you generalize from this case in order to develop an overall approach to dealing with issues similar to the ones raised here?

5 As you analyze the situation, what were the critical decision points?

There are doubtless other themes raised by each case study and a variety of ways to utilize them in a meaningful class discussion. The latter point is the key: cases are meant to bring about discussion. This echoes Plato's belief that we clarify our thinking best when we engage in the public interchange of ideas, adjusting our positions according to the strength of the argument and counterargument.

DISCUSSION STARTERS

1 What are your own expectations about reading a book on business ethics? Are these expectations realistic? What sort of guidance do you feel you need in order to enter the business world?

2 Do you think that today's business activity assumes some of the characteristics of the "state of nature" as Hobbes described it? If so, what are these characteristics? If not, what restraints on business activity reduce its warlike nature?

3 Make a list of issues in business that pose dilemmas. Contrast this list with another that displays a dialectical tension.

4 Look for examples of how popular culture portrays businesspeople. Why is this image of business so prevalent?

5 Are there commonly accepted values for business activity assumed in this country? If so, what are they?

NOTES

1 Not all philosophers use the term "nature" as does Hobbes, for whom the state of nature is the beginning point for human development. Others, such as Aristotle, use the term "nature" to refer to the source of change that develops as we mature, thereby expressing our true nature as creatures possessing reason. A discussion of the variation in the philosophical use of the term can be found in Ronald Hepburn, "Nature, Philosophical Ideas of," in *The Encyclopedia of Philosophy,* vol. 5, pp. 454–458.

2 Hobbes, *Leviathan,* p. 162.

3 The term "self-interest" can be taken in several senses. As a variety of egoism, it can mean either that people do in fact always seek their own good (psychological egoism) or that they should always seek their own good (ethical egoism). Enlightened self-interest is a variety of the latter and seeks

to understand what is in the best interest of the individual by considering such variables as long-term versus short-term benefits, mental as well as physical well-being, and the importance for the individual of human community, interpersonal concord.

4 Kurt Baier, *The Moral Point of View* (New York: Random House, 1965), p. 96.

5 For example, Mill treats this issue at length in Chapter 5 of his *Utilitarianism.*

6 "Ethical Theory and Applied Ethics," in *Medical Ethics: A Reader* (Englewood Cliffs, NJ: Prentice-Hall, 1991), p. 13. The role of theory in applied ethics is developed more here with the assistance of my coauthors Arthur Zucker and Donald Borchert, and some of this analysis is included in the paragraphs that follow.

7 NYT, Feb. 10, 1993.

8 Robert C. Solomon and Kristine Hanson. *It's Good Business* (New York: Atheneum, 1985).

9 This point is thoroughly debated in the article by Albert Z. Carr, "Is Business Bluffing Ethical," and Timothy B. Blodgett's response, "Showdown on 'Business Bluffing'." Both are included in the collection of articles from the *Harvard Business Review: Ethics in Practice: Managing the Moral Corporation,* eds. Kenneth R. Andrews and Donald K. David (Boston: Harvard Business School Press), pp. 99–118.

10 John Passmore, "Logical Positivism," in *The Encyclopedia of Philosophy,* vol. 5, p. 56.

11 I owe the observation that Smith used the phrase "invisible hand" only once in *The Wealth of Nations* to Robert C. Solomon, *Ethics and Excellence* (New York: Oxford University Press, 1993), p. 86.

12 Ibid.

13 Milton Friedman, *Capitalism and Freedom* (Chicago: University of Chicago Press, 1962).

14 Friedman's well-known article from the *New York Times Magazine,* "The Social Responsibility of Business Is to Increase Its Profits," can be found in Hoffman and Moore, *Business Ethics,* 2nd ed. (New York: McGraw-Hill, 1990), pp. 153–157.

15 Friedman, *Capitalism and Freedom,* p. 25.

16 The French philosopher Paul Ricoeur has made this use of dialectical tension a central feature of his own philosophical methods. To see how he uses this approach, consult his book, *The Conflict of Interpretations* (Evanston, IL: Northwestern University Press, 1973).

17 C. Roland Christensen, *Teaching and the Case Method* (Boston: Harvard Business School, 1987), p. 16, citing Alfred North Whitehead, *Essays in Science and Philosophy* (New York: Philosophical Library, 1947), pp. 218–219.

18 In assembling some of these questions, I drew on insights supplied by the article "Teaching with Cases at the Harvard Business School" in Christensen, *Teaching and the Case Method.*

CASE STUDY

Discussions of moral principles sometimes remain abstract until they are brought to bear on specific examples. Case studies are one way to do this, and they are effective in helping to identify morally relevant issues within actual experience. A word of caution: textbook discussions of theory are tidy and clear; examples from experience are messy and ambiguous. One should not approach a case study expecting to find that only a single ethical issue is at stake or that an appeal to a single moral theory will clarify the issues being encountered.

The case study "Dayton Hudson Corporation: Conscience and Control" offers a description of a corporate takeover and raises the issue of whether this kind of behavior between corporations is akin to Hobbes's state of nature. If your answer is yes, the next question asks what restraints should be placed on corporate behavior of this kind. If your answer is no, the issue raised is on what grounds such actions can be defended. Throughout the case note the tension engendered between assessing the actions by their consequences and judging them by the motivations and intentions of the principals themselves.

DAYTON HUDSON CORPORATION: CONSCIENCE AND CONTROL

THE DAYTON HUDSON CORPORATION

The Dayton Hudson Corporation described itself as "a growth company focusing exclusively on retailing." Headquartered in Minneapolis, the company operated 475 stores in 34 states at the end of 1986, employing some 120,000 people nationwide (full-time and part-time). In that year it had pretax earnings of $494.2 million on sales of $9,259.1 million.

Operating Structures and Policies

DHC was composed of four operating companies and a corporate headquarters. This structure reflected DHC's fundamental management philosophy, which favored decentralization. The operating companies were:

Target: an upscale discount store chain. In 1986 Target produced 47% of DHC's revenues and 47.4% of pretax profits, with earnings of $311 million on sales of $4,355 million.

Mervyn's: a highly promotional, popularly priced, value-oriented department store company. In 1986 Mervyn's produced 31% of DHC's revenues and 24.4% of pretax profits, with earnings of $160 million on sales of $2,862 million.

Dayton Hudson Department Store Company (DHDSC): the largest traditional department store operation in the United States. In 1986 DHDSC produced 17% of DHC's revenues and 25.2% of pretax profits, with earnings of $166 million on sales of $1,566 million.

Lechmere's: a hardgoods retail store company. In 1986 Lechmere's produced 5% of DHC's revenues and 3% of pretax profits, with earnings of $19.5 million on sales of $476 million.

The operating companies made autonomous decisions about merchandising and buying, and had responsibility for profits and return on investment. . . .

Financial Policies

DHC's stated financial goal was to provide its shareholders with a superior return on their investment while maintaining a conservative financial position. More particularly, the company preferred to own assets where possible, to meet external needs with long-term debt, and to maintain a maximum debt ratio of 45% (including capital and operating leases). The majority of the company's growth was financed through internally generated funds.

In its 1986 Annual Report, DHC stated that its performance objectives were to "earn an after-tax return on beginning shareholders' equity (ROE) of 18%," to "sustain an annual growth in earnings per share (EPS) of 15%," and to "maintain a strong rating of [its] senior debt." The Report also noted that "the incentive compensation of corporate management and the management of each operating company is based on return on investment, as well as growth in earnings."

These goals, however, were not extrapolated from past performance. The ROE had averaged 15.3% in the period 1975–86, and the earnings per share growth had only been above 15% five times in those twelve years.

Though DHC remained a profitable company, 1986 was a disappointing year. Revenues increased by 12% and passed the $9 billion mark, but net earnings per share dropped by 9%. The principal reason appears to have been difficulty with the Mervyn's division, where operating profits fell by more than 34%. DHC's Annual Report for 1986 acknowledged a problem with Mervyn's and attributed the dramatic decline in profits to an organizational restructuring and to a need to reduce margins in order to remain competitive. . . .

Customer Service

DHC was strongly customer-oriented. The stated merchandising objective of each of the operating companies was to fulfill the value expectations of customers more effectively than the competition. They consciously aimed to do this by providing superior value in five categories: assortment, quality, fashion, convenience and pricing. One concrete sign of this orientation was the long-standing corporate policy of accepting the return of merchandise for a full refund, no questions asked. Stories abounded, especially in Minnesota, about the lengths to which the company was willing to go to honor this policy.

Corporate Community Involvement

In 1946 the Dayton Company became the first major American corporation to initiate a policy by which it donated 5% of its federal taxable income to non-profit organizations. (It was a charter member of Minnesota's "5% Club," an organization founded in 1976 whose membership consisted of corporations that donated 5% of their annual taxable income.) This policy had continued without interruption, and in 1987 DHC's contributions totaled nearly $20 million (principally to arts and social action organizations). These contributions were distributed throughout the states in which DHC did business. . . .

DHC's concern for social responsibility extended into other aspects of its business as well. In 1978, for example, Kenneth Dayton (then chairman and CEO of the company) was one of the principal organizers of the Minnesota Project on Corporate Responsibility. This organization sponsored seminars and other programs aimed at encouraging and strengthening a sense of social responsiveness in Minnesota corporations. James Shannon, then executive director of the General Mills Foundation, commented in a guest editorial in the *Minneapolis Star Tribune,* "In a community nationally known for its corporate support of the arts, social services and education, the Dayton Hudson Corp. is the flagship for dozens of other publicly and privately held corporations committed to the proposition that a successful company has an obligation to be a good corporate citizen."

DHC's relations with the public were not always smooth, however. There were times when its concern for communities was questioned. In 1983, for example, Hudson's flagship store in downtown Detroit was closed. From DHC's perspective the store had become old and inefficient, and the business climate in downtown Detroit unsupportive. Mayor Coleman Young's view was different. As he told the *Detroit Free Press,* "I don't think Hudson's demonstrated any sense of responsibility or citizenship after growing in this city and off this city for almost 100 years."

The following year, 1984, Dayton's and Hudson's operations were consolidated into the Dayton Hudson Department Store Company, with a single headquarters in Minneapolis. Once again, Detroit objected since the move resulted in the loss of about 1,000 jobs for the city, many of them well-paid management positions. Ann Barkelew, DHC's vice president for public relations, commented in the *Minneapolis Star Tribune,* "Our decision to bring the headquarters [to Minneapolis] was a business decision. The whole purpose in combining the companies was to do things better."

THE DART GROUP CORPORATION

The Dart Group Corporation's 1987 Annual Report (year ending January 31, 1987) was spartan and no-nonsense. Its only two photographs, which appeared on the first page, were of Herbert Haft, founder and chairman, and Robert Haft, president and Herbert's older son. There were no photographs of the discount retail outlets they operated or of satisfied customers, nor did other members of management or the board of directors appear. Instead, attention was focused exclusively on information about Dart's operations and finances. And not without reason, for Dart's net income more than tripled in fiscal 1987.

According to the Annual Report, Dart operated retail discount auto parts stores through the Trak Auto Corporation, operated retail discount book stores through the Crown Books Corporation, and operated a financial business which dealt in bankers' acceptances. The present company was a successor to Dart Drug, a Washington, D.C., retail drug store chain founded by Herbert Haft. Haft built a chain of stores from one store he opened in 1954 by selling most of his merchandise at discount prices. . . . In 1984, Dart's drug store division was sold to its employees. . . .

Attempts to Acquire Other Businesses

DHC was not the first corporation in which the Hafts took an interest. Between 1983 and 1986 they attempted to acquire Supermarkets General Corp, Jack Eckerd Drug Stores, Revco Inc., Federated Department Stores, May Department Stores, and the giant supermarket chain, Safeway Stores. In each case they failed, but their failures were spectacularly profitable. They realized a $9 million profit on the sale of their Jack Eckerd stock, $40 million in their unsuccessful attempt to purchase Supermarkets General, and $97 million when they failed to take over Safeway. Nor surprisingly, the value of Dart Group stock rose from $10.75 in 1982 to over $150 per share in 1987.

Target companies have seriously questioned, and seriously resisted, the Hafts' attempts to acquire them. Like many other corporate raiders, the Hafts relied on "junk bonds" as part of the financial component of their proposals, and issuers like Drexel Burnham Lambert indicated that they were "highly confident" that financing could be arranged. Yet unlike many other raiders, the Hafts always targeted businesses close to their own experience. They remained in the retail industry and attempted to acquire chains, especially where their low-margin expertise might be valuable. Since they were always unsuccessful in their acquisition attempts, accusations by critics that they intended to sell off the major assets of the target companies were, while speculative, not entirely unreasonable. For their part, the Hafts insisted that they planned to operate, rather than break up, the companies they targeted.

However, even when a takeover attempt failed, the target company could face a difficult time. In 1986, the Dart Group was unsuccessful in an attempt to acquire Safeway Stores. The management of Safeway eluded the Hafts by taking the company private with a leveraged buyout. This involved taking on $4.2 billion in debt in order to purchase outstanding stock. As a result, Safeway, once the largest supermarket chain in the United States, was compelled to sell off profitable British and Australian holdings. In addition, it sold or closed 251 stores in the United States. Many of these stores were in small towns that had complained bitterly about the move. While Safeway's streamlining substantially improved profitability, it was still left with an enormous debt burden to service.

The Events Leading Up to Early June 1987

In 1986, DHC offered its B. Dalton division for sale. At that time B. Dalton, founded by one of the Dayton brothers in the 1960s, was one of the two largest and most successful retail bookselling chains in the United States. However, DHC had decided to pursue a strategy focused on the operation of large stores that offered a broad spectrum of merchandise. The typical B. Dalton store was fairly small and specialized in books and computer software. Among those seriously interested in acquiring B. Dalton was the Dart Group. Ultimately they were unsuccessful, and the division was sold to Barnes and Noble. According to one rumor, the negotiations broke down when personal hostilities flared up between senior executives of DHC and the Hafts.

Nevertheless, in their negotiations the Hafts had the opportunity to become familiar with DHC. While they recognized value in the company, they were critical of DHC's management. . . . In the spring of 1987 when DHC announced its first decline in earnings in sixteen years, the Hafts saw an opportunity. Though the significant drop in DHC's stock price discouraged some investors, the Hafts felt there was good reason to think that the company still had the potential for solid earnings. . . .

By that same spring the legal climate was becoming less conducive to hostile takeovers. Provisions of an Indiana law that gave the state considerable power to restrict such takeovers had been upheld by the U.S. Supreme Court in April. Some Minnesota corporations (though not DHC) had lobbied hard for similar legislation in 1984, but it had failed to pass, partly because many legislators felt that it would not be upheld by the courts. The Supreme Court's decision, however, came too late to influence the 1987 session of the Minnesota legislature, which adjourned on May 18.

[Kenneth A.] Macke [CEO] himself made clear his opposition to a "bust-up" takeover, one that would require breaking up the corporation and selling off parts to repay the debts incurred by the takeover. He and his management team were convinced that it was best for all the corporation's constituencies—stockholders, customers, employees, and communities—that the company remain intact. As the possibilities were discussed, some were set aside rather easily. They found green-mail, in the words of one participant, to be a "repugnant" alternative. They were also repelled by various schemes to take on debt or sell off assets, which, as another participant put it, would involve doing to themselves exactly what they feared the Hafts would do. Nor were they convinced that the financial defenses would be successful. They realized that if they chose to fight a financial battle, the action would take place in New York, where they had less influence. On the other hand, they had considerable influence in Minnesota, but it was not clear how to bring that influence to bear. . . . [A]fter listening to discussion about alternative defenses, Macke had made it clear to his team that the responsibility for the decision would be his. Later that evening, after consulting with the board of directors, he decided to approach the governor regarding a special session of the legislature to strengthen Minnesota's corporate takeover statute. It seemed to be the alternative that took best advantage of the company's strengths, all things considered, and the one most likely to succeed. But many obstacles still lay in the path.

The strategy that DHC laid out with respect to the legislators was simple in theory, but was complicated to execute in such a short time. . . . At the Capitol, a joint meeting of the House Judiciary and Commerce Committees convened. Macke was the first to testify, but, as the *Minneapolis Star-Tribune* reported, his performance was anything but smooth. Out of his element and disconcerted by recent developments, he seemed nervous and abrupt. He told the committees that he not only believed in a free market, but also in a fair market. "During the last three weeks," he said, "30 percent of our stock was traded. This means that 30 percent of our stock is owned by people who have held it for less than three weeks." Later, an attorney representing DHC reported, "in 10 minutes or less, more than 3 percent of the stock changed hands this morning."

But the most startling moment came when Macke announced that another attempt to acquire the company had begun that morning. A $6.8 billion offer had been made by a Cincinnati stock analyst thought to be representing a wealthy Ohio family. In a matter of hours, the paper value of the company increased by nearly a billion dollars. By the afternoon, however, the offer was shown to be bogus and the stock analyst was found to have had a history of mental illness. The incident graphically underscored the volatility of the circumstances in which the company found itself, and drove home the urgency of the situation to the legislators. . . .

The Provisions of the Bill

The bill proposed in the Minnesota legislature aimed to protect companies by addressing the problem of tender offers. It required approval of the majority of disinterested shareholders before a bidder could gain voting rights for a controlling share of the stock. It also required the approval of a majority of the disinterested members of the board of directors (i.e., those who were neither managers nor representatives of bidders) before the bidder could enter any business combination with the target. Furthermore, and perhaps most importantly, it prohibited the sale of a target company's assets to pay debts incurred in financing a hostile takeover for a period of five years.

One of the most controversial provisions of the Minnesota bill, however, was the stipulation that the board of directors of a target company could legitimately take into consideration the interests of a wide range of groups in exercising their "business judgment." In discharging their duties, directors were authorized to consider "the interests of the corporation's employees, customers, suppliers, and creditors, the economy of the state and nation, community and societal considerations, and the long-term as well as short-term interest of the corporation and its shareholders including the possibility that these interests may be best served by the continued independence of the corporation."

Finally, the bill introduced measures which virtually prohibited golden parachutes and the payment of greenmail, but the greenmail provision was not scheduled to become effective until some months afterwards. . . . [T]he bill passed by an overwhelming margin: 120–5 in the House and 57–0 in the Senate.

Macke was angry, and only half-surprised, as he read the letter he just received from Herbert Haft. The raider was back.

The letter, dated July 23, 1987, announced that a new partnership had been formed under Haft's control, the Madison Partnership. The stated intention of this partnership was to purchase in excess of $15 million of outstanding DHC stock over the next twelve months, and perhaps even to acquire a controlling interest in the company. . . . On Friday, the day after the letter was made public, DHC's stock rose $4.37, and closed at $52.00 per share.

In the following weeks, the Hafts took no further public action. Secretly, however, the Madison Partnership continued to purchase DHC stock, but stopped short of the 5 percent level which would have required SEC notification. . . . September 17, 1987. . . . Macke received another letter from Herbert Haft. That same day the contents of the letter were released by the Hafts to the media. In this letter the Hafts proposed a business combination between DHC and a newly formed affiliate of the Dart Group, New Dayton Hudson. Assuming that DHC's board of directors approved, and that the necessary financing could be arranged, the Hafts proposed to pay DHC stockholders $65 in cash for 95% of their shares and stock in New Dayton Hudson for the balance. (The necessary financing included more than $5 billion in bank loans, and the required bond issue was many times larger than any that their investment banker, Paine Webber, Inc., had handled before.)

The Hafts also made three notable concessions. First, they offered to continue DHC's "current policies regarding employees, management, suppliers, customers, community and corporate responsibilities, and support of charities." Second, they proposed that corporate headquarters would remain in Minneapolis. Third, they promised to donate to Minnesota charities any profits they might realize from their ownership of DHC's stock in the event that the shareholders disapproved of the acquisition agreement.

A variety of reactions followed almost immediately. Nearly 5.5 million shares of DHC stock changed hands the following day, up from 770,000 on the 17th, and the price rose from $52.87 to $58. . . .

When DHC's board of directors met, it rejected the Hafts' offer, saying, "We believe that Dayton Hudson's shareholders and other constituencies should continue to have the opportunity to fully realize the benefits of the business we are operating." That day the stock price closed at $59.00 per share.

The following Tuesday, September 29, another letter from Herbert Haft was delivered to Macke. This letter, also released to the media, was substantially the same as the letter of September 17. However, the cash portion of the offer was raised to $68 per share. . . .

On Wednesday, October 14, DHC's board of directors once again rejected the Hafts' proposal. By then the company stock price had fallen to $52.87 per share. The following day DHC filed in U.S. District Court against the Dart Group, charging that the Hafts were in violation of securities laws and regulations, and seeking to prevent them from soliciting proxies for an attempt to remove the members of the board. On October 16, calling the DHC suit "frivolous," the Hafts responded with their own suit, demanding current information about the identity of DHC's shareholders.

As each side prepared to do battle, however, events overtook them both. On Friday, October 16, DHC's stock participated in a sharp drop in prices across the board, and fell to $44.75 per share.

The following Monday, October 19, the New York Stock Exchange experienced the single greatest drop in value in its history. The Dow Jones Index plummeted 508 points, and DHC's stock fell to $30.00 per share. . . .

On Tuesday, October 20, Robert Haft announced that the Dart Group had sold about a third of its shares in DHC and would not pursue its attempt to acquire the company. In an interview with the *Wall Street Journal,* he said, "The markets have changed so dramatically that to continue would not be prudent." . . .

Because of the events of 1987, management realized that both the profile of the company's stockholders and the environment in which the company did business had changed. The stockholders were no longer individuals who shared the values of the company, but were often large institutional investors for whom performance tended to take precedence over good corporate citizenship. . . .

Despite these events, DHC reaffirmed its commitment to its policy of community involvement even when faced with losses or declining growth in profitability. . . .

Following the successful defense of the company, Macke focused management's attention on the goal of creating value for stockholders through improved performance that would be at least equal to the value they would have received from the Hafts. According to a member of his management team, he was convinced that controlling more of the outstanding stock and making corporate community involvement more effective, while critically important, were not sufficient by themselves. The third leg of the tripod had to be the kind of performance that would pay off on his promise that it was best for all concerned that DHC remain independent and intact.

Epilogue

• DHC announced, in July of 1989, that it planned to create an Employee Stock Ownership Plan (ESOP). At the time of the announcement, approximately 77 million shares of common stock were outstanding, and the plan called for the acquisition of up to 7 million shares.

• DHC's revenues for 1989 were $13.6 billion, a 47% increase over revenues for 1986. Earnings per share for 1989 were $5.35, a 104% increase. Return on beginning equity rose to 22%, from 14.5% in 1988 and 13.1% in 1986.

• In February 1990, the Dart Group agreed to settle a complaint filed by the Securities and Exchange Commission which had charged the company with securities law violations. The SEC contended that, over a period of five years, the company had received so much of its income from trading stocks that it should be registered as an investment company, and so be subject to strict disclosure requirements. The settlement, however, did not require the Dart Group to register as an investment company, but did require them to abide by investment company rules and to make their books available for close SEC examination for a period of three years.

• On June 22, 1990, DHC completed the acquisition of the Chicago-based Marshall Field & Company, for just in excess of $1 billion.

• On June 25, 1990, exactly three years after the Minnesota legislature met in special session, DHC's stock closed at $71.38 per share.

Developing Ethical Habits

William C. Byham, Ph.D.

President and Chief Executive Officer, Development Dimensions International and author of *Zapp! The Lightning of Empowerment*

"Business ethics build trust, and trust is the basis of modern business. If an organization's culture is one of "kill the messenger," sugar-coating bad news, taking credit for others' work, lack of collaboration between departments then flattened, empowered, team-oriented organizations cannot operate. A modern organization does not have a long list of rules and books of procedures. The organization uses mutually understood vision and values to guide decision-making and relies on collaboration and trust to get things done."

If we accept the view, argued for earlier, that there are not two moralities—one for individuals and one for business—but a common moral framework for judging both individual and corporate activities, then we can gain some guidance for business behavior by looking at what philosophers have seen as the morally good life. This is a topic as old as Aristotle, whose ethical views have been given renewed interest under the term "virtue theory."

VIRTUE THEORY

Implicit in the ethical approach of virtue theory is the importance of moral development rather than dependence on specific moral rules, with all the attendant difficulties that rule-bound approaches entail. Virtue theory asserts that there is no common agreement in contemporary society on basic moral principles because we have lost a sense of a common cultural tradition from which moral values spring. Today people argue from widely different premises, some that moral values come from the will of God, others that morality is what makes us individually happy ("do your own thing"), others that individual rights take precedence over all other rights, still others that "the individual" is an outmoded ideal and that the good of society should be our primary goal. Without a shared view of a cultural tradition, these differing moral perspectives lead to the mistaken view that ethical issues cannot be decided by rational means at all, but that they are only emotional responses to imponderable issues and that moral discourse is little more than rhetoric. It is for this reason that Alasdair MacIntyre, a contemporary advocate of virtue theory, refers to prevalent moral discussion and moral views as "emotivism": one's feelings instead of rational arguments are used to make moral decisions.[1]

The works of Aristotle provide the source of the moral views MacIntyre defends. As he puts it, "The Aristotelian moral tradition is the best example we possess of a tradition whose adherents are rationally entitled to a high measure of confidence in its epistemological and moral resources."[2] According to Aristotle, the values to be developed are best learned by studying the lives of heroic persons. Societies where such virtues as honesty, fidelity, honor, and generosity are the norm point to great individuals as models that provide the guidance for individual moral action. Aristotle thinks all the virtues are communicated this way. Confused about honesty? Look to stories of honest behavior, in spite of the consequences, as related in sagas and epic poetry. To find out what courage is, examine the lives of brave persons to discover how to act courageously. Virtue theory also emphasizes the importance of history and literature, for they are a society's cultural memory and provide examples of admirable conduct to be copied and of abhorrent conduct to be avoided. So, too, in business, moral values are often communicated by stories about the company's founders or its leaders who remained true to the company's moral ideals even when financial disaster loomed and the temptation was strong to sacrifice values for the bottom line. Increasingly, business journals talk about "corporate culture," a phrase that refers to the way a company does business based on the actions and attitudes of the company's founders and continued by its current executive officers.

A major difficulty in the application of virtue ethics is the question of an increasingly multicultural society. When there is a commonly held cultural ideal, as was the case in Aristotle's ancient Greece, it is easier to understand how a homogeneous society can agree on the shared values that are to be communicated through the deeds and exploits of cultural heroes. But what of a multicultural, multiracial society, to say nothing of the challenges of the increasingly global dimension of business activity? It is hardly possible to conceive of what a common world culture would be like, even if we hold the view that fundamental moral values run as constants through cultural differences. Chapter 10 examines in more detail the problems of *ethical relativism,* the view that standards of right and wrong, good and bad, and moral values generally are defined by a given society and therefore are not applicable universally. Virtue theory seems to imply a relativist position, with its emphasis on shared cultural traditions and the apparent rejection of any grounds for ethics other than a shared cultural tradition.

For the moment let us put aside the challenges of relativism to see where virtue theory leads. A shared set of values, most frequently communicated—as they are in what MacIntyre calls "heroic societies"—through tales and the recounting of heroic deeds of exemplary figures from the past, has an obvious limitation in that it does not provide much guidance for thinking about ethics in novel situations. What standards, for example, should we apply to leveraged buyouts, hostile takeovers, plant closings, restraints on multinational corporations, or the many issues forced on us by the complexities of an emerging global economy? The virtue theory approach provides even less guidance than we have from other ethical theories when dealing with different cultural traditions. Matters of international business ethics are so difficult

---

VIRTUE THEORY

- Derived from a shared cultural tradition
- Values communicated through exemplars
- Limitations:
  Difficult to apply to novel situations
  Lack of guidance in cross-cultural situations

---

precisely because they involve the clash of cultures and differing standards of conduct. Nonetheless, virtue theory provides many important insights into moral decision making, but by itself seems wanting in ethical guidance.

Though he lived more than two millennia ago, and had no knowledge of the intricacies of corporate existence (and didn't even take much interest in commercial activity), Aristotle's keen insights into the nature of the moral life, which is referred to as the good life, are still as valuable for us today as they were when he wrote them. In spite of the technological changes of our world, human needs are virtually unchanged, and the good life remains, as much for us as for Aristotle, a significant pursuit.

The Search for Well-Being

In his analysis of the moral life, Aristotle raises an important yet simple question. What is it that we desire for its own sake? What is that which is good "which is always desirable in itself and never for the sake of something else?"[3] His answer is happiness. By happiness, Aristotle does not mean a passing emotional response but a state of being in which we are ruled by rational considerations. His word for happiness is *eudaimonia*. Happiness, in this sense of the term, is a fulfilled life, one that is lived according to reason and guided by moderation.

There are two important corollaries to Aristotle's analysis. First, happiness is a quality of life that one generates throughout one's life. It is not something that we can say we have achieved in a few months. To seek happiness is a lifetime activity. "One swallow does not make a summer," Aristotle says, "and so too one day, or a short time, does not make a man blessed and happy."[4] To assess your pursuit of happiness requires that you take a long-term rather than a short-term perspective. The second aspect of happiness, according to Aristotle, is that one cannot seek it directly, for happiness is derived from other goals that we can seek directly. For example, if we are to be happy, we must have enough wealth to free us from poverty. We need health and freedom from disease and disability, and we want success in our chosen work. A circle of companions and friends contributes to one's basic sense of well-being.

Friendship is so important to Aristotle that he devotes more discussion to it in his ethical writing than to any other single topic. Human beings are by nature social creatures, he thinks, and to develop our humanness fully requires that we have meaningful relationships with other people. Aristotle, in other words, is not a rugged individualist. He believes that we find fulfillment in mutually satisfying relations, and these contribute to happiness. There is also an important moral dimension to happiness; Aristotle, in fact, defines happiness as "activity in accord with virtue."[5] In other words, we achieve happiness—in this sense of well-being—by achieving moral virtue, by being honest, loyal, and through becoming interdependent human beings.

By making only a few alterations we can use the language of Aristotle to describe the goals and purposes of business. What *eudaimonia* is to the individual, profits are to the business organization. Without profits, a business dies. Without profits, a business cannot offer employment, make products, or pay investors a return on equity. And just as individuals achieve happiness by seeking other goals, there is growing evidence that the business goal of profit can be best sought if a company first pursues such goals as enduring quality of its product, service to its customers, and a commitment to ensuring a stable community and work force.

Virtue as Excellence

The key word for Aristotle is virtue, but what can we make of the phrase "business virtue"? Can you even imagine an article in *Fortune, Forbes,* or *Business Week* praising the *virtue* of the CEO of a major industrial firm? Probably not. Yet business leaders do speak of their commitment to quality and excellence, and these two words are close to what Aristotle means by virtue.

The English word *virtue* is an imperfect translation of a Greek word *aretē*. It can mean not only moral virtue but excellence in a broad sense.[6] Aristotle, in fact, suggests there is an *aretē*, or excellence, for every kind of activity—that is, we can seek excellence in personal relations as well as in business relations, and both would be examples of virtue (understood in the sense of excellence). Even animals can have virtue in the Aristotelian sense, for the term implies quality and excellence appropriate to the kind of activity being described. When business leaders talk about the need for total quality management, when a manufacturing firm claims that "quality is job one," or when a company says its trademark is "the mark of excellence," these are all references to that same concept Aristotle captures in *aretē*.

A consideration of ethics in terms of virtue not only provides a way of discussing business ethics, it is also an important alternative to the rancorous moral debate that seems to dominate our culture. At least this is what Alasdair MacIntyre argues in his book *After Virtue*. "The most striking feature of contemporary moral utterance," he claims, "is that so much of it is used to express disagreements; and the most striking feature of the debates in which these disagreements are expressed is their interminable character." What this means in practical terms, according to MacIntyre, is that "there seems to be no rational way of securing moral agreement in our culture."[7] We are tempted to think that morality is nothing but the expression of personal preferences, what MacIntyre calls "emotivism," the support for which is not reason but rhetoric. The alternative that MacIntyre proposes to this stridency of competing moral claims is a return to an Aristotelian emphasis on virtue. Part of what modern society has lost, MacIntyre says, is the common understanding of our essential human purpose. Here is his description of this loss:

> Within the Aristotelian tradition to call x good (where x may be among other things a person or an animal or a policy or a state of affairs) is to say that it is the kind of x which someone would choose who wanted an x for the purpose for which x's are characteristically wanted. To call a watch good is to say that it is the kind of watch which someone would choose who wanted a watch to keep time accurately (rather than, say, to throw at the cat). The presupposition of this use of "good" is that every type of item which it is appropriate to call good or bad—including persons and actions—has, as a matter of fact, some given specific purpose or function. To call something good therefore is also to make a factual statement. To call a particular action just or right is to say that it is what a good man would do in such a situation; hence this type of statement too is factual. Within this tradition moral and evaluative statements can be called true or false in precisely the way in which all other factual statements can be so called. But once the notion of essential human purposes or functions disappears from

morality, it begins to appear implausible to treat moral judgments as factual statements.[8]

To see what this means let's look a little more closely at Aristotle's views on ethics.

INTELLECTUAL AND MORAL VIRTUES

Aristotle finds virtue, or excellence, to be of two types. One type of excellence you can learn by training: how to run a computer, how to do calculus, how to operate a lathe. These Aristotle calls "intellectual" virtues. Other virtues can only be obtained through habitual behavior; these he calls "moral" virtues and argues that we develop them by engaging in moral activities. As Aristotle puts it, "Men become builders by building and lyre-players by playing the lyre; so too we become just by doing just acts, temperate by doing temperate acts, brave by doing

---

ARISTOTLE ON VIRTUE

Virtue, then, being of two kinds, intellectual and moral, intellectual virtue in the main owes both its birth and its growth to teaching (for which reason it requires experience and time), while moral virtue comes about as a result of habit, whence also its name *ethike* is one that is formed by a slight variation from the word *ethos* (habit). From this it is also plain that none of the moral virtues arises in us by nature; for nothing that exists by nature can form a habit contrary to its nature. For instance, the stone which by nature moves downwards cannot be habituated to move upwards, not even if one tries to train it by throwing it up ten thousand times; nor can fire be habituated to move downwards, nor can anything else that by nature behaves in one way be trained to behave in another. Neither by nature, then, nor contrary to nature do the virtues arise in us; rather we are adapted by nature to receive them, and are made perfect by habit. . . .

We must, however, not only describe virtue as a state of character, but also say what sort of state it is. We may remark, then, that every virtue or excellence both brings into good condition the thing of which it is the excellence and makes the work of that thing be done well; for it is by the excellence of the eye that we see well. Similarly the excellence of the horse makes a horse both good in itself and good at running and at carrying its rider and at awaiting the attack of the enemy. Therefore, if this is true in every case, the virtue of man also will be the state of character which makes a man good and which makes him do his own work well.

Source: Aristotle, *Nicomachean Ethics*, trans. W. D. Ross (New York: Random House, 1941), sections 1103a.15–25, 1106a.15–23.

brave acts."[9] Because we develop moral habits over a lifetime, it matters a great deal how we behave ourselves as we learn what kind of persons we want to become. "It makes no small difference," Aristotle says, "whether we form habits of one kind or of another from our very youth; it makes a very great difference, or rather *all* the difference."[10] Morals, like manners, are part of the training young people receive in a society in order to help them function well and be successful at the business of being a human being.

The Moral Disposition

To put this in an Aristotelian context, consider what we mean by calling someone a moral person. To be moral does not mean that one occasionally performs a moral act; even immoral persons do moral things sometimes, but we would not call such a person moral just because of an occasional good deed. A truly moral person is one who has developed a moral disposition through the development of right habits and whose behavior is, as a result, consistently moral. This Aristotelian point is well summed up by a contemporary writer who points to the difference between *doing* something that is just or temperate and *being* a just or temperate person. It is the difference, he says, between being a good tennis player and merely having a lucky shot now and then. "What you mean by a good player is the man whose eye and muscles and nerves have been so trained by making innumerable good shots that they can now be relied on." In a similar way, he says, a person "who perseveres in doing just actions gets in the end a certain quality of character. Now it is that quality rather than the particular actions which we mean when we talk of 'virtue.'"[11]

As already mentioned, an important feature of a society that emphasizes virtue is that its values are conveyed through storytelling. A virtue-oriented society transmits its values through the telling and retelling of the deeds of the heroes of that cultural tradition. The goal of moral instruction is to develop the character traits similar to those of outstanding individuals, to model one's behavior after the examples of courage, fortitude, honesty, integrity, and loyalty of the tradition's cultural heroes. What does it mean to be honest? A story from our own cultural tradition that would serve as a model is from the life of Abraham Lincoln: while working as a shopkeeper's assistant, he walked several miles after work to return a few pennies to a woman he had inadvertently overcharged. The Horatio Alger stories are also models of how hard work, honesty, and pluck could allow a newspaper vendor to rise from rags to riches. Such stories provide models for developing behavior that is considered ethically upstanding. In contemporary society this storytelling feature has been taken over by popular culture media—films, television, mass market fiction, rap lyrics—and the values they extol may have more influence on the developing attitudes of young people than all the ethics classes offered in all the schools in the country.

How this relates to business contexts is apparent: if society's popular culture presents business leaders as rapacious scoundrels and business activity as opposing the public good, then the message transmitted to young people is that business is not an ethical activity and that to be successful in business demands the suspension of our ordinary standards of conduct. Within companies this same dynamic is at work. If the company's corporate culture is filled with stories of predatory business practices and legal but not necessarily moral activities, the message to employees is clear: do anything you have to do, cut any corners possible, to advance the company's interest.

Intrinsic and Instrumental Goods

Another feature of Aristotle's analysis of ethics is the important distinction between intrinsic and instrumental goods, though these are not the terms he used. An *intrinsic good* is something that is good in itself, like health. We seek health not just because it is good for something else but because it is something we desire for its own sake. Of course, good health allows us to do many other things we would be unable to do were we in poor health, but we don't desire health so we can hold a job, go to school, or take walks in the evening. We value health for its own sake as an intrinsic good. Other activities are important, therefore, because they contribute to health. We might like a steady diet of greasy hamburgers, but we have learned that vegetables are better. Instead of being a couch potato and letting our muscles atrophy, we know that good health requires regular exercise, so we jog, cycle, go to the health club, play basketball, or whatever, to aid our health. These activities are *instrumental goods;* that is, they contribute to our well-being by encouraging good health.

A moment's reflection shows that what is an instrumental good in one context can become an intrinsic good in another. Some joggers claim they find jogging pleasurable in its own right. For these persons,

---

HAPPINESS *(EUDAIMONIA)*

1 An intrinsic good
2 A lifetime pursuit
3 Must be sought indirectly

---

then, jogging is not just an instrumental good that contributes to their health, although they would still agree that health is a good. Aristotle would point out that if jogging is a component of what makes you happy, then it still is an instrumental good that you pursue for the intrinsic good of happiness. Although each of us may have different activities that bring happiness, we would probably all agree with Aristotle that happiness is the chief and intrinsic good for the sake of which we do all these other things. And we would all agree on a range of instrumental goods that are essential for happiness.

Another important aspect of Aristotle's views on happiness is that it is a goal reached by long-term behaviors, not short-term activity. This emphasis on long- versus short-term considerations set Aristotle apart from those—of both his contemporaries and ours—who advocate the immediacy of the reward. If we apply these concerns to a business context, we would have to say that business's intrinsic goal, like happiness, is long-term profitability.

BUSINESS AND PROFITS

The literature of philosophy is filled with discussions of profit, ranging from its eloquent defense by philosophers such as Adam Smith and John Locke to attacks from other philosophers such as Karl Marx (see Chapter 1). Today profit is viewed as potentially a contribution to the public good by providing the basis for job creation, economic growth, and technological innovation. Given the importance of profitability to business success, the question Aristotle helps us answer is what kind of behavior best aids a company's profitability. There are, to be sure, many public policy issues of economic justice and fairness and the proper role for government in attempting to keep the marketplace free.

There are others who disagree with this Aristotelian approach on purely economic grounds, one of the most well known of whom is the economist and Nobel Prize winner Milton Friedman. As was mentioned in Chapter 1, in a newspaper article that has been so widely reprinted that it has assumed something of the status of a classic, Friedman argues that the *only* social responsibility of business is to increase its profits.[12] His claim is based on the assumption that the corporate executive is responsible to the stockholders who entrusted their money to the company in order to gain a return on their investment. The shareholders may use their earnings for whatever social purposes they wish, but it is irresponsible, Friedman argues, for the executive officers to make those decisions for the stockholders by spending their money on a variety of social causes. At one level we could say that Friedman is correct: the intrinsic good for a business concern is to generate profits. But Friedman is in error when he maintains that a business can ignore its other commitments, for these are instrumental goods that contribute to its overall success.

The arguments against Friedman's narrow vision are compelling. Consider, for example, the quality (excellence, *aretē*) of a company's product. A firm might think that it could boost profits by cutting the quality of its product, perhaps in little ways that management thinks no one would notice. Or management might try to improve productivity by imposing harsh work rules on its employees. In their book *In Search of Excellence,* Tom Peters and Robert H. Waterman, Jr., give numerous examples of how successful companies attribute their success to goals other than profits: make a good product, treat your customers fairly, deal with your employees with attitudes of trust and support. In many successful companies, such as Ben & Jerry's, the social goals of the company are so strongly articulated that an observer might think that good works, not profitability, are the intrinsic goods for that company. But that could hardly be the case, because the ability to do good works, or to use Ben Cohen's phrase, "to celebrate our collective humanity," requires that the company be profitable; without profitability, none of the other goods the company seeks would be possible. Yet, in a remarkable interplay, the profitability of the company is improved by the company's commitment to larger social goals.

The research done by Peters and Waterman shows, however, that some managers are not clear on the need to focus on values other than profits. "Some colleagues who have heard us expound on the importance of values and distinctive cultures have said in effect, 'That's swell, but isn't it a luxury? Doesn't the business have to make money first?' The answer is that, of course, a business has to be fiscally sound. And the excellent companies are among the most fiscally sound of all. But their value set *integrates* the notions of economic health, serving cus-

A Case in Point . . .

Ben & Jerry's Homemade, Inc., started out as a single ice-cream parlor in Burlington, Vermont, but quickly caught the attention of investors through its ability to double in size every year through 1986. The company has been the subject of many news reports, including a documentary featured on PBS. What makes Ben & Jerry's remarkable, and an illustration of Aristotle's point, is that making profit and spawning a growth company was not the goal of the founders. Ben Cohen and Jerry Greenfield wanted a socially responsible company, one that valued making a good product and used its corporate influence for good works. When the company went public in order to generate necessary capital that would allow the company to grow, stock was first offered only to residents of Vermont, allowing the community to be the owner of the firm.

The founders view growth as a way of allowing the company to do more good works. Ben Cohen, chairman and co-founder of the company, says that one of the company's goals is "to celebrate our collective humanity and the interconnection of all things." The firm donates 7.5 percent of its pretax income to environmental and other causes, limits the maximum salary paid to executives to seven times the salary of the lowest paid worker, and has developed a corporate culture that puts the welfare of employees above everything else. In an article on a Ben & Jerry's annual meeting, the *Wall Street Journal* noted that "Ben & Jerry's has thrived on doing things differently—and playing it up to customers and shareholders." When the federal government lowered its milk support prices, Ben & Jerry's decided to continue paying a premium to its dairy suppliers to keep them from going under. In defending this strategy, Cohen said, "We refuse to profit off the misfortune of our dairy suppliers due to some antiquated, misguided, convoluted federal system." *Fortune* somewhat condescendingly referred to the company's "oddball blend of political activism and corporate social responsibility," but there is nothing oddball about its annual sales, which exceed $100 million.

Sources: Utne Reader, Jan./Feb. 1989, 64–75; FORB June 3, 1991; WSJ, Apr. 23, 1991, June 29, 1991, May 8, 1992; GQ, Apr. 1994.

tomers, and making meanings down the line." In language that could be straight from Aristotle, the authors go on to report, "As one executive said to us, 'Profit is like health. You need it, and the more the better. But it's not why you exist.' Moreover, in a piece of research that preceded this work, we found that companies whose only articulated goals were financial did not do nearly as well financially as companies that had broader sets of values."[13]

The Individual and the Organization

Consider, too, Aristotle's emphasis on the importance of friendship for the achievement of happiness. There is a business correlate here: although it does not seem appropriate to speak of a business having friends, it can have loyal customers, faithful stockholders, and dedicated workers. Part of the success of Japanese manufacturing has been attributed to its practice of cultivating networks of suppliers and distributors in what is called *keiretsu*. In such relationships, manufacturers and suppliers cooperate to produce the best product at the lowest cost. Lester Thurow, dean of MIT's Sloan School of Management, in his book *Head to Head: The Coming Economic Battle among Japan, Europe, and America,* describes this approach as a kind of preferential treatment that "comes in the form of buyers and sellers who are willing to work together to insure that the Japanese *keiretsu* supplier is in fact the best supplier." There are advantages to this form of social cooperation that translate into enhanced business activity. "As a group, *keiretsu* members have the advantages (size and coordination) of being a conglomerate without the disadvantages (excessive centralization) of being a conglomerate. Member companies pressure each other to grow and can coordinate their planning."[14]

The radical individualism that has characterized much of American business history is now being challenged effectively by systems that emphasize this kind of social cooperation and mutual loyalty of companies and their employees. It is precisely this issue that is at the center of current world competition, according to Thurow. He analyzes two forms of free market capitalism, which he labels "individualistic" capitalism and "communitarian" capitalism. The former characterizes business activity in the United States and Great Britain, the latter the economies of Japan and Germany.

Many of the practices of communitarian forms of capitalism would be considered illegal in the United States, given this country's commitment to antitrust legislation and distrust of large businesses. Thurow sees this contrast most clearly in the values that each form of capitalism encourages: "America and Britain trumpet individualistic values: the brilliant entrepreneur, Nobel Prize winners, large wage differentials, individual responsibility for skills, easy to fire and easy to quit, profit maximization, and hostile mergers and takeovers—their hero is the Lone Ranger. In contrast, Germany and Japan trumpet communitarian values: business groups, social responsibility for skills, teamwork, firm loyalty, industry strategies, and active industrial policies that promote

growth." Thurow thinks that differing attitudes toward business relationships also translate into differing business strategies. "Anglo-Saxon
firms are profit maximizers; Japanese business firms play a game that
might better be known as 'strategic conquest.' Americans believe in
'consumer economics'; Japanese believe in 'producer economics.'"[15]

Mentioning the two forms of capitalism here is not to argue that one
market system is better than the other. In fact, Thurow thinks that the
verdict is still out, that "in the long run history will tell us which theory is right."[16] The point is that value systems, or here we could say
the virtues to which the company aspires, drive business systems, and
one can tell what values a society has by the stories it tells. The radical
individualism of much contemporary thinking would have sounded
somewhat one-sided to Aristotle, for his ethical analysis stresses com-
munal goals, strong families, great city-states. The idea of a loner, in
fact, struck the Greeks as an aberration; they used a word from which
we derive the English "idiot" (from Greek meaning "one's own") to
describe persons who sought to go their own away apart from the
larger society. There are those who argue that the West needs to redis-
cover communitarian values, that the excessive emphasis on individual
achievement was precisely what led to some of the excesses of the
1980s. Robert N. Bellah's book *Habits of the Heart* is one example of
a growing literature that speaks to this theme. In the United States
there also appears to be some softening in the radical individualism of
business practices in the development of what is coming to be called
the "virtual corporation," a business model that links up suppliers and
producers in networks that are assembled for special projects, then
reassembled for different ones.[17]

Both in Aristotle's ethics and in communitarian forms of capitalism,
individuals find meaning in being part of a larger whole. For Aristotle,
this starts with the family, circles of social friendships, then the political entity. Although organized productive enterprises such as the modern corporation were unknown to Aristotle, it is not difficult to extrap-
olate from his writings to see how he would react to modern business
activity. It would have struck him as somewhat unnatural for an individual to feel no loyalty to a business organization or for the business
to feel no loyalty to its workers. In contrasting the two forms of capitalism, Thurow points out that "firms that effectively provide security
to generate group solidarity obtain employees who are more directed in
their focus, more willing to mobilize and prolong their effort to meet
firm goals, more willing to sacrifice immediate self-interests, and more

interested in achieving the goals of the firm." In contrast to this communitarian approach, the "Angle-Saxon-shareholder wealth-maximization view of the firm explicitly denies the legitimacy of the group. Only individual capitalists count. All other humans are simply rented factors of production."[18] This extreme approach to personal business relationships need not characterize Western forms of capitalism; indeed, according to Tom Peters and Nancy Austin, the best-run American companies are already establishing "almost familial relations between suppliers and producers."[19] And there are those who argue that it is time to abandon our fear of interbusiness cooperation and change the laws that discourage such coalition building.

Discussing the differences—the advantages and disadvantages—of individualistic versus communitarian forms of capitalism takes us into the realm of economic theory, social policy, public welfare provisions, even empirically driven decisions on monetary and industrial policies. All these issues, important as they are, go beyond the scope of this discussion. What is clear, from reading both Aristotle as well as the contemporary literature on business practice, is that *people matter*. Whether the people are workers or customers, how businesses treat people is a key to their success. Again, Peters and Waterman are guides here when

---

ARISTOTLE ON MODERATION

Excess	Deficiency	Mean
irascibility	lack of feeling	gentleness
foolhardiness	cowardice	bravery
shamelessness	shyness	modesty
intemperance	insensibility	temperance
envy	(unnamed)	righteous indignation
gain	loss	the just
lavishness	meanness	liberality
boastfulness	self-depreciation	sincerity
habit of flattery	habit of dislike	friendliness
servility	stubborness	dignity
vanity	meanness of spirit	greatness of spirit
extravagance	pettiness	magnificence
cunning	simplicity	wisdom

Source: Aristotle, *Eudemian Ethics*, trans. J. Solomon, in *The Complete Works of Aristotle*, ed. Jonathan Barnes (Princeton NJ: Princeton University Press, 1984), vol. II, p. 1933.

they say, "The excellent companies have a deeply ingrained philosophy that says, in effect, 'respect the individual,' 'make people winners,' 'let them stand out,' 'treat people as adults.'"[20] Perhaps no topic dominates business ethics more than how business treats people, and subsequent chapters in this book deal with this important topic in more depth.

The Role of Moderation

One could argue, that the two value systems are not mutually incompatible, that a middle ground would combine the social cooperation of communitarian forms of capitalism with the initiative of individualistic forms of capitalism, thereby capturing the best features of both. Such an approach would incorporate another Aristotelian theme: moderation in all things through seeking the mean between extremes. Here is how Aristotle defines virtue: "Virtue, then, is a state of character concerned with choice, lying in a mean, i.e., the mean relative to us, this being determined by a rational principle, and by that principle by which the man of practical wisdom would determine it."[21] Applying this principle leads Aristotle, in another work on ethics, entitled *Eudemian Ethics,* to lay out a series of moderate actions that lie between excess and deficiency. Notice how often in discussing ethical issues in business the term "excesses" is used, as when the business press speaks of the "excesses of the eighties" or when taxation is aimed at "excess profits" or "windfall profits." Aristotle's analysis seems to describe an important aspect of ethical behavior when he counsels moderation in all things, although he is quick to point out that not all activities can be so analyzed. There is no moderation possible in murder, theft, or adultery.

Many people seem to think that corporate moral behavior is at complete odds with business survival, that ethical action is opposed to corporate profit goals. Harvard Business School professors Kenneth E. Goodpaster and John B. Matthews, Jr., respond to this misunderstanding in good Aristotelian fashion in their *Harvard Business Review* article "Can a Corporation Have a Conscience?" Replying to the objection that corporations cannot be expected to sacrifice profit for moral responsibility, Goodpaster and Matthews reply, "We must of course acknowledge the imperatives of survival, stability, and growth when we discuss corporations, as indeed we must acknowledge them when we discuss the life of an individual. Self-sacrifice has been identified with moral responsibility in only the most extreme cases. The pursuit of

A Case in Point . . .

Robert Kierlin and several of his friends started a specialty fastener company with $30,000 they scraped together in 1967. The company that resulted, Fastenal, offers a wide range of fastening products and generates more than $60 million in annual sales. The company has located its 190-plus stores mainly in small towns and has developed a corporate culture that emphasizes quality and service. "There is no such answer as 'Sorry, we don't carry it' in Fastenal's lexicon," according to company co-founder Steve Slaggie. Both *Business Week* and *Forbes* have listed Fastenal as among the best small companies. The firm's corporate culture stresses decentralization and equality among management, stockholders, and employees. There are no assigned parking spaces at the company headquarters; when asked why he always got the best parking place, CEO Robert Kierlin replied, "I am always the first one to work." Other stories that embody the company's culture are the example of the executive who drove a delivery truck through a snowstorm to deliver a needed product after all the regular truck drivers had gone home, and the craftsmen in the company factory who worked over a weekend to make a fastener that was delivered Monday morning and saved the customer half a million dollars in production costs. When an interviewer asked the company president how he developed the values he brings to his company, he reported that while growing up he knew several successful business executives who were committed to ethical business practices, and he wanted to be like them.

Sources: Fastenal's 1991 annual report; FORB, Nov. 9, 1992; Rochester (Minnesota) *Post-Bulletin,* May 27, 1989; *Minneapolis Star and Tribune;* interviews by Marty Coady.

profit and self-interest need not be pitted against the demands of moral responsibility."[22]

The theme of moderation also reinforces the Aristotelian emphasis referred to earlier, that one's enlightened self-interest—and, by extension, a company's interest and profitability—can be best served when the individual or company focuses on other values. Happiness, and profit, accompany the achievement of other goals. The testimony of business leaders on this point is compelling. Tom Peters and Nancy Austin cite the following statement from Edson P. Williams, a vice president of Ford Motor Company and general manager of Ford Truck Operations: "I'd have to say that [before the events of the last four tough years] our culture in the Ford Motor Company said that there's one central objective in our business, and that's to earn a return on our investment. I think we've now learned there's something else that's central—and that profits will fall to you if you view this as central: serve the customer." Acknowledging that costs and quality are important, he goes on to add, "But we must always think the customer is the middle of the thrust of what we're trying to do. I think that's what we've learned. I don't think it's more complicated than that."[23]

MORAL DEVELOPMENT

Although Aristotle was convinced that people develop their moral character over time and through habituation, he did not describe how this happens. That kind of descriptive information has been supplied by Harvard psychologist Lawrence Kohlberg, whose experimental data tracking individual moral development provide an interesting corollary to Aristotle's claims. Director of Harvard's Center for Moral Education, Kohlberg centered his research on describing the stages of moral development and the various stages through which individuals pass as they mature in their moral judgments.

Kohlberg divides moral development into three stages which he calls the "preconventional," "conventional," and "postconventional." Each of these has two levels, giving a total of six possible stages of moral development. The preconventional level is the one of punishment and reward. The conventional level is one in which we seek the approval of others and submit to authority. The postconventional level is the highest level of moral development in which people seek the general welfare and act according to universal moral principles.

Equally interesting, however, are several conclusions Kohlberg made about moral development. He found that people move forward, never backward, through these stages (except in the cases of extreme trauma). Also, individuals do not skip stages; that is, they do not go directly from the preconventional to the postconventional, for example. Kohlberg's research also found that persons at one level can correctly classify statements representing the lower levels but not those referring to higher levels of moral development. It also is the case that moral development is in no way correlated with intelligence.[24] Implicit in Kohlberg's view is that some of these levels of moral development are more advanced—such as thinking in terms of universal moral principles—than others whose values are based on reciprocity—"You scratch my back and I'll scratch yours." Conflicts in moral judgments often result from interactions of people who are at different stages of their

KOHLBERG'S MORAL LEVELS

I. Preconventional level

1. *The punishment-and-obedience orientation.* The physical consequences of action determine its goodness or badness. Avoidance of punishment and unquestioning deference to power are valued in their own right, not in terms of respect for an underlying moral order supported by punishment and authority.

2. *The instrumental-relativist orientation.* Right action consists of that which instrumentally satisfied one's own needs and occasionally the needs of others. Human relations are viewed in terms like those of the marketplace. Elements of fairness, of reciprocity, and of equal sharing are present, but they are always interpreted in a physical, pragmatic way. Reciprocity is a matter of "You scratch my back and I'll scratch yours," not out of loyalty, gratitude, or justice.

II. The conventional level

3. *The interpersonal concordance or "good boy–nice girl" orientation.* Good behavior is that which pleases or helps others and is approved by them. There is much conformity to stereotypical images of what is majority or "natural" behavior. Behavior is frequently judged by intention. "He means well" becomes important for the first time. One earns approval by being "nice."

4. *The "law-and-order" orientation.* There is orientation toward authority, fixed rules, and the maintenance of the social order. Right behavior consists of doing one's duty, showing respect for authority, and maintaining the given social order for its own sake.

III. Postconventional, autonomous, or principled level

5. *The social-contract, legalistic orientation.* This has utilitarian overtones. Right action tends to be defined in terms of general individual rights and standards which have been critically examined and agreed to by the whole society. Emphasis upon the legal point of view but with the possibility of changing the law in terms of rational considerations. This is the "official" morality of the American government and Constitution.

6. *The universal-ethical principle orientation.* Right is defined by the decision of conscience in accord with self-chosen ethical principles appealing to logical comprehensiveness, universality, and consistency. These principles are abstract and ethical (the Golden Rule, the "categorical imperative"* of Kant but *not* such concrete rules as the Ten Commandments).

*Kant's view that a moral principle is one that can be made a universal law.

Source: Lawrence Kohlberg, © *Journal of Philosophy,* Oct. 25, 1973. Used by permission.

moral development. You can imagine a conversation between a supervisor who is at the law-and-order orientation stage with an employee who is at the universal-ethical principle orientation level of moral development. Although Kohlberg's research focused only on individual moral development, a company's behavior might also be categorized in terms of place in the hierarchy of moral stages. This notion of a corporate culture, and its impact on the way a company does business, is explored in a later chapter.

DISCUSSION STARTERS

1 Why do you think the term "virtue" has ceased to be a prominent part of our ethical vocabulary? In what ways has the demise of this term signaled a change in our ethical attitudes?
2 List some of the popular stories that communicate moral values. Your list can include stories that embody both good and bad values. What influence do you think these stories have on the development of values in young people?
3 Explore what implications the term "excellence" has for business activity. What would it mean for a corporation to strive for excellence in its products? In its customer satisfaction? Employee attitudes? Shareholder relations?
4 Do you agree with Friedman that "the only social responsibility of business is to increase its profits"? What can be said in support of this view? Against it? If you were arguing against Friedman's statement, what arguments would you give?
5 Is there any sense in which you are convinced that Aristotle's emphasis on friendship is applicable to contemporary business activity? How would you reconcile this with the prevailing view that business is a dog-eat-dog competitive struggle?
6 Show how moderation is a key to applying Aristotle's ethical analysis. What is the role of reason (versus, say, emotion or tradition) in business practice?

NOTES

1 A thorough discussion of virtue theory and its emotive alternatives is given by Alasdair MacIntyre, *After Virtue*, 2nd ed. (Notre Dame, IN: University of Notre Dame Press, 1984). A good source of discussion about virtue theory, and MacIntyre's interpretation of it, can be found in Robert B. Kruschwitz and Robert C. Roberts, *The Virtues: Contemporary Essays on Moral Character* (Belmont, CA: Wadsworth, 1987).
2 MacIntyre, *After Virtue*, p. 277.
3 Aristotle, *Nicomachean Ethics*, 1097a.35.

4 Ibid., 1098a.18–19.

5 Ibid., 1177a.7.

6 For a discussion of the term, see F. E. Peters, *Greek Philosophical Terms* (New York: New York University Press, 1967), p. 25.

7 MacIntyre, *After Virtue*, p. 6.

8 Ibid., p. 59.

9 Aristotle, *Nicomachean Ethics*, 1103b.1–3. W. D. Ross's translation is used throughout.

10 Ibid., 1103b.24–25.

11 C. S. Lewis, *Mere Christianity* (New York: Macmillan, 1952), p. 77.

12 Milton Friedman, "The Social Responsibility of Business Is to Increase Its Profits," *New York Times Magazine*, Sept. 13, 1970.

13 Thomas J. Peters and Robert H. Waterman, Jr., *In Search of Excellence: Lessons from America's Best-Run Companies* (New York: Harper & Row, 1982), p. 103.

14 Lester Thurow, *Head to Head: The Coming Economic Battle among Japan, Europe, and America* (New York: Morrow, 1992), pp. 134–135.

15 Ibid., p. 32.

16 Ibid., p. 151.

17 See BW, Feb. 8, 1993.

18 Thurow, *Head to Head*, pp. 123–124.

19 Tom Peters and Nancy Austin, *A Passion for Excellence: The Leadership Difference* (New York: Random House, 1985), p. 20.

20 Peters and Waterman, *In Search of Excellence*, p. 282.

21 Aristotle, *Nicomachean Ethics*, 1107a.1–3.

22 Kenneth E. Goodpaster and John B. Matthews, Jr., "Can a Corporation Have a Conscience?" HBR, Jan.–Feb. 1982.

23 Peters and Austin, *A Passion for Excellence*, p. 38.

24 See Lawrence Kohlberg, "Stage and Sequence: The Cognitive-Developmental Approach to Socialization," in David A. Goslin, ed. *Handbook of Socialization Theory and Research* (Chicago: Rand McNally, 1969).

CASE STUDY

One of the claims of virtue ethics is that moral values are transmitted through the telling of stories, principally stories about important people. The development of a corporate culture with strong moral values comes about in similar ways, with stories about the company's founders and other executive officers often providing the framework for employees to understand the moral commitments of the company. The Lorain Products Company clearly took on the values and moral commitments of its founder, Paul Stocker. Even through its first merger these qualities remained part of the firm's corporate culture. The parent company, Reliance Electric, was later acquired by an affiliate of Exxon, and subsequently was purchased by management in a leveraged buyout. An important question is what happens to a corporate culture as companies are acquired, merge with other companies, are sold to still other corporate entities, or, as was the case with Reliance Electric, become once again an independent entity.

BUILDING A CORPORATE CULTURE AT LORAIN PRODUCTS

In the late 1930s, the United States was leading the world in the number of telephones, and long-distance calling was increasing at a rate of over 6 percent a year. However, some of the equipment used in local exchanges frequently failed, none more so than the ringing generators that provided power to actually ring the phones. A contributing cause of the frequent breakdowns was the fact that the ringing generators were composed of numerous moving parts.

A young engineer from Ohio named Paul Stocker invented an improved instrument, which he called the Sub-Cycle. It contained no moving parts and was an immediate success in the telephone industry. Its purchasers, which included the Western Electric Company as well as many small telephone cooperatives, reported that the Sub-Cycle seldom needed maintenance and was a great improvement over previous technology. Stocker's company, Lorain Products, based its product line on the production of the Sub-Cycle.

Troubling reports started arriving from purchasers of the Sub-Cycle, first from coastal areas and later from other parts of the country. The complaint was that the starting switches stayed in the closed position after a power failure, and attempts to reenergize the machine were unsuccessful. Stocker and his small engineering staff discovered the problem to be the cadmium plating on a relay. They concluded that the breakdowns would be eliminated by changing to chromium plating. Though the fix was technically possible, replacing defective Sub-Cycles

---

Information for this case and direct quotations are from David Neal Keller, *C. Paul Stocker: His Life and Legacy.* Copyright © 1991, Ohio University Press. Used by permission of The Russ College of Engineering and Technology.

could be a financial disaster for the small company. Nonetheless, Lorain Products placed advertisements in telephone trade publications offering to replace any frozen Sub-Cycle free of charge even if it was out of warranty, with Lorain Products paying freight both ways.

The company was small and had limited resources, and this gesture almost brought the firm to insolvency. Yet Stocker was convinced that the ultimate success of the company depended on the absolute integrity of its operation, and he borrowed money to make good on his guarantee. His commitment to integrity paid off. The reputation of Lorain Products soared, its product line expanded.

In time the company expanded its line as the telecommunications industry grew, and its customers included the U.S. government and some of the largest communications companies in the country, such as Western Electric, General Telephone, and the Bell System. As the company grew, so did its commitment to its employees. In addition to a company-paid retirement plan, it established an employee profit sharing plan with a commitment to distribute 15 percent of pretax profits to employees. The distribution of the profit sharing checks occurred at an annual meeting at which Mr. Stocker presided and attended by all employees. By the mid 1960s the company had enlarged its facilities, and the number of employees had increased to the point that many presidents would have given up on the attempt to maintain personal relations with company employees. Stocker's biographer records that Paul Stocker worked diligently to prevent a rigid hierarchical organization.

> Still adamant in his belief that excess levels of hierarchy worked counter to effective decision making in many corporations, Stocker intended to keep the structure simple and direct at Lorain Products. His door remained open to all employees, and he continued his "walk around" method of management, greeting each person with a "Good morning," regardless of the time of day. When suggestions arose on changing the hours of working schedules, Stocker had employees select alternatives through a company-wide vote.

The Stocker style of management lives on in stories told by executive officers of the company. Frank Borer, a service manager for the company, recalls, "Stocker's intelligence always came through, but he was a very humble man. And you know, people liked that combination. Customers appreciated it. And so did all of us at the company. It was just ingrained in him. He didn't have to act modest; he *was* modest. On one sales trip, the two of us were walking down a street in New York City and he stopped to get us each an apple, then he pulled out that sharp knife of his and cut off slices, eating them as we walked. Things like that made you always feel at ease with your president, but it wasn't playacting. That's just the way he was." Another employee recalled that "Paul seemed surprised that I considered it unusual for him to drive the Bell Telephone System president from the airport to our plant in his Volkswagen Bug."

In 1973 Stocker agreed to a merger with Reliance Electric in a $37 million stock swap. Stocker's health forced him to step down as president, and he was succeeded by Martin Huge, who had been with the company since his graduation from college. When he assumed the presidency of the now wholly owned subsidiary of Reliance Electric, Huge reflected on the company's corporate values in his initial statement to employees as the company's new president.

> Moving into the position of president of Lorain Products is certainly a challenge and an opportunity for which I am most grateful. At the outset I would like you all to know, however, that I do not consider myself as exactly stepping into the shoes of Mr. Stocker. The tremendous job he has done in building Lorain Products into the organization we have today commands a special kind of respect. The name Lorain Products Corporation is closely identified with the name of C. Paul Stocker, and the Lorain Products name today is recognized by customers, suppliers, and employees alike as meaning highest quality and unquestioned integrity in products, in services, and in personal relationships. This is the structure Mr. Stocker has built, and it now becomes not just my responsibility, but *our* responsibility as a team to continue to build on this structure while maintaining its essential qualities. In joining with Reliance Electric Company, we believe we are joining an organization which will enable us to carry on in the Stocker tradition. . . .
>
> If I were to tell you that nothing is going to change under the new setup I would not be completely honest. Not everything can be exactly the same as it has been, but I want to assure you that I am committed to maintain those policies and practices which have helped Lorain Products grow and which have made working here a satisfying experience.
>
> First among these is fair treatment for each person as an individual and the opportunity for each person to be heard when the need arises. We have called this our open door policy. It has worked in the past and we want to keep it working. . . . I hope the spirit of teamwork that has been a Lorain Products tradition will continue and grow. To have a winning team, we need the best efforts of everyone, and we expect to give recognition to contributions to that effort.

In 1979 Reliance Electric Company was purchased by ENCO, Inc., a subsidiary of Exxon Corporation, who was looking for a company that could mass produce an energy-saving device that its own engineers had been developing at its own research labs. The device would improve the efficiency of electric motors through the use of microprocessors. The acquisition occurred, but the project that brought about the acquisition was abandoned. During the slump in oil prices in the early eighties, Exxon announced that it was selling Reliance Electric Company to a group of executive officers who arranged a leveraged buyout through Citicorp Capital Investors and Prudential-Bache Securities for a price of $1.35 billion.

The vice president and general manager of the Lorain Products division was Pete Paradissis, who had been recruited into the company originally by Paul Stocker. Stocker's biographer reports that the corporate culture instilled in the company by its founder continues to be important in the newly independent corporate entity.

> Indeed, the new head of Lorain Products acquired much of his business philosophy from the company's founder, particularly his belief in getting to know employees by visiting them regularly at their jobs.
>
> On the wall of his new office, where he had been interviewed as a prospective employee twenty-eight years earlier, Paradissis hung a plaque he had received from employees of the Canadian plant he headed for two years. Under the bronze replica of a shoe were the words, "MBWA Award 1986–1988.". . . MBWA, of course, stood for Management by Walking Around.

CHAPTER 3

The Ethical Basis of Cost-Benefits Analysis

CHAPTER OUTLINE

UTILITARIANISM
   Utilitarian Theory
   Hedonistic and Ideal Utilitarianism
   Rule and Act Utilitarianism

UTILITARIAN APPLICATIONS IN BUSINESS
   Cost-Benefits Analysis
   Uncertainty of Outcomes
   The Role of Compromise
   Protecting Individuals

UTILITARIAN DEFENSES OF THE FREE MARKET

Richard H. Brown
President and CEO H&R Block, Inc.

"There's a lot more to balance than not falling down. Similarly, business ethics is not merely a defensive strategy—following the law to avoid financial penalties or a stint in jail. It's a positive approach that says we'll see a much better response from our customers and our employees if we treat them honorably."

An old saying sometimes used to justify an action that might otherwise cause ethical discomfort is "the end justifies the means." The ends of an action are the consequences to be obtained; the means are the actions that produce the desired results. In its extreme form the statement "the end justifies the means" would be the claim that the consequences are the only important thing, that if the end to be achieved is good, then anything necessary to achieve that end is good also. Even lying, cheating, stealing, and killing would be considered ethically acceptable so long as the end to be achieved is good.

Put in this form, hardly anyone would agree that the claim "the end justifies the means" states an acceptable principle, for it would imply that the *only* consideration is the end to be achieved. But we need not take such an extreme position; it has been argued that the consequences of an action are ethically significant, that all the best motives in the world are of no value unless a moral result is achieved. Views that claim that consequences are important for assessing the moral worth of an action are called "consequentialist" views, for the obvious reason that they emphasize consequences. There are a variety of consequentialist views, but in this chapter we consider in some detail the view known as utilitarianism and its business applications in the form of cost-benefits analysis. Before looking at the pluses and minuses of applying consequentialist thinking to business decisions, let's examine more closely the theoretical framework of this view.

UTILITARIANISM

Utilitarian Theory

Utilitarianism is the name applied to an ethical theory formulated by such nineteenth-century thinkers as Jeremy Bentham (1784–1832), James Mill (1773–1836), and John Stuart Mill (1806–1873). This approach places the moral worth of an action in the action's consequences and emphasizes the good of the total society, not the benefits accruing to a single individual or even a group of individuals. Utilitarians sought to provide legislators with a clear and scientific method for evaluating legislative options. An early leader of the utilitarian movement, Jeremy Bentham produced a book for legislators entitled *An Introduction to the Principles of Morals and Legislation*, which laid out the utilitarian proposal to base moral judgments on the *principle of utility*. The attractiveness of this formula is that it was quantifiable, or so Bentham argues; one can add up all the positive aspects of a decision, contrast them with all the negative aspects, and then make the decision on the grounds of producing the greatest happiness for the greatest number of people. For Bentham, the matter was simple: pain is bad, pleasure is good. If an action produces a sum total of more pain than pleasure (again, for the greatest number of people), then the only consequence to be considered is the action's tendency to produce pleasure and avoid pain.

As articulated by Mill and Bentham, utilitarianism aims not for the pleasure of the individual but the "greatest good for the greatest number" of people. Refined by its later interpreters, utilitarianism also rejects a simplistic belief in pursuing the most pleasure possible in favor of the view that incorporates qualitative standards and elevates pleasures of the mind over pleasures of the body. The term "happiness" seems to capture this broadened sense best, and utilitarians sometimes call their principle the "greatest happiness principle."

Critics of utilitarianism have charged that it is not a total approach to ethical decision making, for by concentrating on the consequences of

---

JOHN STUART MILL ON HUMAN SOCIETY

Now there is absolutely no reason in the nature of things why an amount of mental culture sufficient to give an intelligent interest in these objects of contemplation should not be the inheritance of everyone born in a civilized country. As little is there an inherent necessity that any human being should be a selfish egotist, devoid of every feeling or care but those which center in his own miserable individuality. . . . Yet no one whose opinion deserves a moment's consideration can doubt that most of the great positive evils of the world are in themselves removable, and will, if human affairs continue to improve, be in the end reduced within narrow limits. Poverty, in any sense implying suffering, may be completely extinguished by the wisdom of society combined with the good sense and providence of individuals. Even that most intractable of enemies, disease, may be indefinitely reduced in dimensions by good physical and moral education and proper control of noxious influences, while the progress of science holds out a promise for the future of still more direct conquests over this detestable foe. . . . All the grand sources, in short, of human suffering are in great degree, many of them almost entirely, conquerable by human care and effort; and though their removal is grievously slow . . . yet every mind sufficiently intelligent and generous to bear a part, however small and inconspicuous, in the endeavor will draw a noble enjoyment from the contest itself, which he would not for any bribe in the form of selfish indulgence consent to be without.

Source: John Stuart Mill, *Utilitarianism,* Chapter II, "What Utilitarianism Is."

UTILITARIAN ETHICS

"Greatest good for the greatest number"

- Emphasis on consequences and outcomes
- Business form is cost-benefits analysis
- Difficulties with:
  Individual rights
  Rights of minorities

---

actions it ignores intentions and motives, which are also important in moral decision making. The limits of utilitarian considerations can also be seen in a business context in what is known as *cost-benefits analysis,* a process wherein the monetary costs of a certain course of action are weighed against the benefits to be gained in contrast to other pos-

---

BENTHAM'S HEDONISTIC CALCULUS

Pleasures then, and the avoidance of pains, are the *ends* which the legislator has in view; it behooves him therefore to understand their *value*. Pleasures and pains are the *instruments* he has to work with. . . .

To a *number* of persons, with reference to each of whom the value of a pleasure or a pain is considered, it will be greater or less, according to seven circumstances:

1 Its *intensity.*
2 Its *duration.*
3 Its *certainty or uncertainty.*
4 Its *propinquity* or *remoteness.*
5 Its *fecundity* [or the chance it has of being followed by sensations of the same].
6 Its *purity* [or the chance it has of not being followed by sensations of the opposite kind].
7 Its *extent;* that is, the number of persons to whom it extends or (in other words) who are affected by it. . . .

Sum up all the values of all the *pleasures* on the one side, and those of all the pains on the other. The balance, if it be on the side of pleasure, will give the *good* tendency of the act . . . if on the side of pain, the *bad* tendency of it upon the whole.

Take an account of the number of persons whose interest appears to be concerned, and repeat the above process with respect to each. Sum up the numbers . . . the same process is alike applicable to pleasure and pain, in whatever shape they appear, and by whatever denomination they are distinguished.

Source: Jeremy Bentham, *Introduction to Principles of Morals and Legislation,* Chapter 4.

sible actions. Utilitarianism also faces limitations in its seeming inability—on the grounds of the greatest happiness principle alone—to deal adequately with the rights of individuals and minority groups. If, for example, the greatest happiness of the greatest number of people can be secured by denying rights to small groups, then the utilitarian principle would seem to be unable to reject this unethical conclusion. John Stuart Mill responds to some of these criticisms in Chapter 5 of his work *Utilitarianism,* giving attention especially to the concept of justice, which he claims can be derived from considerations of utility. In addition, recent interpreters of utilitarianism have modified it in an effort to avoid these problems, although there is still disagreement over whether these attempts are successful. Regardless of the outcome of the debates among philosophers regarding utilitarianism's ability to embrace standards of rights and justice, all philosophers agree that these two important ethical principles must be part of an overall approach to ethics, and we devote additional considerations to them in the following chapter.

Perhaps the best-known advocate of utilitarian views, and the one whose work *Utilitarianism* is taken as the definitive statement of this approach to ethics, is John Stuart Mill. In this work he sums up the basic principle of utilitarianism as follows:

> The creed which accepts as the foundations of morals Utility, or the Greatest Happiness Principle, holds that actions are right in proportion as they tend to promote happiness, wrong as they tend to produce the reverse of happiness. By happiness is intended pleasure and the absence of pain; by unhappiness, pain and the absence of pleasure.

Like the ancient Greek philosopher Epicurus, the utilitarians are hedonists, that is, they see pleasure as the intrinsic good. Also like Epicurus, they argue that many factors enter into the estimation of the pleasure-pain equation: the long-term effects of an action, its tendency to promoting additional pleasure rather than producing pain, its certainty or uncertainty, and its intensity, duration, and the difficulty or ease of achieving it. In the second edition of *Introduction to Principles of Morals and Legislation,* Bentham even includes a bit of doggerel that he thought summed up his moral philosophy nicely:

Intense, long, certain, speedy, fruitful, pure—
Such marks in *pleasures* and in *pains* endure.
Such pleasures seek, if *private* be thy end;
If it be *public,* wide let them *extend.*

Such *pains* avoid, whichever be thy view;
If pains *must* come, let them *extend* to few.[1]

Unlike Epicurus and other hedonists, however, the utilitarians do not look toward an individual's pleasure but seek instead the greatest good for society as a whole. They see themselves as social reformers and have tried, in some cases successfully, to influence legislation that would promote the common good.

As you first read the utilitarians it may seem that there is great similarity between their views and Aristotle's analysis of pleasure and that good at which all other human activities aim. Although both the utilitarians and Aristotle are, in some broad sense, consequentialists in ethics (that is, they judge the morality of actions by their outcomes), there the similarity ends. Aristotle's ethical theory is based on a complex worldview that determines the excellence of an object by how well it fulfills its intended function and reflects its unique nature. The essential function of human beings is reason, and the ethical life is one that is ruled by reason and that tends toward moderation in all things. Aristotle's ethics are developmental as well, emphasizing the formation of moral habits over a long period of time and a lifestyle emphasizing those most human aspects of our nature. Utilitarian views imply that the considerations of utility could be used without the development of a moral disposition as Aristotle proposes.

It still sounds like we are back with Aristotle: the utilitarians insist on pleasure as the measure of the good life; Aristotle argues for happiness as the goal of life. Are the two synonymous? At first glance it might seem that they are, as pleasure could be seen as bringing happiness. Or does it? Remember that Aristotle argues that happiness describes a much longer time frame than does pleasure. A second, and perhaps more important, difference is that Bentham emphasizes only quantitative measures, whereas Aristotle's pursuit of happiness involves qualitative measures that call for a cognitive judgment. We may not be

---

DIFFERENCES BETWEEN PLEASURE AND HAPPINESS

1 Pleasure is quantitative; happiness is qualitative.
2 Happiness is a lifelong goal.
3 Happiness requires a cognitive judgment.
4 Pleasure is not essential to achieving happiness.

able to say at any given moment whether we are happy or not, but we certainly know whether we are feeling pleasure or feeling pain. For Aristotle, happiness, in the sense of total well-being, is the goal of life, and it may even be the case that pleasure is unnecessary to achieve that goal, or at least is incidental to it.

Hedonistic and Ideal Utilitarianism

The initial appeal of utilitarianism is its apparent straightforward simplicity: pain is bad, pleasure is good. Actions that provide the greatest good for the greatest number are moral. As ethical theory, however, Bentham's utilitarianism has several flaws. Throughout Bentham's writings is an emphasis on quantifiable calculations. Indeed, his approach has sometimes been called a "hedonistic calculus." But there is a difficulty with this approach that becomes obvious, given a moment's reflection: How does one measure pleasure? And aren't some pleasures better than others? Bentham is unbending in his insistence on the sheer quantity of pleasure as the only important variable in his hedonistic calculus. "Pushpin is as good as poetry," he says. Pushpin was a kind of simple child's game, and the pleasures of such a pastime are as legitimate as are those of the finest poetry, or so Bentham thinks. Because of his emphasis on the quantity of pleasure as the measure of goodness, Bentham's version of utilitarianism later came to be called "hedonistic utilitarianism."

It seemed to other utilitarians, such as John Stuart Mill, that there is an important difference in the *quality* of various pleasures. Which is better, the pleasure of cheap wine or the enjoyment of a bottle of cabernet from a vintage year? We would want to say the latter, or at least those familiar with wines would. Mill also argues that the pleasures of the mind are superior to those of the physical side of our nature: "It is better to be a human being dissatisfied than a pig satisfied; better to be Socrates dissatisfied than a fool satisfied. And if the fool, or the pig, is of a different opinion, it is because they know only their side of the question." Mill's form of utilitarianism, which recognizes qualitative distinctions, not just the quantitative measures advocated by Bentham, has come to be called "ideal utilitarianism."

The introduction of qualitative distinctions, which seemed to be required to respond to one set of critics of the theory, led to another problem. Utilitarianism was supposed to be based on empirical principles. If you want to know what gives people pleasure, ask them. But now, with the introduction of qualitative distinctions, we are forced to

include the judgments of experts, those who know what the finer pleasures are. Even if a majority of people think a certain experience brings
them pleasure, the expert can say, "I realize all of you think that this
will bring you pleasure, but you are mistaken. The real pleasure is
something quite different. Just trust me." The empirical foundations of
the theory are undercut by the introduction of qualitative distinctions.
Yet J. S. Mill inserts qualitative distinctions into the theory to defend it
against those who claim utilitarianism is a degrading view that does
not include in its calculus the higher pleasures requiring human intellectual capacities—reason, aesthetic enjoyment, and the pleasure
derived from good conversation and lasting friendships.

MILL ON DISTINCTIONS OF QUALITY

When I am asked what I mean by difference of quality in pleasures, or what makes
one pleasure more valuable than another, merely as a pleasure, except its being
greater in amount, there is but one possible answer. Of two pleasures, if there be
one to which all or almost all who have experience of both give a decided preference, irrespective of any feeling of moral obligation to prefer it, that is the more desirable pleasure. If one of the two is, by those who are competently acquainted with
both, placed so far above the other that they prefer it, . . . we are justified in ascrib-
ing to the preferred enjoyment a superiority in quality so far outweighing quantity as
to render it, in comparison, of small account. . . .

From this verdict of the only competent judges, I apprehend there can be no
appeal. On a question which is the best worth having of two pleasures, or which of
two modes of existence is the most grateful to the feelings, apart from its moral
attributes and from its consequences, the judgment of those who are qualified by
knowledge of both, or, if they differ, that of the majority among them, must be admitted as final. . . .

According to the greatest happiness principle, as above explained, the ultimate
end, with reference to and for the sake of which all other things are desirable—
whether we are considering our own good or that of other people—is an existence
exempt as far as possible from pain, and as rich as possible in enjoyments, both in
point of quantity and quality; the test of quality and the rule for measuring it against
quantity being the preference felt by those who, in their opportunities of experience,
to which must be added their habits of self-consciousness and self-observation, are
best furnished with the means of comparison. This, being according to the utilitarian
opinion the end of human actions, is necessarily also the standard of morality which
may accordingly be defined "the rules and precepts for human conduct."

Source: John Stuart Mill, *Utilitarianism,* Chapter II, "What Utilitarianism Is".

A Case in Point . . .

In the 1960s the American automotive industry was facing stiff competition from German imports, the Volkswagen "beetle." To mount a credible challenge against this foreign invasion, Lee Iacocca, then vice president at Ford Motor Company and the executive responsible for the highly successful Ford Mustang, took on the task of beating the Germans at their own game. The plan: to make a subcompact car that would weigh 2,000 pounds and sell for $2,000, and to bring the auto into production in two years rather than the usual three and one-half years. The car was called the Pinto.

During the Pinto's development, Ford built and tested prototypes especially with a view toward proposed federal regulations that would require all automobiles built after 1972 to be able to withstand a 20-mile-per-hour impact without fuel spillage. The standards were to increase to 30 miles per hour in 1973. Ford engineers found that the prototypes, when struck from the rear at 20 miles per hour, suffered a ruptured fuel tank due to the tank's being driven forward onto the differential housing.

In a 1977 article in *Mother Jones,* writer Mark Dowie charged that Ford executives based their decision to go ahead with production on a cost-benefits analysis that contrasted the cost of fixing the fuel tank problem with accepting the legal settlements that would result from manufacturing the car with the known defect. The article charged that Ford analysts used statistics from the National Highway Traffic Safety Administration which estimated $200,000 as the social cost of a traffic death. The article further charged that Ford executives used this figure in a cost-benefits analysis that justified going ahead with production of the automobile rather than spending $11 per vehicle (which would have amounted to $137 million over the production life of the model). Ford denied both charges.

A notable trial in California focused attention on the case of Richard Grimshaw, a 13-year-old boy who was riding in a 1972 Pinto Hatchback owned by Mrs. Gray when it was hit from the rear after it stalled on a California freeway. The Pinto caught fire, and both Gray and Grimshaw were badly burned. Mrs. Lily Gray died a few days later, and Grimshaw had to undergo extensive surgery and skin grafting over a ten-year period. Mrs. Gray's car was stalled, hence stationary, when struck from the rear by a large truck traveling more than 40 miles per hour. Even severe critics of Ford have pointed out that no car could have survived such a crash without serious injuries to the occupants. A California jury awarded Grimshaw $2.5 million in compensatory damages and $125 million in punitive damages (reduced to $3.5 million by the appeals court). The heirs of Mrs. Gray were awarded slightly more than half a million dollars.

The jury's decision seems to have been due in large part to the evidence brought out in the trial that engineers had proposed over ten different ways of remedying the design defect, most of which cost less than the $11 Ford used in its analysis and some of which cost under $3. The inference drawn was that, because of the expense that would be required to make the car safer, the company was willing to put people at risk. Ford's defense was that it was obeying all applicable laws and was making an automobile as safe as any others of its size and type. The jury disagreed. In the aftermath of this and other suits, Ford spent millions in lawsuits and out-of-court settlements.

Sources: App., 174 Cal. Trpt. 348; *Mother Jones,* Sept./Oct. 1977; W. Michael Hoffman, in *Case Studies in Business Ethics* (Englewood Cliffs, NJ: Prentice-Hall, 1984); William H. Shaw, *Business Ethics* (Belmont, CA: Wadsworth, 1991); press release by Herbert L. Misch, vice president—Environmental and Safety Engineering Staff, Ford Motor Company, 9/26/77; Lee Iacocca, *An Autobiography* (New York: Bantam, 1984), pp. 161–162; and conversations with Jerry Sloan, former executive director of public affairs, Ford Motor Company.

Rule and Act Utilitarianism

The application of utilitarian theory has other problems as well. For example, it is entirely conceivable that an unethical action could be defended on utilitarian grounds. If we could demonstrate that society as a whole would benefit by severely restricting the rights of a minority of the population, there is little in utilitarian theory that could argue against it. Or if we could show that the greatest good would be enhanced by breaking a law, then it would be difficult to give utilitarian reasons against proceeding with the action. Our own history contains examples of just such kinds of conduct. During World War II, the United States government interned thousands of Americans of Japanese ancestry and relocated them to deserts in the American West, even though they had done nothing wrong and gave no evidence of even intending to be disloyal to the war effort. The rationale for this action was that it was in the interest of national defense. The government of the United States has since officially apologized and made token reparations to those affected by its actions. More recently, those who sought to subvert the will of Congress by diverting funds to Central American rebels were also doing it in the name of national security. In the case of the internment of Japanese Americans, basic human rights were being violated for the sake of the good of society. In the case of arms for rebels, the will of Congress, a constitutional and representative assembly, was subverted in the name of national security.

Mill addresses these issues in the last chapter of *Utilitarianism,* for they are obvious difficulties in utilitarian theory. Mill also wrote an impassioned defense of liberty and a book advocating the equality of women.[2] In both cases he argues that no amount of general good for society would justify infringements of personal liberty or the restriction of women's rights. In his arguments Mill sets up the outline of a modification of utilitarian thought that has, since his time, come to be called "rule utilitarianism." According to rule utilitarians, we should not use utilitarian principles on a case-by-case basis. Not only would this take an enormous amount of time, it would also open the door to abuses of the kind mentioned above. Utilitarian principles should be used to develop and defend rules that will bring about the best consequences for society in the long run and provide the stability and security desired both by individuals and by the business community.[3] Rules like "always tell the truth," "obey the law," and "respect the rights of others at all times" are examples.

The version of utilitarianism that did not appeal to general rules but judged the rightness or wrongness of each act by its tendency to bring about the greatest good for the greatest number came to be called "act utilitarianism." In its more recent forms, rule utilitarianism begins to sound a lot like the kind of ethical theory that is introduced in the next chapter, the deontological approach, which judges the morality of an action by whether it conforms to the demands of duty and whether the action can be judged to be universalized without contradiction.

UTILITARIAN APPLICATIONS IN BUSINESS

There are several ways that utilitarian thinking enters into business decisions, and we will examine two in detail: the application of consequentialist modes of thinking as cost-benefits analysis and the utilitarian analysis and defense of the free market.

Cost-Benefits Analysis

Cost-benefits analysis is an accepted technique for decision making in business. Indeed, it is hard to consider how business could function without such a decision procedure. The calculation of the costs of a decision and the benefits of that decision, expressed in monetary terms, is at the heart of the pursuit of the bottom line. Such thinking is like utilitarianism in three ways. First, it is consequentialist in its orientation, directed toward a desired outcome. Second, it is concerned with producing the maximum benefits. A decision analysis using costs and benefits may not use the language of utilitarianism ("the greatest good for the greatest number"), but clearly the company is interested in maximizing sales to the greatest number of people possible and providing them the best product at the price that will bring them into the marketplace. Third, like the practice of some utilitarians, the costs and benefits are expressed in quantitative terms, usually in dollars. Cost-benefits analysis ordinarily will not factor into the equation many qualitative considerations at all, so in this sense cost-benefits analysis is more like Bentham's utilitarianism than it is like Mill's version.

The earlier brief discussion of utilitarian theory showed some of the vulnerabilities of consequentialist thinking when it is not complemented by other considerations. Although utilitarians were concerned with the effects of actions on people, they were left in the somewhat uncomfortable position of not having a strong defense against the claim that the interests of the majority should prevail over the rights of a minority. Mill again argued against this outcome in his *Essay on Liberty* in which he attempted to defend individual liberty on grounds of utility. It is a continuing matter of debate among philosophers whether this defense is successful on the basis of utilitarian considerations alone. That this debate continues shows that individual rights and liberty form an important part of our ethical thinking regardless of whether they can be defended effectively by utilitarian standards alone.

Utilitarianism is also criticized by its opponents for basing the moral significance of an action on outcomes when it is notoriously difficult to predict the outcome of an action. We will examine more closely each of these limitations to consequentialist ways of thinking as they are applied in the context of business.

Uncertainty of Outcomes

The difficulty of predicting outcomes in specific cases led later utilitarians to move away from the view that each act should be evaluated in terms of the greatest happiness principle to the notion that utilitarian considerations should be used to develop rules that, in the aggregate and in the long run, produce the greatest good for the greatest number. Such rules as tell the truth, do not defraud others, do not limit the freedoms of minorities for the sake of the majority, and so forth, give broad directives to decision making and disallow decisions that might, in a single instance, produce greater happiness for the majority but in the long run would be destructive of social harmony. Even if one did not know for certain whether telling the truth or telling a lie would produce the greatest happiness for the greatest number of people, the rule that says "always tell the truth," a rule justified on utilitarian grounds quite apart from this specific instance, guides decision making in every case. The adoption of the form of consequentialist thinking embodied in rule utilitarianism is a good corrective to the uncertainties of trying to apply utilitarian considerations to each specific act.

If cost-benefits analyses are based on act-utilitarian forms of consideration, they will be open to the kinds of problems discussed. All business decisions face the uncertainty of outcomes: Will the product hold up as tests indicate? Will efforts to add to the company's product line make the company more productive? Will moving a manufacturing facility to a new location and building a more modern facility produce the desired increase in efficiency and profitability? Ethical choices in business would be easy if one could be assured that one would make only safe products, would pursue only those policies that increase profits and protect the jobs of workers, or would always know how much to invest in new product and process development so as to fend off competition. These are some of the reasons, according to rule utilitarians, that we should be guided by broad, general principles rather than a case-by-case cost-benefits analysis.

If we always knew the outcomes of our actions, ethical decisions would not be as difficult as they usually are. Several current business practices are controversial precisely because it is not known whether they are beneficial or harmful to society. Consider hostile takeovers. Defenders of the practice, such as Sir James Goldsmith, a British businessman who has attempted several takeovers in the United States, argues that he serves as a kind of cleansing agent, cleaning up inefficiency and waste and making companies more profitable than they were before. The result is a more productive and competitive company, one that is better able to survive in an increasingly worldwide marketplace.[4] Critics of the practice respond with the argument that takeovers focus only on short-term gains, not long-term productivity; they also destroy productive companies in the name of individual greed, and they cause unemployment for displaced workers and contribute to community economic decline. Who is correct in this debate? No one knows for sure at this point in business history.

The Role of Compromise

It is also the case that many business decisions, and certainly most engineering decisions, are the result of a series of compromises. It is possible for engineers to design an automobile that would be much safer than those currently available. Imagine, though, the design requirements and the cost of an automobile that was built to be as safe as is technically possible. First, it would be well protected against collision, even against larger vehicles such as trucks, making the car extremely heavy and therefore requiring a larger engine, which would burn more fuel. And if the goal was to make it as reliable as possible, engineering tolerances would have to be minute and testing extensive, as currently the case with aircraft airframes and engines. Everything about the auto would be expensive—from the larger tires required to support the extra weight to the additional redundancies built into the design, to the thicker window glass, and on and on. Seeking ever greater margins of safety, the company would be forced to price the automobile out of reach of most purchasers. No company could afford to mass-produce such a product, and automobile ownership would be restricted to the wealthy few. Because of the limited number of automobiles, there would be little public spending on roads and highways, inadequate incentives for oil companies to search for new fuel supplies, and limited facilities to repair and maintain the vehicles. To bring automobile ownership to a majority of the people (the greatest good for the greatest number), manufacturers seek to make the best products for the lowest cost so that they will enjoy the largest market and produce the greatest profit to the companies. This is cost-benefits analysis at work, and without it, modern economies would be impossible.

Protecting Individuals

Business decisions are caught in a dialectical tension between the obvious desirability for a company to produce an absolutely safe product and the need to make the product available to the widest possible market at the lowest possible cost. This dialectical tension is not easily resolved. Resolving it in favor of one of the poles of this dialectic will produce disaster for a business enterprise: either the company's products will not find a niche in the marketplace, with attendant consequences to the company, or its product will cause injury or death to users, resulting in losses to the company in the form of damage suits and litigation costs.

This feature of cost-benefits analysis was underscored in the Ford Pinto case, a perfect illustration of the dynamics with which business executives have to grapple. The apparent willingness of company executives to trade off individual safety against corporate profits so offended the moral sensibilities of the jurors that, in one now-famous case, they awarded the largest punitive damage award ever given up to that time by an American jury.[5] The message communicated by the jury is that cost-benefits analyses cannot ignore the rights of individuals in an unrestrained way.

So how are we to judge when cost-benefits analyses get out of hand? Here are some of the ways this might be done. This is not an exhaustive list, but it is at least a start toward thinking about how to ensure that consequentialist thinking encompasses individual concerns.

1 Does the action, though justifiable on cost-benefits terms, violate an ethical norm, such as lying, cheating, or stealing? There is a philosophical debate lying behind this observation. The response of early twentieth-century philosophers, such as G. E. Moore, to the nineteenth-century utilitarian approach to ethics was to emphasize the intrinsic nature of moral goodness. Just as we recognize the color red when we see it, so we can also recognize moral goodness when we encounter it, and no amount of rational analysis destroys that recognition.[6] So when our rational analysis, whether it be cost-benefits calculations or some other rationalized approach to decision making, leads us to violate one of these intrinsic moral norms, we know we have gone too far.

2 Will the action produce serious, perhaps irreversible, consequences? Rule utilitarians would argue that a needed limit to cost-benefits analysis is of rules that prohibit actions that would cause pain, loss of life, or serious injury to individuals. Societies that live by such rules will be more peaceful and happier than will societies that willynilly trample on the rights of individuals, and the sum total of happiness for everyone will be maximized.

3 Would I be willing to have the decision apply to me (or would I be willing to have this product used by me and my family)? This question brings up an insight that can reveal when an action violates an important moral principle: Would you want to be one of the individuals whose rights are infringed? If not, the action could not be justified on moral grounds. That some Ford engineers testified under oath that they were willing to drive a Pinto, and had in fact bought them for family use, was instrumental in persuading an Indiana jury to find Ford not guilty of criminal homicide in another suit against the Ford Motor Company involving a Pinto fire.

4 Is the analysis one that I would be willing to defend publicly? The test here is not just that of bringing the decision under wider scrutiny, it also involves a sense of making the judgment a universal principle. If the decision works best when kept secret, then it may be masking conflict of interest or even blatant self-interest that could not survive public scrutiny.

UTILITARIAN DEFENSES OF THE FREE MARKET

It is important not to conclude that utilitarian modes of thinking are to be avoided at all costs. That a theory has limitations does not discredit the theory but, rather, shows the extent to which it has legitimate applications and where additional considerations must be brought to bear. Consequentialist considerations, in their utilitarian forms, can provide a powerful way of thinking about business activity, and no clearer evidence of this can be found than in defense of the free market itself.

The free market approach to national economic policy is being embraced around the world for one principal reason: it seems to be the best way of unleashing the productive capacities of a society in a way that will create the kind of flow of goods and services that will benefit the most people. In short, free market economies are the most productive, and this means that more people benefit than under any other economic scheme that has been devised. By being the engine for economic growth, the free market creates a greater totality of wealth that is, at least in principle, available for distribution to a greater number of people. In a free market economy more people will have more goods and services and be able to participate more fully in the economic life of the society. As applied to business practices, this argument implies that companies must honor the freedom of the marketplace, and any attempt by a company to manipulate the market so as to reduce this freedom is unethical. Examples of this include price-fixing, collusion to restrict the supply of goods and services, and other anticompetitive practices.

The problems with free market economies parallel the practical problems of the utilitarian approach to ethics. The free market alone seems unable to deal with the issue of economic justice and the needs of individuals who do not benefit from or are unable to participate in the free market. It cannot deal with the problems of the homeless and the plight of those who, due to limited intelligence, education, or resources, cannot compete in the market. Just as utilitarian theory needs to be supplemented by concern for individual rights, so a free market economy requires something more than the forces of supply and demand to provide for those individuals who are not benefited by the free market: workers who lose their jobs due to market forces, those who lack the skills to find their niche in the market, or those the market rejects as too old, too sick, or too poorly educated. These functions are usually assigned to government; but how much the government should intrude into the marketplace, and the form of that intrusion, are subjects of ongoing debate and lead quickly into matters of social policy.

As we continue to look at issues in business ethics, however, we will return again and again to the important role of the free market. With all its imperfections, the free market does seem to be the best way of organizing society's productive capacities to provide the greatest good for the greatest number of people. Key to this utilitarian function of the market is the freedom of the marketplace, but when people attempt to manipulate the market illegally or unfairly for their own, not society's, benefit, they have crossed over the line from ethical to unethical behavior.

DISCUSSION STARTERS

1 Do you think that most CEOs would agree that their decisions are more or less shaped by utilitarian concerns? If so, can you give examples? If not, do you think they should be?

2 One of the ongoing debates in consequentialist ethics is over the difference between pleasure and happiness. How would you characterize the difference, if any, between the two? A business organization can experience neither happiness nor pleasure, so are these categories useless in discussing business conduct?

3 To what extent do you think that legislators appeal to utilitarian principles when enacting laws? Would following utilitarian standards for legislation (as Bentham proposed) result in generally good laws? Why or why not?

4 Even if you think that the free market is an imperfect system of allocation of a society's goods and services, can you use utilitarian considerations to defend the claim that the free market is nevertheless a morally defensible arrangement?

5 Discuss how utilitarian arguments might be used for or against the following contemporary business practices: leveraged buyouts; insider trading; hostile takeovers; downsizing of companies to increase efficiency; closing profitable plants in order to shift resources to even more profitable endeavors; and offering businesses tax abatements in order to influence their decision to locate in a certain area.

NOTES

1 Found in Chapter 4 of Introduction to *Principles of Morals and Legislation.* There are many editions of this work, but a convenient source of this and other writings of utilitarian philosophers is *The English Philosophers from Bacon to Mill,* ed. E. A. Burtt (New York: Modern Library, 1939).

2 These were his famous essays *On Liberty* and *On the Subjection of Women.*

3 For a good explanation of rule utilitarianism, and the defense of the claim that Mill was really a rule utilitarian at heart, see Anthony Quinton, *Utilitarian Ethics* (LaSalle, IL: Open Court, 1988), especially pp. 47–49. Quinton also provides a good and readable summary of contemporary utilitarian thought in the epilogue to his book.

4 He argues this in a panel discussion in a videotaped discussion entitled "Anatomy of a Corporate Takeover," one of the programs of the "Ethics in America Series" produced by the Annenberg Foundation.

5 Cited by W. Michael Hoffman in *Case Studies in Business Ethics,* 2nd ed., eds. Thomas Donaldson and A. R. Gini (Englewood Cliffs, NJ: Prentice-Hall, 1984), p. 181.

6 See G. E. Moore's *Principia Ethica* (Cambridge: Cambridge University Press, 1903).

CASE STUDY

Producing products that provide the greatest value for the greatest number of people is at the heart of the market system. As noted in the discussion of cost-benefits analysis, every manufacturing decision is, in a real sense, a compromise. It will always be possible to build a safer product—but at what cost? Could large numbers of people purchase a product that carried no risks at all? Is it even possible to determine accurately the consequences of a design decision? These are important questions raised by the ongoing discussion in the United States of the desirability of air bags in automobiles.

AIR BAGS AND AUTOMOBILE MANUFACTURERS

In 1966 the U.S. Congress passed the National Traffic and Motor Vehicle Safety Act and established the National Highway Traffic Safety Administration (NHTSA) to administer the act. The purpose of the act was to develop a coordinated national safety program. One of the major thrusts of the legislation and the subsequent regulations and directives issued by the administration was the development and enforcement of safety performance standards for motor vehicles.

One of the NHTSA's first notices, entitled "Inflatable Occupant Restraint Systems," was published in 1969. It emphasized use of the controversial "air bag." It required that the air bag be installed in all vehicles manufactured in the United States. This notice, Motor Vehicle Safety Standard (MVSS) 208, was opposed by the automobile industry. Detailed questions were raised about safety research, engineering designs, financial burdens, and possible legal violations in order to postpone required implementation from 1972 yearly for a decade. By 1981, MVSS 208 appeared doomed. During the period from 1969 to 1981, millions of dollars had been spent by the automobile industry, automobile insurance companies, public interest groups, and the government to promote their various views and to fight those of the opposition. . . .

Proponents of air bags cite research on the effectiveness of passive restraints and the desirability of reducing fatalities by whatever means available as reason enough for requiring air bags; automobile manufacturers and their allies, by contrast, contend that there are many unresolved problems in the implementation of this technology. While air-bag critics agree with the desirability of reducing traffic fatalities, they see the increased use of seat belts, through either public education or legislation, as the preferred means of achieving that goal. Historically, seat-belt usage in the United States has been low. In 1974, 26 percent of all motorists used seat belts. The level dropped to 14 percent in 1983.[1] Supporters of air-bag legislation cite a DeLorean Corporation study that found "[b]elt usage is, and may be expected to be . . . inadequate to allow benefits or payoffs equal to those predicted for air cushion-lap belt systems."[2]

Opponents of air bags have claimed that air bags could be a hazard and a potential *cause* of accidents in the case of accidental inflation. Research on this problem under test conditions has shown, however, that while people do demonstrate a "startle" reaction to unexpected bag inflation, "drivers retained good control of the test vehicle" and "were able to see to guide their car in spite of the minimal obstruction of vision produced by the inflated air bag."[3] General Motors experimented with inflating air bags without warning as test subjects drove on straightaways and turns at speeds up to 45 mph. General Motors reported that "without exception, the subject retained control of the automobile."[4]

Some concern also has been expressed over the propellant used to inflate the air bags. It is the chemical sodium azide, a class B poison (in the same category as insecticides). In solid form it is toxic, but the process of firing it involves a chemical reaction that causes it to become nontoxic hydrogen. Passengers do not in theory come into contact with sodium azide at any time, but critics fear that damage to the container or residual particles in the bag after firing might endanger passengers. The NHTSA firmly believes the current propellant container can be used without fear due to its strength and inaccessibility.[5]

Industry opposition to the air bags as revealed in Congressional hearings, court testimony, and lobbying efforts has focused on the cost of the system, the costs and difficulties in retooling the industry for this addition, the performance of the bag in real-life situations, and has complained about government "paternalism" and overregulation. Industry representatives see such government behavior as an unwarranted restriction on their freedom to design and produce automobiles.

The automakers consistently cite cost-of-production changes required to make and install the air bags. This argument gained force in 1973–74 when the energy crisis shifted public and government focus from safety to fuel economy. Redesigning and retooling to make smaller and more fuel-efficient cars took precedence for automakers over redesigning and retooling to make automobile air bags. As the decade wore on, the increasing competition from fuel-efficient foreign cars, coupled with a general recession and the automobile industry's increasingly dismal economic situation, supported the auto manufacturers' contention that (1) they could not afford to absorb the cost of retooling for air bags and (2) they could not pass the additional cost on to consumers and remain competitive.

Driver-side air bags were offered as standard equipment in all Mercedes Benz autos for the 1987 model year. This feature added roughly $1,350 to the price of each car.[6] Ford simultaneously offered driver-side air bags as optional equipment in two of its lines for approximately $815.[7] The cost to the consumer should be much less if mandatory legislation were passed requiring installation in *all* cars, because production levels would be substantial if air bags were produced for every automobile.[8] The U.S. Department of Transportation has estimated the cost of full front-seat systems to be around $350.[9] Although the automakers maintain that seat belts are the best safety feature, they have recognized that there is a market for air bags and passive belts. Consequently, the automakers, especially Ford, plan to make passive restraints available for voluntary purchase on virtually all models.

Air-bag regulations have been supported by the automobile insurance industry, which is convinced that the bags save lives and health and insurance costs. The Insurance Institute for Highway Safety provided funds and technical expertise to counter auto industry arguments. Allstate Insurance Company was particularly active in support of air bags, providing favorable advertising and support before congressional committees, and offering discounts on insurance premiums for air-bag equipped cars. A pamphlet issued by Allstate in 1976 stated, "Allstate advocates the use of lap belts, used in conjunction with air bags. This system offers the best protection feasible now and within the foreseeable future in most types of crashes—air bags to reduce injury and lap belts to prevent ejection in rollovers."[10]

Allstate was joined by a number of consumer interest groups. They maintain that air-bag technology is adequate, affordable, and lifesaving. These groups contend that the government's duty to protect the public interest entails required passive restraints. They point out that there is more at risk than the consumer's personal safety. The safety of passengers not directly involved in the purchase decision is clearly at risk.

There is also some evidence that the public supports air bags. . . . *Newsweek* magazine conducted a survey in 1986 of people who purchased automobiles in November or December of 1985. When asked whether "air bags should be standard equipment on all new cars" the response was 34 percent strongly agree, 53 percent somewhat agree, 8 percent disagree, and 5 percent strongly disagree.[11] . . . There is some consumer dissent concerning mandatory passive restraints. Some consumers resent being forced to purchase safety devices. While most agree that the government has some responsibility to the public to make sure that they purchase well-made automobiles, they do not think they should be unwillingly burdened with costs. Consumers suggest that insurance companies bill drivers according to the automobile safety devices they purchase. These consumers feel the freedom to choose also includes the freedom to make a wrong choice. . . .

In October 1981, the NHTSA issued a final rule calling for the complete rescission of passive restraints and amended Modified Standard 208 accordingly. The end result was a standard identical to the 1968 standard, requiring manual seat belts in all motor vehicles. Within a month, on November 25, 1981, the National Association of Independent Insurers (NAII), representing 509 insurance companies, filed suit in a federal court seeking to overturn this order, which would repeal all rules requiring either air bags or automatic seat belts. The insurance companies were particularly upset by the way the matter had been handled in the Transportation Department (DOT): Raymond Peck, administrator of the NHTSA, said that the opposition of U.S. automobile companies had killed the air-bag policy. Peck said his decision was based on the fact that all of the major auto companies intended to comply with the detachable, automatic seat belts, coupled with his firm belief that most motorists would simply disconnect the activating systems. He preferred a voluntary seat-belt campaign, but said he would try to revive interest in the development of better air bags. Mr. Peck's decision had been unanimously opposed by his senior staff, but it was praised as professionally sound by the three leading U.S. automobile manufacturers.[12]

The NAII suit challenged the claim that air bags and belts would be disconnected by owners, and argued that Mr. Peck did not understand the several different designs well enough to appreciate that it would be extremely difficult to dismantle properly engineered systems.[13] . . .

The court found that the NHTSA's reasons for rescinding Modified Standard 208 were insufficient. However, the agency was given thirty days to present a schedule for resolving the questions raised in the case leading either to an ultimate rescission or to implementation of the standard. The standard was not rescinded.

In July of 1984, then Secretary of Transportation Dole added a new twist to the struggle. She announced that if states representing two-thirds of the population pass mandatory seat-belt laws that meet predetermined federal standards, she would rescind the passive restraint requirement. States were given five years, until April 1989, to get these laws on their books. In the interim, automakers were to begin phasing in passive restraints (air bags or automatic seat belts on the driver's and the passenger's sides) in the following percentages for each model year: 10 percent in 1987, 25 percent in 1988, 40 percent in 1989, and 100 percent in 1990. This phase-in could be stopped by the secretary at any time after the mandatory seat-belt law coverage attained the two-thirds level. A special incentive was given to the auto manufacturers to use air bags. One car equipped with air bags would count as 1.5 cars towards this requirement.[14]

After this announcement, interest groups changed their focus. They mobilized to influence state legislatures. Auto companies formed "Traffic Safety Now," whose express purpose was to lobby state legislatures to pass mandatory seat-belt laws. Proponents of air bags were left in a quandary. Should they lobby for strong mandatory seat-belt legislation and risk rescission of the passive requirements? Or should they lobby against seat-belt legislation, knowing that seat belts decrease deaths and injuries in all types of crashes, with the hopes of getting federal passive restraint regulations in place eventually?

The insurers went to court a second time. This time they challenged the secretary and the DOT on three issues: (1) safety standards must be uniform, (2) state laws are not substitutes for federal regulation, and (3) the secretary does not have the authority to influence state legislation. In September 1986, a three-judge panel of the U.S. Court of Appeals ruled the issues were "not ripe for decision" at this time. In essence, they decided not to decide. The judges found that of the twenty states currently with mandatory seat-belt laws, none met federal standards. With this evidence, they concluded that the two-thirds level would not be met by 1989, and the passive restraint standard would not be rescinded. However, the judges stated at several points that insurers would have new recourse if states modify seat-belt legislation to meet federal standards and/or states presently not covered by mandatory seat-belt legislation pass laws that comply with federal standards (achieving the two-thirds level by 1989). Under these circumstances, the insurers could file suit again and the court would make a definite ruling on each of the issues. Should the plaintiffs find the conditions about to be met they could refile and the judges would decide on the issues at that time.[15]

Because the required level of coverage of state seat-belt laws was not met, the phase-in procedure for the passive restraint rule began as of September 1, 1986. After that date an increasing number of automobiles must be equipped with passive restraints on both the driver and the passenger sides of the vehicle. Passive restraints could be air bags, passive seat belts, or protective interiors (padded dashboards, shock-absorbent steering columns, etc.).

In November 1986, the Department of Transportation proposed to delay the full front-seat automatic restraint systems requirement until model year 1994 in response to a petition from the Ford Motor Company. However, in May 1988 the Chrysler Corporation announced that it had started putting driver-side air bags as standard equipment in six of its car lines (24 percent of total sales). The corporation projected that it would meet the federal standard in all of its passenger cars by 1990.

NOTES

1 NHTSA study as quoted in Robert W. Crandall, *Regulating the Automobile* (Washington, D.C.: Brookings Institution, 1986), p. 54.

2 Richard Hodgetts, "Air Bags and Auto Safety," in *The Business Enterprise: Social Challenge, Social Response* (Philadelphia: W. B. Saunders Co., 1977), p. 138.

3 H. Haskell Ziperman and G. R. Smith, "Startle Reaction to Air-Bag Restraints," *Journal of the American Medical Association* 233 (August 4, 1975), p. 440.

4 General Motors study, as quoted in Anne Fleming, *About Air Bags* (Washington, D.C.: Insurance Institute for Highway Safety, 1987), p. 7.

5 U.S. House Committee on Interstate and Foreign Commerce, "Department of Transportation Automobile Passive Restraint Rule," *H. Rpt.* 502-35 (Washington, D.C.: Government Printing Office, 1977).

6 Gary Williams, Manager, Owner Services, Mercedes-Benz of North America, personal interview, Washington, D.C., October 1, 1986.

7 Dave Zoia, "Some Wait to Decide on Passive Restraints," *Automotive News* (September 15, 1986), p. 1.

8 Hodgetts, "Air Bags and Auto Safety," p. 142.

9 U.S. Department of Transportation statistic adjusted for inflation, as quoted in Fleming, *About Air Bags,* p. 8.

10 Quoted by Hodgetts, "Air Bags and Auto Safety," p. 136.

11 "1986 Buyers of New Cars: Summary Report," research report, *Newsweek* (New York, 1986), Table 67.

12 "Insurers Sue for Return of Passive Restraint Rule," *Baltimore Sun,* November 26, 1981, and Peter Behr, "U.S. Halts Effort to Require Use of Car Air Bags," *Washington Post,* October 24, 1981, sec. A, pp. 1, 24.

13 Ibid.

14 Zoia, "Some Wait to Decide on Passive Restraints," p. 1.

15 U.S. Court of Appeals, District of Columbia Circuit, No. 84-1301. *State Farm Mutual Automobile Insurance Co.* v. *Elizabeth Dole, Department of Transportation.*

Rights and Duties

Richard Lancaster
President
RBI Precision

"*In all relationships trust is the basic element. Trust is created from honesty. Honesty is one of the most difficult qualities of character to achieve in business, family, or any other arena where one's self-interest competes with that of the other party. Yet, as we learned while we were young, in every case it is always the best policy. Most of us in business have a mission and related plans. As we direct our resources and energy towards achieving our mission we develop covenants along the way. Employers depend upon employees, customers depend upon suppliers, banks depend upon borrowers and in each case the latter party depends on the former party while the list of parties goes on and on. Therefore we find that the businesses of quality and long tenure tend to be those where all relationships are built upon honesty and trust.*"

Contemporary business practice takes place in the midst of a sea of rights claims: Employees claim the right to organize and bargain collectively with employers. Business executives speak of management rights, including the right to hire and fire employees who are considered employed "at will," or in other words, only so long as management wishes them to be. Environmentalists claim that all of us have the right to clean air, clean water, and an environment free from pollutants. Animal rights activists invoke the rights of all living creatures and protest the use of animals in drug and cosmetic research and the sale of fur. Human rights activists may urge boycotts of countries that have a poor human rights record. Right-to-life groups organize their own boycotts of businesses they view as proabortion. And businesses' healthcare benefits may well be transformed by a belief in a national right to medical care. How are we to evaluate these various rights claims? What is the ethical course of action when claims collide? The first task in answering these questions is to try to develop an understanding of the notion of rights. We begin with some of the fundamental issues that lie at the heart of rights.

MORALITY AND RIGHTS

The philosophical issue that is fundamental in any discussion of rights is the question of justifying fundamental rights claims and providing a rational analysis of how the notion of rights comes about. A philosopher whose work was pivotal in this regard was Immanuel Kant (1724–1804). As a member of the philosophy faculty at the University of Königsberg, Kant was a teacher of logic, and in his moral philosophy he wanted to bring the same standards of clarity to ethical analysis as one finds in logical analysis. It also seemed clear to Kant that the rightness or wrongness of an action is not really determined by the action's consequences but by the intentions and motives of the moral agent. Kant's view on this matter is even reflected in our prephilosophical thinking about ethics, when, for example, we hold a person less morally responsible for causing an accidental death than we do a person who deliberately and "with malice aforethought" takes the life of another person.

Another similarity to logical thinking that Kant seeks in ethics is the universality of its judgments. The canons of logic are the same no matter where and when they are invoked, and they should apply equally to all arguments. The same standard should be applied to the fundamental principles of ethics: they should apply equally to all rational persons. If this were not the case, Kant argues, there would be no way rational persons could converse about ethical matters, and the hope of achieving any kind of agreement in ethics would disappear. The two standards Kant proposes are universality and necessity. *Universality* is the principle just discussed, that ethical standards should apply to all equally. *Necessity* is a logical term that implies the inner consistency of a principle. Without universality and necessity, ethics will never be fully grounded on rational principles.

Kant's contribution to the discussion of ethics is in providing a way of understanding that the moral obligation arises when we articulate standards of morality for every rational being. The search for universality of judgments led Kant to the principle he called the "categorical imperative." The phrase itself may seem somewhat unusual, but the concepts it embodies are not. To say that a moral principle is "categorical" is to claim that it is without exceptions and not iffy or provisional. To describe it as an "imperative" means that it is a command that we as rational beings not only give to ourselves but impose on all rational persons. Here is the most widely cited form of the categorical imperative: *act on that principle that you can will to be a universal law.* Because this principle is a principle of reason, it is our duty as rational beings to obey. Moral views such as Kant's that stress duty and obligation are called "deontological."

Like the formulas of logic, the categorical imperative is a formal principle; that is, it has no specific content. It is general enough to provide direction through the maze of often conflicting cultural traditions and allows one to determine one's moral duty even when the consequences of the action are unclear. But precisely because Kant's approach ignores outcomes it is open to the charge of being incomplete and inadequate by itself to provide total moral guidance. Outcomes are important, yet Kant's theory does not give them standing in moral analysis.

Kant's approach also does not provide much guidance when we are faced with conflicting moral obligations, and the most difficult ethical decisions we face are those where we are forced to choose between rival duties: Should we tell a lie to save a life? How should we balance our duties to stockholders with our obligations to the community, to workers, and to customers? Are there ever cases when individual rights should be sacrificed for the sake of a greater good? Should we place restrictions on hateful speech, even though it violates our commitment to free speech?

ETHICS OF DUTY

• Emphasis on motives and intentions
• Inherent dignity and equality of every rational being
• Limitations:
  Ignores outcomes
  Little guidance relative to conflicting obligations

MORAL REASONING

Kant's view differs from other approaches to ethics in three important ways. First, Kant denies the view that we have a special faculty for making moral decisions, whether it be called moral intuition, a moral sense, or conscience. He argues that we use the same mental faculty for making ethical judgments that we use when we obtain knowledge of the world. This faculty, *reason,* functions differently when making moral judgments, but it is nevertheless the same faculty.

This emphasis on reason leads to a second difference: Kant's search for a logical basis for ethics tried to bring the same standards to ethical principles as apply to logical principles. Just as logical principles apply to all arguments, and are unaffected by who and where these arguments are constructed, so ethical principles apply to all people at all times (the characteristic of universality). Another logical criterion is consistency. If I expect everyone to follow a moral principle but fail to follow it myself, then I am being inconsistent. One might advocate the ethical principle that everyone should always tell the truth, but for oneself tell the truth only when it is to one's benefit. This would be an example of a failure of consistency. Kant argues that we can apply such tests to ethical judgments at the level of fundamental ethical principles, which are *formal* (which means they have no specific content). A logical formula can have different applications because its principles are justified by formal analysis, not by their content. Similarly, Kant presents formal principles for ethics that can be used to test the morality of a variety of contemplated actions.

A third difference is Kant's rejection of consequences as significant in assessing the moral worth of an action. The philosophers we have encountered thus far—Hobbes, Aristotle, Bentham, Mill—despite their differences, all emphasize that the consequences of actions are significant for judging an action's moral worth. Kant's criticism of consequentialism in ethics is that it cannot provide the universality and consistency that ought to characterize moral judgments. Additionally, it cannot capture the importance of intentions as essential to understanding the morality of an action. We would want to say, for example, as our legal system does, that there is a major difference between premeditated murder and accidental homicide. Consequentialist ethics cannot easily capture this distinction.

We have already mentioned Kant's defense of the principle of ethics known as the categorical imperative. Although there is but a single categorical imperative, Kant argues, it can be understood as having several dimensions.

The Principle of Universality

An imperative is a command, but there are several types of commands. A categorical imperative is a command that applies in all circumstances, without exception. In contrast, a *hypothetical* imperative is a conditional command, an if . . . then directive. *If* I want to seek the greatest good for the greatest number, *then* I will have to do those things that will maximize utility. Any view based on consequences can only be derived from hypothetical imperatives. The truly moral imperative involves being able to will that principle of one's action into a universal law. To do this, Kant argues that we must first isolate the principle on which we are acting (he called this the "maxim"). Then we apply the consistency test to see whether we could make this maxim, or principle, one that everyone could follow. There are two ways in which the maxim could fail this test. One is when making the principle universal undercuts its own possibility. Borrowing money (from a bank or a friend) on the promise to repay the loan is possible when keeping promises is made a universal law. But suppose the maxim were something like this: "I will promise to repay only when convenient for me." This could not be made a universal law because, were everyone to follow this maxim, borrowing and lending would soon disappear. An individual promising to repay a loan, but having no intention of keeping the promise to repay the loan, can act in this way only because most people do keep promises. This is an example of how a principle fails the test of consistency.

A maxim can also fail the test of universal application when a person is inconsistent in applying it. There are some maxims that can be made universal without the kind of contradiction just mentioned. Kant's example is that of helping people in need. Suppose the maxim were something like "People should only have what they themselves earn," a maxim that could be described as a principle of self-sufficiency. There is no self-contradiction in making this a universal law, but there would be a change in the attitude of the person following the maxim were that person's situation to change. For example, when individuals find themselves in need, they would modify the maxim of self-sufficiency. In its modified version it might be something like the following: "People should only have what they themselves earn, except when circumstances beyond their control make it necessary to receive help from others." But this is a very different maxim from the original one, and this change shows that the first maxim could not be made a universal law without exception because the individual using this maxim would change it to reflect changing circumstances. A command involving such a maxim fails to be categorical and is an example of not meeting the test of universality.

It is not difficult to think of business examples to illustrate the principle of universality. If in advertising a product I decide to lie about it, then my principle or maxim would be something like the following: "Lie about your product in order to increase sales." Could this principle be made a universal law? Of course not, because advertising needs credibility in order to be useful as a sales medium, and advertisers themselves are consumers of others' products and would not wish to grant others the right to lie to them. False advertising fails as a universal activity because applying the maxim would not only destroy the credibility of advertising, but also the purveyor of false advertising would not want to be the recipient of false advertising.

In order to capture these two senses of what it means to make one's principle of action universal, the contemporary business ethics writer Manuel Velasquez suggests the terminology "universalizability" and "reversibility." Although this is not Kantian terminology, it does capture Kant's meaning. Here is how Velasquez puts it:

Universalizability. The person's reasons for acting must be reasons that everyone *could* act on at least in principle.

Reversibility. The person's reasons for acting must be reasons that he or she would be *willing* to have all others use, even as a basis of how they treat him or her.[1]

Basic, then, to Kant's analysis of moral rights are the notions of consistency and fairness. *Consistency* is another way of addressing the criterion of making our principle universal, and *fairness* means, in some important sense, that we are willing to play by the same rules we apply to everybody else. We will see later on in this chapter how contemporary philosophers use these terms in articulating Kantian principles to a modern audience, but notice how these two moral principles seem to operate at a fundamental, almost intuitive, level of human interaction. Children are quick to complain, "That's not fair," and it does not take much interpersonal experience to spot inconsistencies in the way we are treated and label such treatment as wrong. When Kant set out to provide a formal statement of the foundations of morality, he did not think he was making a new discovery but, rather, was stating with philosophical precision those principles of morality of which we are long aware. As Kant puts it, "What distinguishes philosophy from common rational knowledge is its treatment in separate sciences of what is confusedly comprehended in such knowledge."[2]

The Principle of Respect

These Kantian principles easily lead to a second formulation of the categorical imperative. As rational beings we demand to be treated with respect. To give respect to someone, Kant says, is to acknowledge worth without price; we cannot put a dollar value on human worth. If I demand respect from others, the categorical imperative directs me to extend this same demand to others, to make the rule I apply to myself a universal law. Therefore it is rational to demand that we treat humanity, whether it be my humanness or that of others, as ends and never as a means *only*. Kant's point here is frequently misunderstood, for we all treat other people as a means. A teacher serves as a means of providing an education, a clerk in a store is a means of delivering service, a worker in a factory is a means of production. There is nothing wrong with this as long as we do not treat other persons as means only—that is, as long as our treatment of them does not deny their basic humanity and inherent dignity. This is, after all, how we expect others to relate to us, and we thus are obligated to treat them in the same way.

The Principle of Autonomy

Also basic to Kant's view is the principle of autonomy, literally self-rule, and this leads to the third formulation of the categorical impera-

KANT ON MORAL RIGHTS

Thus the moral worth of an action does not lie in the effect which is expected from it or in any principle of action which has to borrow its motive from this expected effect. . . . Therefore, the pre-eminent good can consist only in the conception of the law in itself (which can be present only in a rational being) so far as this conception and not the hoped-for effect is the determining ground of the will. This pre-eminent good, which we call moral, is already present in the person who acts according to this conception, and we do not have to look for it first in the result.

But what kind of a law can that be, the conception of which must determine the will without reference to the expected result? Under this condition alone the will can be called absolutely good without qualification. Since I have robbed the will of all impulses which could come to it from obedience to any law, nothing remains to serve as a principle of the will except universal conformity of its action to law as such. That is, I should never act in such a way that I could not also will that my maxim should be a universal law. . . .

I do not, therefore, need any penetrating acuteness in order to discern what I have to do in order that my volition may be morally good. Inexperienced in the course of the world, incapable of being prepared for all its contingencies, I ask myself only: Can I will that my maxim become a universal law? If not, it must be rejected, not because of any disadvantage accruing to myself or even to others, but because it cannot enter as a principle into a possible universal legislation, and reason extorts from me an immediate respect for such legislation. . . . To duty every other motive must give place, because duty is the condition of a will good in itself, whose worth transcends everything.

Source: Immanuel Kant, *Foundations of the Metaphysics of Morals* (New York: Library of Liberal Arts, 1959), pp. 17–18, 19–20.

tive. Kant argues that it is essential to a moral action that it be willingly done; no one can force you to be moral. Again, this point corresponds with our ordinary, commonsense view of morality. Freedom of choice lies behind the common saying that we cannot legislate morality. We can certainly legislate that people act in accordance with moral rules, but such actions, if done from a fear of punishment, or only because the law says we have to, is not morally significant. To act morally means that we freely choose the action, that it is done because we will it. If someone forces us to act in a certain way, our action is done for reasons other than moral ones, and Kant calls this acting under *heteronomy* rather than autonomously.

At first it might seem that Kant is giving us contradictory insights with his emphasis, on the one hand, on universal laws and absolutes and, on the other hand, his claim that the only moral act is a free act. But, remember, Kant is not claiming that to know the right thing to do is to do the right thing. We might be fully aware of the moral course of action but fail to act on that knowledge because of fear of failure, conflict with our own self-interest, or simply lack of will to carry out our intentions. None of these considerations argues against Kant's point in the least; if knowing the right thing to do led us inevitably to do the right thing, the moral worth of the action would disappear. Our actions have moral worth only when they are done *for moral reasons*. Individual autonomy is basic. Take that away, Kant thought, and you remove morality as well. There are two senses, then, in which autonomy is important. The first is that we freely choose to do the morally right thing. The second is that free choice is a basic demand of reason, and no action—or system—can be said to be moral unless it honors the principle of autonomy or free choice.

To summarize, there are three forms of the categorical imperative, each of which captures an important aspect of moral action. Kant insists repeatedly that even though the categorical imperative can be stated differently, there is but one categorical imperative. What he means is that one statement leads logically into the others. The principle of universality leads us to apply our maxims to ourselves as well as others. This is also true of respect, which we demand from others and which we owe to others. Finally, moral actions are those freely chosen; if a moral action is one that I will to be a universal law, then an action forced on me by the law of someone else is not my moral act. Here, then, are three forms of the categorical imperative as Kant stated them.

First formulation. Act only according to that maxim which you can at the same time will that it should become a universal law.

Second formulation. Act so that you treat humanity, whether in your own person or in that of another, always as an end and never as a means only.

Third formulation. The principle of autonomy of the will in contrast to all other principles . . . is thus the basis of the dignity of both human nature and every rational nature.[3]

We could say that the first formulation captures the importance of consistency, the second that of fairness and respect, and the third that of free choice. These are all three important aspects of the notion of rights.

A Case in Point . . .

Illustrating the difficulty of deciding among rights claims is the case of Johnson Controls, Inc., a Milwaukee firm that makes lead batteries in several plants scattered around the country. The air inside these plants contains small particles of lead and lead oxide. Although these are dangerous substances, the company claimed that emission levels are safe for adults but cited guidelines from the Occupational Safety and Health Administration (OSHA), which held that these substances were at a critical level for women who plan to bear children.

As a result the company instituted a policy barring fertile women from working in battery manufacturing areas, even if women said they did not plan to bear children. Only women past the age of childbearing or who had surgically been rendered unable to bear children were given these jobs. The company reasoned that pregnancies are often unplanned and that the risk to children was too great. Not only would it put its female employees at risk, birth defects blamed on working conditions could subject the company to costly lawsuits. A company representative said, "You can't turn aside our concern for a child's health. That's at the center of our position. At the same time, we have a legitimate position in protecting our shareholders' interest."

The United Auto Workers sued, claiming that the company's policy was discriminatory against women and therefore illegal under Title VII of the Civil Rights Acts of 1964. The union demanded that the company reduce lead exposure for everyone, a goal that management claimed was not possible. Female employees claimed the company policy caused them to lose promotions to younger men and that they were forced to seek sterilization to keep their jobs.

Both a district court and a federal appeals court upheld the company's policy, but the union took the case to the U.S. Supreme Court.

Many other groups rallied to the employees' cause. Women's rights advocates claimed that this was just another excuse for "keeping women in their place." One spokeswoman for the ACLU said, "The attitude of Johnson Controls is: 'We know better than you. We can't allow women to make this decision. We have to make it for them.'" Others pointed out that as many as 20 million women are employed in hazardous jobs: health-care providers, flight attendants, construction workers, just to name a few.

In March 1991, the U.S. Supreme Court reversed the appeals court by deciding that the company's policies violated Title VII of the Civil Rights Act as amended by the Pregnancy Discrimination Act of 1978. In its statement the Court concluded, "Congress mandated that decisions about the welfare of future children be left to the parents who conceive, bear, support, and raise them, and concerns about the next generation were not part of the essence of the employer's business."

Sources: 499 U.S. (1991), 113 L.Ed. 2d 158; NYT, Sept. 2, 1990; *Washington Post,* Jan. 7, 1990; *Vogue,* May 1990.

RIGHTS AND FAIRNESS

One of the most significant efforts to apply Kant to issues of contemporary society is found in the work of Harvard philosopher John Rawls, who takes the Kantian demand for fairness as central to any attempt to deal with questions of social justice. Rawls suggests that a truly fair society would be established according to rules determined by reasonable and unbiased persons. But how can we ensure that such persons act truly in an unbiased way? Rawls suggests that we create a thought experiment whereby we see what kinds of rules such persons would enact if they placed themselves behind a "veil of ignorance"— that is, without knowing where they would be in the social structure or organizational setup. For example, how high would you be willing to allow CEO compensation to rise if you thought you might someday be CEO? Conversely, what minimum salaries would you agree to if you truly thought you might be a minimum wage earner? Given this veil of ignorance, what principles would you as a free, disinterested, and rational person choose? Rawls argues that you would, first of all, choose a principle that guards your right to liberty. That is, nothing is worth exchanging for your freedom, not a high-paying job, not social status, nothing. So the basic and most important principle is that "each person is to have an equal right to the most extensive basic liberty compatible with a similar liberty for others." This Rawls calls the first principle of justice, and we can see here Kant's notion of universalizing the principle, extending it to everyone, not just ourselves.

Rawls's second principle of justice is less obvious and is the one that has caused the most debate. He includes in it a provision for differences in outcomes (not all of us can be CEOs, and not all of us will be at the bottom of society or of a business organization). How unequal are we to allow our society to be and still be able to claim that it is fair? Rawls says that the second principle will regulate this as follows: "social and economic inequalities are to be arranged so that they are both (a) reasonably expected to be to everyone's advantage, and (b) attached to positions and offices open to all."[4] In an organization the positions requiring higher levels of training, skills, or abilities will require higher levels of compensation. Everyone will benefit—stockholders, employees, managers, the community—if an organization is staffed with capable individuals of varying abilities who receive varying levels of compensation. These positions, however, should be open to all: no "glass ceilings" on advancement because of gender or race, no exclusion from higher-compensated positions. Rawls makes clear in his analysis that

---

RAWLS ON FAIRNESS

My aim is to present a conception of justice which generalizes and carries to a higher level of abstraction the familiar theory of the social contract . . . that the principles of justice for the basic structure of society are the object of the original agreement. They are the principles that free and rational persons concerned to further their own interests would accept in an initial position of equality as defining the fundamental terms of their association. . . . In justice as fairness the original position of equality corresponds to the state of nature in the traditional theory of the social contract. . . .

I shall now state in a provisional form the two principles of justice that I believe would be chosen in the original position. . . .

The first statement of the two principles reads as follows.

First: each person is to have an equal right to the most extensive basic liberty compatible with a similar liberty for others.

Second: social and economic inequalities are to be arranged so that they are both (a) reasonably expected to be to everyone's advantage, and (b) attached to positions and offices open to all. . . .

These principles are to be arranged in a serial order with the first principle prior to the second. This ordering means that a departure from the institutions of equal liberty required by the first principle cannot be justified by, or compensated for, greater social and economic advantages. The distribution of wealth and income, and the hierarchies of authority, must be consistent with both the liberties of equal citizenship and equality of opportunity.

Source: John Rawls, *A Theory of Justice* (Cambridge, MA: Belknap Press of Harvard University Press, 1971), pp. 11, 12, 60, 61.

---

we cannot justify trading off the basic liberty interests of anyone for the sake of an overall good. This is a response to the utilitarian's lack of emphasis on individual rights. To summarize, Rawls's two principles of justice are as follows:

The basic liberty principle. Each person is to have an equal right to the most extensive total system of equal basic liberties compatible with a similar system of liberty for all.

The difference principle. Social and economic inequalities are to be arranged so that they are both (a) to the greatest benefit of the least advantaged, and (b) attached to offices and positions open to all under conditions of fair equality of opportunity.

Rawls's principles are useful for thinking about fairness not only within an organization but also as a way of thinking about the fairness of the marketplace itself.

THE MORALITY OF THE MARKETPLACE

The debate between consequentialists and deontologists in many respects parallels the ongoing discussion in contemporary society about how to promote fairness and what should be the proper role of both government and business in a free society. This tension between the sometimes rival demands of outcomes and rights is not limited to business; it is embedded in the founding documents of the American republic. The Declaration of Independence begins with the statement that all people have certain unalienable rights: life, liberty, the pursuit of happiness. But notice that the pursuit of happiness is directed toward consequences, and when the Constitution of the United States was written, it scarcely mentioned rights at all. Instead it was concerned with establishing a "more perfect union" (consequences), "insuring domestic tranquility" (consequences), and "providing for the common good" (again, consequences). The Constitution then turns to processes of government that will bring about these consequences, with little attention being given to individual rights. It was only through the addition of the first ten amendments to the Constitution, the "Bill of Rights" as it came to be called, that this important document provided for such individual rights as free speech, religious freedom, the right to assemble, the right to freedom from arbitrary searches, the right not to be forced into self-incrimination, and so on.

Achieving desirable consequences while balancing rights claims in a modern economic system seems at first difficult, and indeed it is, given the complexities of modern economic systems. Some contemporary philosophers, however, think that Rawls's Kantian approach can provide valuable insights in this regard. In broad terms we can distinguish between the two principal kinds of systems by using terms that come from economics: command economies and demand economies. *Command* economies are those economic and social arrangements whereby a central authority allocates resources, directs the productive capacities of a society, and sets up rules for the distribution of the products coming from business and industry. During times of national emergency, such as World War II, the United States had a command economy, but for most of its history the nation has had a demand economy. In *demand* economies, the forces of supply and demand provide the means of allocating resources and pricing goods. Evoking again the phrase coined by the eighteenth-century philosopher Adam Smith, these forces act as an "invisible hand" to guarantee that resources are allocated to those industries most responsive to consumer demand.

Prices, too, reflect consumer demand. If a company is inefficient and therefore has to price its products accordingly, a competing firm that more efficiently produces its products for sale at a lower price will gain the larger share of the market, thereby forcing greater efficiencies on the industry as a whole. We see something of this process at work currently in the automotive industry, where firms that can offer a product with greater quality at a lower price are forcing competitors either to improve their product or to leave the marketplace.

Now that command economies, especially as they existed in Marxist countries, have fallen out of favor, the demand approach to economy seems to be on the rise, although there are different versions of free market economies, as was discussed in Chapter 2. It is possible, however, to add to the free market approach an element of command through national industrial policy and through cooperative arrangements among manufacturers and suppliers.[5] These variations aside, demand economies seem best to satisfy some of the moral dimensions of rights claims. In demand economies people are free to make their own choices of what employment they pursue, how they spend their money, and in general how they allocate their time. Another feature of demand economies is that they create a greater supply of goods and services than do command economies; that is, they generate more wealth than command economies do, and this greater overall wealth could, in principle, be available to help those in society who are the least well off—the sick, disabled, chronically unemployed, the homeless—though how best to make this help available is not an easy question to answer. Demand economies, then, are able to qualify as moral arrangements for society, provided that they remain free from manipulation and unfair use of the marketplace. Here is how Velasquez applies Rawls's principles to the notion of a free market, demand economy:

> Rawls claims that the more productive a society is, the more benefits it will be able to provide for its least advantaged members. Since the difference principle obliges us to maximize benefits for the least advantaged, this means that business institutions should be as efficient in their use of resources as possible. If we assume that a market system like ours is most efficient when it is most competitive, then the difference principle will in effect imply that markets should be competitive and that anticompetitive practices like price-fixing and monopolies are unjust. In addition, since pollution and other environmentally damaging "external effects" consume resources inefficiently, the difference principle also implies that it is wrong for firms to pollute.[6]

Note how the notion of fairness enters into the discussion of the free market. Fairness, this good Kantian notion of being willing to apply a principle both universally and to our own actions, leads to the conclusion that attempts by individuals or groups to manipulate the market to their own advantage violate this fundamental ethical norm. If I conspire with my competitors to agree upon a fixed price so that we all make money and are not forced to compete in the marketplace, then I have acted unethically by limiting the freedom of the marketplace. If I lie in my advertising and make false claims about my product, I have acted unfairly by lying to my customers, thereby depriving them of the truth on which to base a free choice as informed buyers. A major aspect of public policy debate, then, is over how best to ensure that the market remains truly free. Some argue that the market is more free when the government stays completely out of it in a laissez-faire policy, but this conclusion might not follow from the application of Rawls's rules.

Keeping the Free Market Free

The tension between utilitarian and rights approaches to ethics is reflected to some degree in the differences between two major views on the proper role of government in society. Those who consider themselves conservatives would argue that the best approach is to allow the marketplace to operate independently, keep the government out of the marketplace as much as possible, and encourage businesses and investors to spend their money to create jobs that will benefit society as a whole. Liberals are less convinced that an unregulated market will remain competitive. As a popular economics column puts it, liberals believe that competition "breeds monopoly and unfairly distributes wealth and power into too few hands. Thus they generally favor unionization as one way to neutralize that power and assure that those who produce the products also can afford to buy them."[7] Conservatives would generally argue that the market itself will force unscrupulous vendors out of business and that those who mistreat their workers will find it hard to get good employees; thus the forces of the market will encourage both ethical behavior and good treatment of workers. Liberals argue that the forces of government must be brought to bear in order to protect the rights of workers and to restrain the excesses brought about by an unfettered market. Without a framework of law, minority rights would be compromised, women would continue to be treated unfairly by employers, and the rights of consumers would not be protected. Liberals argue "that the desire to maximize profits may not translate into safe and reliable products being produced in the best possible working conditions."[8]

A Plea for Moderation

Who is correct in this debate? We most likely will want to say that both are, in spite of the disagreements. In Chapter 1 we encountered the notion of dialectical tension, which prevents our surrendering to either pole completely. Applied to ethics, this dialectical tension leaves us with the sometimes uneasy tension between utilitarian and rights approaches. Each view emphasizes important moral insights, but neither seems adequate by itself. Stressing the morality of outcomes does seem to be an important ethical consideration; good intentions alone are not enough, and it does appear to be the case that a free market produces the best overall total of goods and services for a society. Yet it is also important to guard individual rights and to protect the environment, even if it means reducing somewhat the forces of competition and increasing the role of government in the marketplace. The tension between these two views can be creative by preventing us from pursuing the greatest good at the expense of individual rights or building entitlements so deeply into the system that nothing gets done. This leads us back to Aristotle's plea for moderation, for a reasoned approach to behavior that recognizes the importance of individuals as well as the demands of the larger society. It is not always easy to know how to balance these rival ethical demands, but we should never give up the attempt to do so.

DISCUSSION STARTERS

1 Make a list of all the rights that persons claim in contemporary society. Then categorize them by whether they are moral, legal, or institutional rights. Are we, as a society, sometimes unsure whether a right is a legal or moral one? If so, give examples.

2 Kant thought that the categorical imperative was a philosophical statement of a moral insight that can also be expressed in other, nonphilosophical terms. What are some of the ways this moral principle is expressed?

3 An important aspect of treating someone in a moral way is to avoid treating the person as a means only, according to Kant. Cite some examples of how business practices fall into this error. How could businesses change their behavior to avoid these actions?

4 There is a current debate surrounding what many consider to be excesses in executive compensation. Can you use Rawls to help clarify this debate?

5 Give a Kantian argument for a free market economy. Compare this argument with the utilitarian argument for a free market economy. In what respects do the two approaches agree? In what respects do they disagree?

NOTES

1 Manuel G. Velasquez, *Business Ethics: Concepts and Cases,* 3rd ed. (Englewood Cliffs, NJ: Prentice-Hall, 1992), pp. 80–81.
2 Immanuel Kant, *Foundations of the Metaphysics of Morals,* trans. Lewis White Beck (New York: Liberal Arts Press, 1959), p. 6.
3 Ibid., pp. 39, 47, 51, 54.
4 John Rawls, *A Theory of Justice* (Cambridge, MA: Belknap Press of Harvard University Press, 1971), p. 60.
5 Lester Thurow, *Head to Head: The Coming Economic Battle among Japan, Europe, and America* (New York: Morrow, 1992), p. 32.
6 Velasquez, *Business Ethics,* p. 99.
7 Ross M. LaRoe and John Charles Pool, "The Instant Economist," CD, Aug. 15, 1992.
8 Ibid.

CASE STUDY

The Johns-Manville Company has become synonymous with behavior that is not only detrimental to employees but to the corporation as well. The company was charged with ignoring employee health and safety over several decades; legal claims finally brought the firm into Chapter 11 bankruptcy. As you read this case, ask yourself whether the utilitarian concerns outweighed the concern for individual rights and what changes in the corporate culture would have called for preventive action much sooner than it occurred.

LIVING AND DYING WITH ASBESTOS

Asbestos is a fibrous mineral used for fireproofing, electrical insulation, building materials, brake linings, and chemical filters. If you are exposed long enough to asbestos particles—usually ten or more years—you can develop a chronic lung inflammation called asbestosis, which makes

Source: William H. Shaw, *Business Ethics.* © 1991 Wadsworth Publishing Co. Used by permission.

breathing difficult and infection easy. Also linked to asbestos exposure is mesethelioma, a cancer of the chest lining that sometimes doesn't develop until forty years after the first exposure. Although the first major scientific conference on the dangers of asbestos was not held until 1964, the asbestos industry knew of its dangers over fifty years ago.

As early as 1932, the British documented the occupational hazards of asbestos dust inhalation.[1] Indeed, on September 25, 1935, the editors of the trade journal *Asbestos* wrote to Sumner Simpson, president of Raybestos-Manhattan, a leading asbestos company, asking permission to publish an article on the dangers of asbestos. Simpson refused and later praised the magazine for not printing the article. In a letter to Vandivar Brown, secretary of Johns-Manville, another asbestos manufacturer, Simpson observed: "The less said about asbestos the better off we are." Brown agreed, adding that any article on asbestosis should reflect American, not English, data.

In fact, American data were available, and Brown, as one of the editors of the journal, knew it. Working on behalf of Raybestos-Manhattan and Johns-Manville and their insurance carrier, Metropolitan Life Insurance Company, Anthony Lanza had conducted research between 1929 and 1931 on 126 workers with three or more years of asbestos exposure. But Brown and others were not pleased with the paper Lanza submitted to them for editorial review. Lanza, said Brown, had failed to portray asbestosis as milder than silicosis, a lung disease caused by long-term inhalation of silica dust and resulting in chronic shortness of breath. Under the then-pending Workmen's Compensation law, silicosis was categorized as a compensible disease. If asbestosis was worse than silicosis or indistinguishable from it, then it too would have to be covered. Apparently Brown didn't want this and thus requested that Lanza depict asbestosis as less serious than silicosis. Lanaza complied and also omitted from his published report the fact that more than half the workers examined—67 of 126—were suffering from asbestosis.

Meanwhile, Sumner Simpson was writing F. H. Schulter, president of Thermoid Rubber Company, to suggest that several manufacturers sponsor further asbestos experiments. The sponsors, said Simpson, could exercise oversight prerogatives; they "could determine from time to time after the findings are made whether we wish any publication or not." Added Simpson: "It would be a good idea to distribute the information to the medical fraternity, providing it is of the right type and would not injure our companies." Lest there should be any question about the arbiter of publication, Brown wrote to officials at the laboratory conducting the tests:

It is our further understanding that the results obtained will be considered the property of those who are advancing the required funds, who will determine whether, to what extent and in what manner they shall be made public. In the event it is deemed desirable that the results be made public, the manuscript of your study will be submitted to us for approval prior to publication.

Industry officials were concerned with more than controlling information flow. They also sought to deny workers early evidence of their asbestosis. Dr. Kenneth Smith, medical director of a Johns-Manville plant in Canada, explained why seven workers he found to have asbestosis should not be informed of their disease:

It should be remembered that although these men have the X-ray evidence of asbestosis, they are working today and definitely are not disabled from asbestosis. They have not been told of this diagnosis, for it is felt that as long as the man feels well, is happy at home and at work, and his physical condition remains good, nothing should be said. When he becomes disabled and sick, then the diagnosis should be made and the claim submitted *by the Company*. The fibrosis of this disease is irreversible and permanent so that eventually compensation will be paid to each of these men. But as long as the man is not disabled, it is felt that he should not be told of his condition so that he can live and work in peace and the Company can benefit by his many years of experience. Should the man be told of his condition today there is a very definite possibility that he would become mentally and physically ill, simply through the knowledge that he has asbestosis.

When lawsuits filed by asbestos workers who had developed cancer reached the industry in the 1950s, Dr. Smith suggested that the industry retain the Industrial Health Foundation to conduct a cancer study that would, in effect, squelch the asbestos-cancer connection. The asbestos companies refused, claiming that such a study would only bring further unfavorable publicity to the industry and that there wasn't enough evidence linking asbestos and cancer industry-wide to warrant it.

Shortly before his death in 1977, Dr. Smith was asked whether he had ever recommended to Johns-Manville officials that warning labels be placed on insulation products containing asbestos. He provided the following testimony:

The reasons why the caution labels were not implemented immediately, it was a business decision as far as I could understand. Here was a recommendation, the corporation is in business to make, to provide jobs for people and make money for stockholders and they had to take into consideration the effects of everything they did, and if the application of a caution label identifying a product as hazardous would cut our sales, there would be serious financial implications. And the powers that be had to make some effort to judge the necessity of the label vs. the consequences of placing the label on the product.

Dr. Smith's testimony and related documents have figured prominently in hundreds of asbestos-related lawsuits, totaling more than $1 billion. In March 1981, a settlement was reached in nine separate lawsuits brought by 680 New Jersey asbestos workers at a Raybestos-Manhattan plant. Several asbestos manufacturers, as well as Metropolitan Life Insurance, were named as defendants. Under the terms of the settlement, the workers affected will share in a $9.4 million court-administered compensation fund. Each worker will be paid compensation according to the length of exposure to asbestos and the severity of the disease contracted.

By 1982, an average of 500 new asbestos cases were being filed each month against Manville (as Johns-Manville was now called), and the company was losing more than half the cases that went to trial. In ten separate cases, juries had also awarded punitive damages, averaging $616,000 a case. By August, 20,000 claims had been filed against the company, and Manville filed for bankruptcy in federal court. This action froze the lawsuits in their place and forced asbestos victims to stand in line with other Manville creditors. After more than three years of legal haggling, Manville's reorganization plan was finally approved by the bankruptcy court. The agreement set up a trust fund valued at approximately $2.5 billion to pay Manville's asbestos claimants. To fund the trust, shareholders were required to surrender half the value of their stock, and the company had to give up much of its projected earnings over the next twenty-five years.[2]

NOTES

1 See Samuel S. Epstein, "The Asbestos 'Pentagon Papers,'" in Mark Green and Robert Massie, Jr., eds., *The Big Business Reader: Essays on Corporate America* (New York: Pilgrim Press, 1980), 1154–65. This article is the primary source of the facts and quotations reported here.
2 See Robert Mokhiber, *Corporate Crime and Violence* (San Francisco: Sierra Club Books, 1988), 285–86; and Arthur Sharplin, "Manville Lives On as Victims Continue to Die," *Business and Society Review* 65(Spring 1988):27–28.

PART **TWO**

BUSINESS AND ITS RELATIONSHIPS

"This might not be ethical. Is that a problem for anybody?"

Business and Customers

CHAPTER OUTLINE

Glenn E. Corlett

Chief Operating Officer and
Executive Vice President
N. W. Ayer Incorporated

"In advertising a product, it is sometimes tempting to bend or break the truth in order to increase sales quickly; however, in the long run, advertising only succeeds when it creates customer loyalty by building trust and confidence. Our objective is to enjoy a long-term relationship with our client. This can only be achieved through the use of strategies for which both the client and we can be proud."

Business needs customers. After all, what point is there in making a product unless there is someone to sell it to? Or why offer a service unless there are those who want that service? To use a biological metaphor, businesses and customers exist in a *symbiotic relationship:* the public depends on business to deliver the necessities for survival and to offer discretionary goods and services. Businesses, in turn, depend on the continued support of their clients and customers in order to ensure their survival.

The number of topics that can be included under the rubric of business and its customers is vast, but this chapter focuses more narrowly on advertising practices and product safety and liability concerns. First, however, we take a look at some of the philosophical issues that will guide our discussion of these topics.

BUSINESS AND LONG-TERM CONSIDERATIONS

As we saw in Chapter 2, the search for profits is best achieved when a business gives its highest priorities to values other than the sought-for profits. As Aristotle argued, we seek happiness for its own sake, but happiness occurs as we search for other virtues. In a similar way, profit is an intrinsic good for a business, but a business can best enhance its profits by emphasizing instrumental goods—that is, things that are not good in themselves but good because they lead to other good things. There is another dimension to this discussion of the goals of actions, and that is the importance of long-term versus short-term goals. No philosopher has better explored this important distinction than Epicurus, a Greek philosopher of the third century B.C.E.

Epicurus champions the pursuit of pleasure as the supreme goal of life, but this does not mean the unrestrained pursuit of excesses of any kind. Instead, Epicurus argues for a life of sober restraint and moderation in all things. He shares with Aristotle the belief that a life lived according to rational principles is the best life, one that would be free from the pain that comes from excesses. Epicurus' name survives in the term "epicurean," which is used to refer to someone with elevated tastes and a lifestyle centered on pleasure. But, as a survey of his writings shows, Epicurus counsels a way of life very different from what the popular use of the term implies. Although his view is a form of "hedonism," a term derived from the Greek word for "pleasure," the pleasures Epicurus recommends are those that are easy to achieve and simple in nature. Chief among these is the pleasure to be gained from a life lived according to reason.

Central to Epicurus' analysis is the conviction that we must distinguish between short-term and long-term pleasures. Against the predictable human tendency to accept the pleasures of the moment, Epicurus argues that a rational calculation of one's long-term good is better than acting on short-term pleasures. The prolonged pursuit of pleasure is best achieved by restraint and enlightened choice. A moment's reflection shows that a person who makes decisions on the basis of short-term gain would not be acting very reasonably. Should I spend the evening drinking with friends rather than study for the exam? Should I drop out of college now rather than pay all that tuition and still have to hunt for a job? Should I ignore that sharp pain in my side, hoping that it will go away? Should I indulge myself and buy that expensive car even though I do not know whether my job is secure?

EPICURUS ON PRUDENCE

And since pleasure is the first good and natural to us, for this very reason we do not choose every pleasure, but sometimes we pass over many pleasures, when greater discomfort accrues to us as the result of them: and similarly we think many pains better than pleasures, since a greater pleasure comes to us when we have endured pains for a long time. Every pleasure then because of its natural kinship to us is good, yet not every pleasure is to be chosen: even as every pain also is an evil, yet not all are always of a nature to be avoided. Yet by a scale of comparison and by the consideration of advantages and disadvantages we must form our judgment on all these matters. For the good on certain occasions we treat as bad, and conversely the bad as good. . . .

When, therefore, we maintain that pleasure is the end, we do not mean the pleasures of profligates and those that consist in sensuality, as is supposed by some who are either ignorant or disagree with us or do not understand, but freedom from pain in the body and from trouble in the mind. For it is not continuous drinking and revellings, nor the satisfaction of lusts, nor the enjoyment of fish and other luxuries of the wealthy table, which produce a pleasant life, but sober reasoning, searching out the motives for all choice and avoidance, and banishing mere opinions, to which are due the greatest disturbance of the spirit.

Of all this the beginning and the greatest good is prudence. Wherefore prudence is a more precious thing even than philosophy: for from prudence are sprung all the other virtues, and it teaches us that it is not possible to live pleasantly without living prudently and honourably and justly, nor, again, to live a life of prudence, honour, and justice without living pleasantly.

Source: "Epicurus to Menoeceus," in *The Stoic and Epicurean Philosophers,* ed. W. J. Oates (New York: Modern Library, 1940), p. 32.

The point is, acting for the sake of short-term goals only is not very smart, either for individuals or for businesses.

No philosopher ever understood or stated this better than Epicurus, and it does not take too much of an extrapolation to apply the wisdom of Epicurus to business activity. Profitability is best served by taking into consideration many variables, including the long-term loyalties of satisfied customers who return again and again to a business for goods and services. In the short run, perhaps, a business can succeed by ignoring customers, but the long-run success of the company is put in peril by such attitudes.

THE COMPANY AND THE CONSUMER

One way some observers choose to express the relationship between company and consumer is embodied in the Latin expression *caveat emptor*, "let the buyer beware." As a principle it means something like this: "the buyer assumes all the risks when making a purchase, and it is the buyer's responsibility to be assured of the suitability and dependability of the product. The one offering the goods or services has no particular responsibility to tell the truth and certainly has no ongoing responsibility to the consumer." A contemporary metaphor for this description of the relation between company and consumer is that of the poker game, which Albert Z. Carr used in his widely reprinted article "Is Business Bluffing Ethical?" "Poker's own brand of ethics is different from the ethical ideals of civilized human relationship," Carr claims. "The game calls for distrust of the other fellow. It ignores the claim of friendship. Cunning deception and concealment of one's strength and intentions, not kindness and open-heartedness, are vital in poker. No one thinks any the worse of poker on that account. And no one should think any the worse of the game of business because its standards of right and wrong differ from the prevailing traditions of morality in our society."[1]

Carr's article stirred up a storm of protest and, according to *Harvard Business Review* managing editor Timothy B. Blodgett, "few articles . . . aroused a response as great and as vociferous."[2] Commenting on the short-term implications of Carr's attitude, one business executive wrote, "All of us in business know that 'playing the game' yields only short-term rewards. We'll admit our faults, but not endorse them as part of our philosophy. To do so would bring the house of business down on itself."[3] A sales representative for a national corporation also wrote, "My advice to Mr. Carr would be to read Aristotle again, and

A Case in Point . . .

The *Wall Street Journal,* in a feature on the L. L. Bean Company, related an incident that tested the company's customer-satisfaction principles. A woman returned a sweater, unworn but obviously not a currently stocked item, with a note saying that she would like a refund for the purchase her husband had made 32 years earlier. According to her note, her husband never wore it, never liked it, and as she was going through his things after his death she found the sweater. The L. L. Bean Company sent a refund.

The company states its guarantee in each of its catalogs: "All of our products are guaranteed to give 100% satisfaction in every way. Return anything purchased from us at any time if it proves otherwise. We will replace it, refund your purchase price or credit your credit card, as you wish. We do not want you to have anything from L. L. Bean that is not completely satisfactory."

The company's passion for quality and customer service has driven its corporate culture from the firm's beginning. Leon L. Bean's first product was the Maine hunting boot, an invention of his own design that he sold to other hunting enthusiasts. When the boot proved to be defective, Bean personally refunded the purchase price and made a commitment to quality and customer satisfaction that continues to dominate the decisions of the company. The current president, Leon Gorman, grandson of the founder, even scaled back the company's growth plans lest growth diminish the company's ability to provide quality products and services. Such commitments pay off, as the company's annual sales of more than three quarters of a billion dollars attest.

Sources: WSJ, Dec. 5, 1973, supplemented by an oral report from Paul Sampson, educational director of the Direct Marketing Association; WSJ, July 31, 1989; *Boston Globe,* Mar. 7, 1991; *Chicago Tribune,* Dec. 26, 1985; FORT, Apr. 5, 1993.

he will find that Aristotle was correct in his observation that much of our being is formed by personal, self-imposed discipline. If we permit ourselves to be weak in one area, it flows into our personality in other areas. Man cannot make excuses in one area by saying this is a game, and then become a strong, moral creature in other things—we just were not made that way."[4]

Relating the issue to the importance of building strong consumer loyalty, an employee relations counselor wrote, "In the long run, deception cannot compete against quality. Fortunately, we are beginning to see the emergence of business organizations which recognize that people have had their bellyful of shoddy merchandise. (And shoddy merchandise is the inevitable byproduct of a business that operates on the ethic of bluffing.)" "The fallacy in Carr's line of thinking," this reader claims, is "the fact that business ultimately must rely on the consuming public. The public may not be interested in joining the poker game when it finds it can get full value from a business enterprise that puts its time and effort into developing a product worthy of people."[5] Again, Epicurus provides wise counsel: long-term success demands behavior that ignores short-term gain.

CRITICISMS OF ADVERTISING

Epicurus' counsel to avoid unnecessary desires is echoed in the criticisms of advertising offered by John Kenneth Galbraith, who blasted the industry in his book *The Affluent Society,* for creating what he called "the dependence effect." His basic complaint about advertising is that it stimulates wants that are unnecessary, desires that, to be filled, require that disproportionate amounts of our time be devoted to the acquisition of privately produced goods. The loser in this constant spiral of acquisition is the public, for the more we spend on the acquisition of things, the less is available to help relieve poverty or to improve the quality of our common life by building parks, hospitals, roads, and schools. In a particularly vigorous metaphor, Galbraith likens the power of advertising to the effect of demons.

> Were it so that man on arising each morning was assailed by demons which instilled in him a passion sometimes for silk shirts, sometimes for kitchenware, sometimes for chamber-pots, and sometimes for orange squash, there would be every reason to applaud the effort to find the goods, however odd, that quenched this flame. But should it be that his passion was the result of his first having cultivated the demons, and should it also be that his effort to allay it stirred the demons to ever greater and greater effort, there would be question as to how rational was his solution. Unless restrained by conventional attitudes, he might wonder if the solution lay with more goods or fewer demons.[6]

In a rationally ordered society, Galbraith argues, less of the productive capacity of society would be directed toward satisfying wants, many of which are unnecessary and are created by the power of advertising itself. "If the individual's wants are to be urgent," Galbraith says, "they must be original with himself. They cannot be urgent if they must be contrived for him. And above all they must not be contrived by the process of production by which they are satisfied."[7]

Notice the value judgments Galbraith is making: it would be *better* for society if its productive capacity were turned away from the satisfaction of contrived wants (contrived by the power of advertising) and devoted to more socially useful products and services. We could even interpret this as a sort of hidden utilitarian argument, that the greatest good of society would be addressed by directing society's productive capacity to social goods. But this claim is open to the same objections made to Mill's introduction of qualitative judgments into the utilitarian formula. Utilitarianism is based on the claim that the test of the desirability of anything is its tendency to promote pleasure and decrease pain. But to have someone else—an expert, a social critic, an economic planner—decide that most people are wrong when they find pleasure in responding to advertising is inconsistent with utilitarianism's basic premise.

To be fair to critics of advertising, such as Galbraith, we have to admit that Epicurus would doubtless agree with them. It very well may be the wisest course of action to turn ourselves away from the mindless acquisition of material things to other goods, such as improving family life, enriching relationships, cultivating the life of the mind, enjoying the pleasures of friends and companions, and even stopping to "smell the roses." It is the mark of prudence, Epicurus argues, to be able to distinguish between those desires that are for necessary things and those desires that are for unnecessary things. One should also be aware of the difference between natural desires (for food, shelter, companionship) and unnatural desires (fame, fortune, power) and concentrate one's effort on the natural and necessary desires. Here is how he put it:

> We must consider that of desires some are natural, others vain, and of the natural some are necessary and others merely natural; and of the necessary some are necessary for happiness, others for the repose of the body, and others for very life. The right understanding of these facts enables us to refer all choice and avoidance to the health of the body and the soul's freedom from disturbance, since this is the aim of the life of blessedness. For it is to obtain this end that we always act, namely, to avoid pain and fear. And when this is once secured for us, all the tempest of the soul is dispersed, since the living creature has not to wander as though in search of something that is missing, and to look for some other thing by which he can fulfil the good of the soul and the good of the body.[8]

How ironic that the man whose name is now synonymous with extravagant dining (we call such a person an *epicure*) actually counseled the opposite behavior and even urged freedom from such desires. He argues that if we have only a few things, we will enjoy them more than if we had many things, and if we do not become used to rich and expensive foods, then simple fare, which is easier to obtain, will satisfy us more. "And so plain savours bring us a pleasure equal to a luxurious diet," Epicurus says, "and bread and water produce the highest pleasure, when one who needs them puts them to his lips. To grow accustomed therefore to simple and not luxurious diet gives us health to the full, and makes a man alert for the needful employments of life."[9] Clearly, Epicurus could not have made a career on Madison Avenue.

Although the wisest of us might follow Epicurus' advice, there is nothing particularly unethical about manufacturers attempting to entice us to buy their products, even though prudence would say we should not let such messages stimulate unnecessary desires. Defenders of advertising give a powerful counterargument to the kinds of criticisms that Galbraith makes. If we assume that we, as individuals, should be free to make our own decisions (the principle of autonomy), we cannot very well allow an expert, be it Galbraith or anyone else, to make our decisions for us by deciding what should and should not be presented to us—(assuming that advertising is directed to responsible adults; advertising directed to children is quite another matter). And if we accept the conclusion argued for in Chapter 4 that the free market is the fairest way of distributing society's goods and services, then restraint of advertising would be a restraint on the freedom of the market and therefore unethical.

Another argument for advertising is that it disseminates information, allowing for more and better informed choices. It also forces manufacturers to keep prices as low as possible in order to compete with other suppliers of the same good or service. Without price advertising, so the argument goes, we would lose a valuable basis for comparing one product with another. It is interesting, though, that these same arguments are currently raging about the advertisement of legal services. Defenders of such advertisement say that it keeps prices down by forcing legal professionals to compete with each other in the marketplace. Critics say just the opposite: it stimulates unnecessary desires and appeals to our baser feelings ("Have you been recently injured? There is a possibility that you have money coming to you. Call us for a free consultation").

Who is right in this debate that has one side arguing that we should limit advertising because it has an overall harmful effect on society and the other side arguing that advertising promotes free choice and allows individuals to exercise their freedom and autonomy? This question has already been answered in part by public policy, which now limits the ability of manufacturers to advertise certain products—no cigarette or liquor advertisements on television (except for beer)—and sets requirements that producers of both products include warning messages on labels and in print advertisements; makes restrictions on how long a manufacturer can claim that a product is "new and improved" (six months); puts limits on the health claims made by drug companies for over-the-counter drugs, and is involved in a growing furor over nutritional claims made about foods. The list could go on and on, but the point is that public policy, in the name of public good, places limits on the rights of individual manufacturers to advertise some products.

We see here another example of the tension between deontological and utilitarian principles. Utilitarian arguments would stress the need to restrain the individual excesses of greedy advertisers for the overall public good. Deontological arguments would point to the rights of individuals to be free to make their own choices, a freedom that is abrogated by the decision of someone else to keep certain kinds of product claims off the market. In trying to balance these rival values, we face an ethical dilemma. Still, there are certain conclusions we can reach about what is unacceptable in advertising.

ETHICAL PROBLEMS IN ADVERTISING

Misrepresentation

Advertising must be truthful. On this, both sides in this ethical discussion would agree. The utilitarian argument goes something like this: the free market is the fairest way of distributing society's goods and services; anything that interferes with that freedom is a distortion of the market and therefore unethical. Making false claims about a product is precisely such a distortion, because consumers cannot make good choices on the basis of unreliable information. Therefore, false advertising is unethical. A similar conclusion can be reached by deontological considerations: each person who makes a claim must be able to say that this behavior could become universal law. But if advertisers lied when convenient to them, no one would believe any advertisements and this would destroy the entire advertising industry. Therefore, false claims in advertising are immoral.

In short, advertising works because most people believe its claims. An advertiser can contemplate lying in advertising only because most

A Case in Point . . .

Two men who happened to observe a Volvo ad being made in a rodeo arena in Austin, Texas, saw something they did not like. Dan White, described as "an unemployed Volvo buff," and Don Horne, father of Dan's friend, heard the sound of an abrasive saw cutting steel. Upon closer investigation they discovered that workers were cutting through the support pillars on all of the cars in the demonstration except for the Volvo, which was reinforced with wood and steel. When the ads were filmed, a six-ton monster truck rolled over a line of cars, crushing the roofs of all, except for the Volvo. White and Horne reported what they saw to the Texas attorney general's office. Four months later, when Volvo ran the ads, the attorney general's office took action.

As part of its settlement with the Texas attorney general's office, Volvo apologized publicly in corrective statements in *USA Today* and other newspapers, changed advertising agencies, and paid a fine of $316,250. In its public apology, Joseph L. Nicolato, president and CEO of Volvo Cars of North America, said: "Volvo has built its reputation on honesty and candor. It was not the intention of Volvo to produce an advertisement which deceived or misled." The defense he gave for the behavior of the film team making the ad was that it was done "to enable the filming to be done without threatening the safety of the production crew." How much did the deception cost Volvo? The fine is a known quantity. The loss in consumer confidence is harder to give a dollar value. An *Adweek* writer summed it up in the following words: "With a single faked spot, Volvo has tarnished an image of trust and safety that took two decades to build."

Sources: USA, Nov. 6, 1990; NYT, Nov. 6 and 14, 1990; WSJ, Nov. 8 and 14, 1990; *Austin* (Texas) *American Statesman,* Nov. 6, 1990; *Adweek,* Nov. 12, 1990.

people do not lie. To be sure, we expect a certain amount of puffery in advertising, but not outright lying. A pattern of lying in advertising would destroy it as a sales medium.

Manipulation

Another important criterion for ethical advertising and marketing strategies is the avoidance of manipulative tactics. Tom L. Beauchamp, a noted writer on issues in business ethics, defines manipulation as "a broad category that includes any successful attempt to elicit a desired response from another person by noncoercively altering the structure of

available choices or by nonpersuasively altering the person's percep-
tions of those choices." He includes in the notion of manipulation such
activities as "indoctrination, propaganda, emotional pressure, irra-
tional persuasion, temptation, seduction, and deception."[10] Probably
no product calls for the use of more of the string of efforts just mentioned than does the advertising of cigarettes.

Think about it. How would you like to try to entice people to buy
the following product? It tastes bad, will make one sick the first time it
is tried, stinks up everything with which it comes in contact, stains fin-
gers and teeth, produces bad breath, destroys one's sense of taste,
causes fires—sometimes with fatal results—prompts others to ask you
not to use it in their presence, and contributes to death by cancer. In
spite of all these drawbacks, the sale of cigarettes continues. Advertising for this product focuses on status ("You've come a long way
baby"), image ("What does it take to be a smooth character?"), and
pleasure ("Come to where the flavor is").

Sometimes, though, these strategies come under attack. One manufacturer of cigarettes, R. J. Reynolds, a unit of RJR Nabisco, found
itself attacked from all sides for developing advertising plans for a cigarette named Uptown aimed especially at African-Americans. Secretary
of Health and Human Services Louis Sullivan accused the company of
using "slick and sinister advertising" and "promoting a culture of cancer." The head of the American Cancer Society unit in Philadelphia,
where the test marketing was to occur, said of the company, "Here
comes R. J. Reynolds, with a business-as-usual attitude and no feeling
of social or moral responsibility and targets the community with
death."[11]

STANDARDS OF PRACTICE OF THE AMERICAN ASSOCIATION
OF ADVERTISING AGENCIES

First adopted October 16, 1924—Most recently revised September 18, 1990

We **hold** that a responsibility of advertising agencies is to be a constructive force in
business.

We **hold** that, to discharge this responsibility, advertising agencies must recognize an obligation, not only to their clients, but to the public, the media they employ,
and to each other. As a business, the advertising agency must operate within the
framework of competition. It is recognized that keen and vigorous competition, honestly conducted, is necessary to the growth and the health of American business.

However, unethical competitive practices in the advertising agency business lead to financial waste, dilution of service, diversion of manpower, loss of prestige, and tend to weaken public confidence both in advertisements and in the institution of advertising.

We **hold** that the advertising agency should compete on merit and not by attempts at discrediting or disparaging a competitor agency, or its work, directly or by inference, or by circulating harmful rumors about another agency, or by making unwarranted claims of particular skill in judging or prejudging advertising copy.

To these ends, the American Association of Advertising Agencies has adopted the following *Creative Code* as being in the best interests of the public, the advertisers, the media, and the agencies themselves. The A.A.A.A. believes the Code's provisions serve as a guide to the kind of agency conduct that experience has shown to be wise, foresighted, and constructive. In accepting membership, an agency agrees to follow it.

Creative Code

We, the members of the American Association of Advertising Agencies, in addition to supporting and obeying the laws and legal regulations pertaining to advertising, undertake to extend and broaden the application of high ethical standards. Specifically, we will not knowingly create advertising that contains:

a False or misleading statements or exaggerations, visual or verbal
b Testimonials that do not reflect the real opinion of the individual(s) involved
c Price claims that are misleading
d Claims insufficiently supported or that distort the true meaning or practicable application of statements made by professional or scientific authority
e Statements, suggestions, or pictures offensive to public decency or minority segments of the population

We recognize that there are areas that are subject to honestly different interpretations and judgment. Nevertheless, we agree not to recommend to an advertiser, and to discourage the use of, advertising that is in poor or questionable taste or that is deliberately irritating through aural or visual content or presentation.

Comparative advertising shall be governed by the same standards of truthfulness, claim substantiation, tastefulness, etc., as apply to other types of advertising.

These Standards of Practice of the American Association of Advertising Agencies come from the belief that sound and ethical practice is good business. Confidence and respect are indispensable to success in a business embracing the many intangibles of agency service and involving relationships so dependent upon good faith.

Clear and willful violations of these Standards of Practice may be referred to the Board of Directors of the American Association of Advertising Agencies for appropriate action, including possible annulment of membership as provided by Article IV, Section 5, of the Constitution and By-Laws.

Scarcely had the furor over the cigarette Uptown died down when the company found itself in the midst of another controversy, for its plans to direct a new cigarette toward a target population of "poorly educated white women," which the company called "virile females." The typical "virile female" was described as an 18- to 24-year-old woman "with no education beyond high school, whose favorite television roles are Roseanne . . . and whose chief aspiration is to get married in her early 20s and spend her free time 'with her boyfriend doing whatever he is doing.'" Secretary Sullivan again attacked the company: "It is especially reprehensible to lure young people into smoking and potential lifelong nicotine addiction, and the risk that smoking specifically poses for women adds another tawdry dimension to any cigarette marketing effort aimed at younger women."[12] In the face of all the adverse publicity, RJR withdrew plans to market both brands.

Similar pressures mounted against the advertising strategies of a brewery that attempted to market ale named after Crazy Horse, a Sioux chief. Surgeon General Antonia Novello attacked the company saying, "These types of targeting products just keep coming back. . . . When will it stop?"[13] The brewery denied that it was targeting minority groups, insisting that its product honored the Indian heritage, although Native American leaders reject that claim. "Crazy Horse thought alcohol would destroy the Indian people," according to Gregg Bourland, chairman of the Cheyenne River Sioux tribe in South Dakota. The surgeon general wants Congress to ban alcoholic products that "disparage cultural symbols and appeal to Indians and the urban poor."[14]

Manipulative tactics include overstating the effectiveness of the product, failing to give full disclosure of the risks of using the product, and setting up unrealistic expectations of what the product can do. Government increasingly steps in to protect consumers from misleading or high-pressure tactics by giving consumers time to back out of purchases of products sold door-to-door or land offers for retirement property. Misleading practices, although unethical because they deceive and mislead, may boost corporate profits in the short run, but in the long run such practices undermine the confidence consumers have in the products being offered in the marketplace and in the claims made about them.

Paternalism

The issue becomes somewhat more complicated, however, when we view advertising in light of another important value, that of avoiding paternalism. Paternalism can best be described as the attitude that tries to protect consumers from things that someone else deems harmful. Paternalism is not intrinsically a bad thing. As the term itself implies, parents have such a relationship with their children. Most would agree that parents not only have the right but the duty to protect their children from harmful and dangerous influences. The reason for this is that children, by virtue of their age and inexperience, are not in a position to make sound judgments, so it is the parents' responsibility to impose adult judgments. Paternalism becomes an ethical issue when it is applied to relationships between rational adults. Paternalism overrides autonomy, the value of letting persons make up their own minds and decide for themselves.

Here again we see a conflict between ethical values. On the one hand we value the right of unrestricted speech and the freedom of consumers to make their own choices without the paternalistic voice of government telling them what they can and cannot buy. On the other hand, a utilitarian standard would argue for restrictions on certain kinds of advertising in the name of the public good. How to balance these competing moral claims produces ethical conflict that we do not clearly know how to resolve. The issue of tobacco marketing in general (even setting aside the controversial strategies mentioned earlier) has become so prominent in this national debate that the *Journal of the American Medical Association* devoted its December 11, 1991, issue to the topic, with heavy emphasis on marketing strategies aimed especially at young people. In its editorial statement, *JAMA* said, "The success of the tobacco industry is dependent on recruiting people who don't believe that smoking kills. Enticing children, Third World populations, and disadvantaged members of our own society to smoke is the only way for tobacco companies to make up for the number of smokers who quit or die." *JAMA* continued, "We should be especially alarmed at the tobacco industry's effort to recruit children to nicotine addiction . . . but young people do not have the information and experience to recognize the dangers of smoking cigarettes."[15]

The government has acted in a paternalistic way in requiring warning labels on cigarettes and alcoholic beverages. But when do we cross the line from offering important information to consumers and acting paternalistically toward them? This issue is further complicated in that all advertising strategies, in a sense, are attempts to get consumers to act in a way different from the way they would act without advertising. The question is one of fairness, and it is not always easy to decide what kinds of advertising behavior avoid paternalistic attitudes and at the same time respect individual autonomy.

The notion of autonomy (from Greek words that literally mean "self-ruled") includes both the notions of freedom and responsibility. If a person is free to choose an action, that person is therefore responsible for it. As we have already seen, Immanuel Kant argued persuasively that the only moral act is a free act. One cannot force another to do a moral thing. By extension, if a person is not free to act rationally (such as a child would be, or a person with severe mental limitations), then it makes no sense to hold that person morally responsible for the action. Any advertising that takes advantage of individuals does not respect the individual's autonomy.

Taking Unfair Advantage

Advertising that is directed solely at children is increasingly coming under scrutiny. The problem results from the fact that children, due to their limited ability to assess the claims made by advertisers and to their intellectual and emotional immaturity, are not able to exercise responsible choices. Those who might reject paternalism in relations among adults call for it here. Appeals for government regulation of broadcasters' right to direct advertising to children were not encouraged by the Federal Communications Commission as a result of the climate of deregulation that dominated Washington during the 1980s. Congress likewise debated the issue, with the terms of discussion often divided along partisan lines. The debate itself brought to light several advertising practices aimed at children that critics challenge as being unethical:

• The National Association for Better Broadcasting, a public interest group located in California, charged in a complaint to the Federal Communications Commission that a Los Angeles television station agreed to a barter arrangement for showing a television program that was provided by a toy manufacturer whose product was prominently featured in the program.

• Increasingly, weekend programs for children are product-generated shows that some critics, such as an organization called Action for Children's Television, say are really nothing but "program-length commercials." One trade magazine acknowledged in a report on government attempts to regulate advertising to children that "children's programming has become just one long product tie-in."

• Networks seem unwilling to place restrictions on the amount of television programming devoted to commercials. Government proposals to limit advertising on children's programs to 10.5 minutes per hour on weekends were opposed by the Association of National Advertisers as amounting to ad censorship. Falling into a "slippery slope" fallacy (the claim that if one begins a course of action, there is no stopping point until the extreme has been reached), a spokesperson for the American Advertising Federation said, "If the would-be censors are allowed to ban or restrict truthful ads for any legal consumer product, the first step will have been taken down the road to the loss of commercial speech for all products." The 10.5 minutes per hour was the more lenient of two congressional bills, the other of which, originating in the Senate, would have lowered the limit to 9.5 minutes per hour.

An advertising trade journal, not too enthusiastic about legislative restraints on advertising, admitted that the industry's failure "to enforce meaningful standards itself" in limiting advertising directed toward children is virtually inviting government regulation.[16] The industry might learn from Epicurus that its long-term good depends on its willingness to temper its short-term interests. This no doubt explains the reasons why many companies are willing to devote advertising dollars to associate their organizations with environmental awareness, increase public awareness of certain social concerns, and reaffirm the companies' commitment to customer satisfaction.

CONSUMER SAFETY AND PRODUCT LIABILITY

By now you have probably seen a pattern emerging. A predictable response to questionable business practices is a call for government regulation and restriction. This usually results in the establishment of a government agency, a profusion of regulations, and a mechanism for imposing sanctions or assessing penalties. A partial listing of such agencies concerned with worker and consumer protection includes the following:

Federal Trade Commission	Regulates advertising practices
Food and Drug Administration	Regulates safety of drugs and purity of foods
Consumer Products Safety Commission	Provides consumer protection against unsafe products
Nuclear Regulatory Commission	Regulates nuclear energy and consumer access to radioactive materials

Occupational Health and Safety Administration	Protects worker safety
Federal Communications Commission	Regulates all aspects of the communications industry and imposes practice standards to protect consumers

Empowering these and other agencies are specific laws defining unacceptable business practices. Among some recent ones are the Federal Hazardous Substances Labeling Act (1960), the Truth in Lending Act (1968), the Magnuson-Moss Warranty Act (1975), the Consumer Leasing Act (1976), the Fair Debt Collection Practices Act (1978), and the Toy Safety Act (1984). The Consumer Product Safety Act of 1972 established standards for consumer products and penalties for companies that manufacture hazardous products.[17]

Consumers are protected from hazardous or defective products not only as a result of legislation; the courts are being increasingly used as an avenue for consumer redress. The awards given by courts in civil suits for damages and injury have gotten so broad that many critics are calling for reform of liability laws. In the early years of the United States, courts applied a standard of "common and ordinary care," which demanded that individuals exercise reasonable care and prudence in their conduct.[18] By the middle of the nineteenth century, courts had already begun to move away from an "all or nothing" attitude about negligence toward a doctrine of comparative negligence in which a person's ability to recover damages was due in large part to the negligence of the party causing the harm. In a system of comparative negligence, liability is apportioned as each party contributes to the injury.

By the early twentieth century the courts moved even farther toward protecting the consumer. In a now famous case, decided in 1916, *MacPherson v. Buick Motor Co.*, the U.S. Supreme Court concluded that the manufacturer assumed responsibility to the consumer by the act of placing a product on the market. This expectation on the part of consumers was increased by a landmark case in 1960, *Henningsen v. Bloomfield Motors, Inc.* Henningsen was driving a new Plymouth automobile when there was a loud noise, and the steering wheel jerked out of her control. The car swerved to the right and Henningsen was injured when the car struck a brick wall. The trial court found the manufacturer responsible in large part for Henningsen's injuries on the grounds that when purchasing something as complex as an automobile, the consumer "must rely on the manufacturer who has control of its construction, and to some degree on the dealer who, to the limited extent called for by the manufacturer's instructions, inspects and services it before delivery."[19] The court reasoned that the consumer expects the manufacturer to produce safe products, that compensating consumers for injury caused by a manufacturer's products is a cost of doing business, and that businesses have a special duty to produce safe products.

In another case, also from the 1960s, *Greenman v. Yuba Power Products, Inc.,* the trial court defined the notion of strict liability when it found that "a manufacturer is strictly liable . . . when a product he places on the market, knowing that it is to be used without inspection for defects, proves to have a defect that causes injury to a human being."[20] The doctrine of strict liability is the prevalent view in most courts, though some states, notably Colorado, Idaho, Michigan, and Washington, have adopted comparative responsibility statutes that modify the strict liability approach. Comparative responsibility divides responsibility between plaintiff and defendant when both are negligent.

Whether legislatures define product liability in terms of comparative responsibility or strict liability turns in large part on social policy. In a complex industrial society where consumers use many products the safety and reliability of which they must trust others to guarantee, a strict liability policy is a way of spreading damages across society at large. Whenever a jury awards a damage settlement to a consumer, the costs of that award are borne by subsequent consumers, who will pay a higher price for the product. The higher price is caused not only by the cost of liability insurance but also by the costs associated with remedying the defect in future products. One could argue, in good utilitarian fashion, that the doctrine of strict liability is justifiable because it ultimately causes safer products to be available, thus preventing injury to consumers. On the other hand, it does not seem reasonable for manufacturers to be held responsible for stupid or careless use of their products. Here, again, is a conflict between paternalism and autonomy; and currently the balance, as enforced by the courts, seems to be shifting toward paternalism.

Nothing shows more clearly the ongoing conflict in public policy between deontological and consequentialist criteria. Should a company be found at fault when someone is injured by a product as a result of its misuse? The deontological standard stresses intention: If the company did not knowingly and deliberately put a faulty product into the stream of commerce, then should it be held responsible for the injury of someone using it? The consequentialist standard points to the overall good produced by principles of strict liability: If a company makes a product that injures someone, shouldn't it be held responsible? The debate about which of these two ethical principles should be applied to product liability issues is a classic instance of the ongoing tension between ethical principles.

DISCUSSION STARTERS

1 Do you think Epicurus rationally applied the principles of a hedonistic approach to behavior? Discuss this, especially in terms of his distinction between long-term and short-term pleasures.

2 Epicurus claimed, "It is not possible to live pleasantly without living prudently and honourably and justly." How would you argue for this claim? Against it?

3 What arguments can you marshal against Carr's claim that there should be a separate set of ethical principles for the "game" of business?

4 Do you agree with Galbraith that advertising stimulates unnecessary desires? What defense can you give for Galbraith's view about advertising?

5 Applying ethical standards, what limitations would you advocate for advertising directed at children? The marketing of tobacco products? Using tie-ins with minority groups to sell products?

6 Which standard for product liability seems more ethically defensible, comparative responsibility or strict liability?

NOTES

1 Albert Z. Carr, "Is Business Bluffing Ethical?" *Harvard Business Review* (Jan./Feb. 1968).

2 Timothy B. Blodgett, "Showdown on Business Bluffing," in *Ethics in Practice: Managing the Moral Corporation,* ed. Kenneth R. Andrews (Boston: Harvard Business School Press, 1989), p. 109.

3 Ibid., p. 111.

4 Ibid., p. 114.

5 Ibid., p. 115.

6 John Kenneth Galbraith, *The Affluent Society* (New York: Houghton Mifflin, 1958).

7 Ibid.

8 *The Stoic and Epicurean Philosophers,* ed. W. J. Oates (New York: Modern Library, 1940), p. 31.

9 Ibid., p. 32.
10 Tom L. Beauchamp, "Manipulative Advertising," in *Ethical Theory and Business*, 3rd ed., eds. Tom L. Beauchamp and Norman E. Bowie (Englewood Cliffs, NJ: Prentice-Hall, 1979), p. 425.
11 WSJ, Jan. 20, 1990; and NYT, Jan. 20, 1990.
12 CD, Feb. 19, 1990.
13 CD, May 20, 1992.
14 Ibid.
15 JAMA, Dec. 11, 1991, p. 3185.
16 The information and examples are taken from *Television/Radio Age*, Aug. 8, 1988, and Aug. 7, 1989; *Broadcasting*, Mar. 27, 1989; and *Adweek's Marketing Week*, July 17, 1989.
17 This listing of federal acts came from O. C. Ferrell and John Fraedrich, *Business Ethics* (Boston: Houghton Mifflin, 1991), p. 75.
18 See *Butterfield v. Forrester*, 103 Eng.Rep.926(K.B.1809). I am grateful to Ann Stewart for the research used in discussing the issue of liability.
19 32N.J.358, 161 A.2d69 (1960).
20 *Greenman v. Yuba Power Products, Inc.*, 59Cal.2d57, 377P.2d897, 27 Cal.Rptr.697(1963).

CASE STUDY

The case of the A. H. Robins Company and its product, the Dalkon Shield, illustrates the ongoing tensions in applying the standards of utility and maximizing the effects of a business strategy on stockholders, employees, and customers while being mindful of rights of a minority, the users of the product. The difficulty of predicting consequences, the duty of the company to individual claimants, and the courses of action open to a company with major claims of product defect show the interplay of deontological and utilitarian standards.

A. H. ROBINS: THE DALKON SHIELD

On August 21, 1985, A. H. Robins of Richmond, Virginia—the seventeenth largest pharmaceutical house in America and corporately rated as number 392 in the Fortune 500—filed for reorganization under Chapter 11 of the 1978 Federal Bankruptcy Code. On the surface, Robins seemed to be a thriving company. Its popular products, includ-

Excerpted from a case study written by A. R. Gini, © Loyola University, and T. Sullivan, DePaul University. Reprinted by permission of the authors.

ing Robitussin cough syrup, Chap Stick lip balm, and Sergeant's flea and tick collars for cats and dogs, generated record sales in 1985 of $706 million with a net income in excess of $75 million. Robins' petition for protection under Chapter 11 stems directly from the "blitz of litigation" over a product it has not produced since 1974, the Dalkon Shield intrauterine birth control device. At the time it filed for bankruptcy Robins had been deluged with more than 12,000 personal injury lawsuits charging that the Dalkon Shield was responsible for countless serious illnesses and at least 20 deaths among the women who used it. . . .

The A. H. Robins Company is essentially a family owned and operated organization. The original company was founded by Albert Hartley Robins, a registered pharmacist, in 1866 in Richmond, Virginia. His grandson, E. Claiborne Robins, built and directed the company into a multinational conglomerate which was able to obtain Fortune 500 status by the middle of the twentieth century. . . . Both the family and the company take pride in having "always gone by the book" and always giving their customers a good product at a fair price. In its 120 years of operation the company had done business without having a single product-liability lawsuit filed against it. Critics now claim that Robins has been involved in a directly ordered, prolonged institutional cover-up of the short- and long-term effects of the use of the Dalkon Shield. Moreover, many critics claim that, more than just stonewalling the possible side effects of the Shield, Robins is guilty of marketing a product they knew to be relatively untested, undependable, and therefore potentially dangerous. . . .

IUDs are among the most ancient forms of contraception, known for more than two thousand years. Exactly how an IUD prevents conception is not known. It may interfere with the fertilization of the eggs, but most experts believe that when inserted into the uterus it prevents pregnancy by making it difficult for a fertilized egg to attach itself to the wall of the uterus. Over the centuries the materials used in the fabrication of IUDs include ebony, glass, gold, ivory, pewter, wood, wool, diamond-studded platinum, copper, and plastic.[1] The Dalkon Shield was developed by Dr. Hugh J. Davis, a former professor of obstetrics and gynecology at the Johns Hopkins University, and Irwin Lerner, an electrical engineer. In 1970 they sold their rights to the Shield to Robins, who agreed to pay royalties on future sales and $750,000 in cash. Between 1971 and 1974 Robins sold 4.5 million Dalkon Shields around the world, including 2.85 million in the United States.

By the late 1960s large numbers of women had become concerned about the safety of the Pill. These women formed an ever-growing potential market for an alternative means of birth control. Many of these women switched to "barrier" methods of birth control, particularly the diaphragm, which, when used with spermicidal creams or jellies, can be highly effective, though inconvenient. Others turned to IUDs, which, although convenient, previously had been considered unsafe—causing pelvic infections, irregular bleeding, uterine cramps, and accidental expulsion. . . .

In January 1971 Robins began to sell the Dalkon Shield, promoting it as the "modern, superior," "second generation" and—most importantly—"safe" intrauterine device for birth control. The Shield itself is a nickel-sized plastic device that literally looks like a badge or a shield with spikes around the edges and a thread-sized "nylon tail string," which allowed both the wearer and the physician a means to guarantee that the device had not been expelled. The Shield was relatively inexpensive. The device itself sold for between $3.00 and $4.50 (its production costs were an incredibly low figure of $.25 a Shield). The only other cost associated with the Shield was the doctor's office fee for insertion and a recommended yearly pelvic examination. Dr. Hugh Davis claimed that the Dalkon Shield was the safest and most effective IUD because it is "the only IUD which is truly anatomically engineered for optimum uterine placement, fit, tolerance, and retention."[2] Davis was able to persuade a large number of physicians of the effectiveness of the Shield in an article he published in the "Current Investigation" section of the *American Journal of Obstetrics and Gynecology* in February 1970. The article described a study conducted at the Johns Hopkins Family Planning Clinic involving 640 women who had worn the Shield for one year. His analysis was based on 3,549 women-months of experience. Davis cited five pregnancies, ten expulsions, nine removals for medical reasons, and three removals for personal reasons. His startling results: tolerance rate (nonexpulsion) 96 percent; pregnancy rate, 1.1 percent. The A. H. Robins Company reprinted no fewer than 199,000 copies of the Davis article for distribution to physicians.[3]

While various executives strongly recommended that other studies be commissioned to validate Davis's results, in January 1971 Robins began to market and sell the Shield on the basis of Davis's limited analysis. Robins's decision to produce and sell the Shield based on Davis's statistics may not coincide with the highest standards of scientific research, but it did not violate any FDA statutes and was therefore perfectly legal. At the time Robins produced the Shield, FDA had no regulatory policies in force regarding IUDs of any kind. While FDA had the authority to regulate the production, testing and sales of all new prescriptions, it could only *recommend* testing on new medical devices. It could not monitor, investigate, or police a device unless charges of lack of effectiveness, injury, or abuse were formally leveled against the device or the producer.

In December 1970 Robins commissioned a major long-term study to reinforce Davis's results. The study concentrated on ten clinics. . . . Between December 1970 and December 1974 (six months after Robins suspended domestic sales) 2,391 women were fitted with the Shield. The first results came out in November 1972, with only about half of the women enrolled in the study. The statistics showed a sixteen-month pregnancy rate of 1.6 percent. The Robins home office was more than pleased and immediately communicated this information to its sales staff. Thirteen months later, with all the women now participating in the program, less happy figures began to show up. The pregnancy rate after six months was 2.1 percent; after twelve months, 3.2 percent; after eighteen months, 3.5 percent; and after twenty-three months, 4.1 percent. In a final report published as a confidential internal document in August 1975 the final figures and results were even more devastating. The pregnancy rate after six months was 2.6 percent; after twelve months, 4.2 percent; after eighteen months, 4.98 percent; and after twenty-four months, 5.7 percent. Two of the scientists involved in this project submitted a minority report claiming that the Shield was even less effective than these already damaging figures indicated. They claimed that the pregnancy rate during the first year was much higher: after six months, 3.3 percent; and after twelve months, 5.5 percent. This twelve-month pregnancy rate is exactly five times *higher than* the rate Robins advertised and promoted—1.1 percent—to catapult the Shield to leadership in the IUD business.[4] This minority report was never disclosed to the medical community by Robins. Nor did Robins communicate these results to its own sales force. It did report some of these findings to FDA in July 1974, but only after the company had suspended domestic sales earlier that June. . . .

At the same time that the Robins Company was receiving research results pointing to poor statistical effectiveness of the Shield, they also began to receive more and more "single physician experience" reports warning and complaining about some of the medical consequences from using the Shield. These physician reports plus the statistics generated from controlled clinical reports began to portray the Shield as neither effective nor safe.

The primary cause of concern for Shield users proved to be a much higher incidence of uterine/pelvic bacterial infections. PID (pelvic inflammatory disease) is a highly virulent and very painful, difficult to cure, life threatening infection, which more often than not impairs or destroys a woman's ability to bear children. Of those women who conceived with the Shield in place (approximately 111,000 in the United States), an estimated 60 percent of them miscarried after suffering severe bacterial infections (PID). In 1974 FDA reported that over 245 women in their fourth to sixth month of pregnancy suffered the relatively rare bacterially-induced miscarriage called septic spontaneous abortions. For fifteen women, these septic abortions were fatal.[5] . . .

Scientists now believe that the systemic cause for these virulent forms of bacterial infection is the nylon tail of the Shield itself. The Dalkon Shield tail string runs between the vagina, where bacteria are always present, and the uterus, which is germ free. It then passes through the cervix, whose cervical mucus is the body's natural defense against bacterial invasion of the uterus. Robins claimed that cervical mucus would stop all germs from entering and infecting the uterus. To the naked eye, the Dalkon Shield tail string is an impervious monofilament, meaning that bacteria on it could not get into it. Actually, however, it is a cylindrical sheath encasing 200 to 450 round monofilaments separated by spaces. While the string was knotted at both ends, neither end was actually sealed. Therefore, any bacteria that got into the spaces between the filaments would be insulated from the body's natural antibacterial action while being drawn into the uterus by "wicking," a phenomenon similar to that by which a string draws the melting wax of a candle to the flame. Scientists believe that the longer the Shield and its string/tail is in place, the greater the chances of its deterioration and infiltration, thereby inducing infection in the uterus. Scientists now also contend that the "syndrome of spontaneous septic abortions" that occurred to women who had the Shield in place in the early second trimester of their pregnancy was caused by the tail string. That is, radical and sudden infection occurred when the uterus expanded to the point where it tended to pull the tail string into itself, thereby bringing on instant, often lethal, contamination.[6]

In the summer of 1983 the Centers for Disease Control in Atlanta and the FDA recommended that all women still using the Shield should contact their physicians and have it immediately removed. The Agencies found that women using the Shield had a fivefold increase in risk for contracting PID as compared to women using other types of IUDs. No change in contraceptive practice was recommended for women using any other type of IUD.[7] In April 1985 two studies funded by the National Institute of Health announced yet another dire warning. These studies showed that childless IUD wearers who have had PID run a higher risk of infertility if their devices were Shields than if they were other makes.[8] . . .

The company's response to all claims of faulty product design and limited testing procedures has been counterassertions or counterclaims regarding the faulty or improper use of the product by the user or the physician. The company has steadfastly maintained that there were no special dangers inherent in the device. In a report to FDA they stated: "Robins believes that serious scientific questions exist about whether the Dalkon Shield poses a significantly different risk of infection than other IUDs." Their continuous theme has been that doctors, not the device, have caused any infections associated with the Shield. The company was committed to the notion that pregnancy and removal rates could be kept extremely low by proper placement of the Shield. They also contended that user abuse played a part in the Shield's supposed malfunctioning. They defined user abuse as poor personal hygiene habits, sexual promiscuity or excessive sexual activity, or physical tampering with the device itself.

According to three different independent investigative reports[9] the company's public face of calm denial and counterargument masked an internal conspiring to conceal information from the public, the court system, and the FDA. . . . By May 1974 Robins could no longer avoid the evidence presented to it by FDA implicating the Shield in numerous cases of spontaneous septic abortions and in the death of at least four women as a result. These findings were disclosed in a letter sent by the company to 120,000 doctors. In June 1974 Robins suspended the U.S. distribution and sale of the Shield. In January 1975 Robins called back and completely removed the Shield from the market. The company termed the action a "market withdrawal," not a recall, because it was undertaken voluntarily and not at the direct order of FDA. In September 1980 Robins again wrote the medical community suggesting as a purely precautionary measure that doctors remove the Shield from their patients. In October 1984 Robins initiated a $4 million television, newspaper, and magazine advertising campaign warning and recommending that all women still wearing the device have it removed at

Robins's expense. In April 1985 Robins publicly set aside $615 million to settle legal claims from women who had used the Shield. This reserve is the largest provision of its kind to date in a product liability case. In May 1985 a jury in Wichita, Kansas, awarded nearly $9 million to a woman who had charged that the use of the Shield caused her to undergo a hysterectomy. The award was the largest ever made in the history of litigation involving the Shield. Officials of the Robins Company felt that adverse decisions of this magnitude could mean that their $615 million fund would prove to be inadequate. On August 21, 1985, Robins filed for Chapter 11 protection, citing litigation relating to the Shield as the main cause for its actions. Company spokesmen said that it hoped that the Federal Bankruptcy Court in Richmond would set up a payment schedule that would enable it to survive while insuring that victims "would be treated fairly." E. Claiborne Robins, Jr., called it "essential that we move to protect the company's economic viability against those who would destroy it for the benefit of a few."[10] The intriguing financial irony in all of this is that when Robins filed for Chapter 11 it had already spent, at a conservative estimate, $500 million in settlements, litigation losses, and legal fees for a product it had only manufactured for three years and from which it had only realized $500,000 in real profits![11] . . .

To the extent that Robins is using Chapter 11 as a shelter against the rush of product-liability litigation, the company is nevertheless taking a gamble. . . . For example, as part of their reorganization arrangement with the court, Robins agreed to a class action procedure in which they would begin a 91 nation advertisement campaign to announce to all former users their right to file a claim for compensation for any health problems that may have been caused by the Shield. As of June 1986 more than 300,000 claims have been filed against Robins![12] Numbers such as these may completely overwhelm the bankruptcy court's ability to reorganize and reestablish the company on a sound financial basis.

There are several lessons lurking in this case. The first of them has to do with the dangers held by the combination of a legalistic society and a highly technological one—or, perhaps more clearly, in a society based upon notions of individual freedom suddenly caught up in rapid innovation. Generally speaking, we hold, in America, that that which is not specifically prohibited is permitted. The danger comes when technology continually creates inventions for which there are no categories and hence no rules. FDA clearly is charged with safeguarding health and monitoring the pharmaceutical industry, among others. The

Dalkon Shield is clearly a contraceptive capable of creating physical good or ill, and yet because it is a device, neither a food nor drug, and because neither FDA nor A. H. Robins would act at the outset on anything other than the exact literal definition of the rules, no real consideration was given to the medical consequences of the Shield. FDA felt it lacked the authority and A. H. Robins felt no moral imperative that was not specifically imposed upon them. We have left all interpretations of intention, all exercise of reasonableness, to the court systems—experts and de facto agents. The second lesson can be found in that the Dalkon Shield itself may have been a genuinely safe, useful product, even a breakthrough, as the first effective IUD. The danger was ancillary to the device—the "wicking" action of the tail string—and had Robins followed the usual FDA approval guidelines for drugs, this flaw might have been discovered, and perhaps eliminated. It was in adhering only to the letter of the regulations and in using this exclusion of devices to rush into production and quicker profits that the company began a course which may end in its own demise.

Given all of this conflicting data, perhaps there is only one thing we can say with certainty in regard to Robins's production of the Dalkon Shield: "In the pharmaceutical world, products that fail can cripple companies as well as people."[13]

NOTES

1 Morton Mintz, *At Any Cost* (New York: Pantheon Books, 1985), p. 25.
2 Ibid., p. 82.
3 Ibid., pp. 29–31.
4 Ibid., pp. 86–88.
5 *FDA Consumer,* May 1981, p. 32.
6 Mintz, *At Any Cost,* pp. 131–48 and 149–72.
7 *FDA Consumer,* July–August 1983, p. 2.
8 *Wall Street Journal,* April 11, 1985, p. 1.
9 Mintz, *At Any Cost.* Sheldon Engelmayer and Robert Wagman, *Lord's Justice* (New York: Anchor Press/Doubleday, 1985). Susan Perry and Jim Dawson, *Nightmare: Women and the Dalkon Shield* (New York: Macmillan Publishing, 1985).
10 *New York Times,* August 22, 1985, pp. 1, 6.
11 *Time,* November 26, 1986, p. 10.
12 *Wall Street Journal,* June 26, 1986, p. 10.
13 *U.S. News & World Report,* September 2, 1985, p. 12.

Business and Employees

CHAPTER OUTLINE

Gordon H. Brunner
Senior Vice President—Research
& Development
Procter & Gamble

*"Our long held view is that the factor most responsible
for Procter and Gamble's success is the character of its
people. An integral part of that character is ethical values—honesty, integrity, fairness and a respect and concern for others. We will never tolerate efforts or activities to achieve results through illegal or unfair dealings
anywhere in the world. We charge our people to always
try to do what is right and have no doubt that ethical
behavior ultimately pays off at the bottom line."*

Employees regularly evaluate their bosses and are encouraged to write reviews of their organization's business practices. There is little sense of hierarchy, and employees are given time off—at company expense—to do volunteer work. A university run by its faculty? A commune left over from the '70s? A religious community stressing brotherhood and mutual responsibility? The correct answer is, none of the above. The description is of a fast-growing cosmetics business, The Body Shop, whose worldwide sales exceed half a billion dollars. Started in England in 1976, the company has over 260 outlets in the United States; and the view of its founder, Anita Roddick, is that young people "don't want to work for a company that doesn't have a social conscience, or that is passive."[1] The company's attitude toward everything is shaped by its ethical commitments. According to Roddick, "first and foremost are the values."[2]

Nucor Steel, headquartered in Charlotte, North Carolina, provides production bonuses to its employees, offers worker stock plans, and for twenty years has avoided layoffs. In bad economic times, everyone, from CEO to the newest employee, takes a pay cut, and when times improve everyone shares in the profits. In addition to its Charlotte plant, the company operates other steel minimills in eight states and defies the trends in other segments of the steel industry by being a growth company whose stocks are highly valued on Wall Street.[3]

EMPLOYEES: A COMPANY'S ASSETS

According to a *Business Week* editorial writer, practices such as those just described would not be considered unusual in Japan. Alan Blinder, economic columnist, observes that "finance-dominated capitalism too often forgets that a business organization is made up of people and can function no better than they do. The Japanese rarely forget this. Indeed, Japanese managers commonly believe that the company's employees, not its machines, are its most important assets and are therefore to be valued, nurtured and—except in extremis—retained."[4] Ask an American company who the most important officer is after the CEO, and the answer you will get is probably the chief financial officer, according to Lester Thurow, dean of MIT's Sloan School of Management. In contrast, he notes, "The post of head of human resources management is usually a specialized, off-at-the-edge-of-the-corporation job, and the executive who holds it is never consulted on major strategic decisions and has no chance to move up to chief executive officer

(CEO)." The contrast between the two corporate attitudes is even greater, due to the fact that "in Japan the head of human resources management is usually the second most important person after the CEO. To become CEO, it is a job that one must have held."[5]

These views are reiterated by Thomas J. Peters and Robert H. Waterman in their book *In Search of Excellence* in which they recount a conversation with a senior Japanese executive who said, "We are very different from the rest of the world. Our only natural resource is the hard work of our people." Such an attitude, according to Waterman and Peters, permeates the entire Japanese corporate ethos. "Treating people—not money, machines, or minds—as the natural resource may be the key to it all. Kenichi Ohmae, head of McKinsey's Tokyo office, says that in Japan organization and people (in the organization) are synonymous. Moreover, the people orientation encourages love of product and requires modest risk taking and innovation by the average worker."[6] These lessons are not being lost on American companies that face the challenges of competing in a global economy.

Attitudes toward employees such as these reflect what The Body Shop's Anita Roddick calls "empowerment of employees,"[7] an outlook that sees them as important contributors to the bottom line, not just another commodity to be factored into a cost-benefits analysis of a business. "Productivity through people," is what Waterman and Peters call it. They quote Bill Hewlett, founder of Hewlett-Packard, who underscores this point from his personal experience: "I feel that in general terms it is the policies and actions that flow from the belief that men and women want to do a good job, a creative job, and if they are provided with the proper environment they will do so. It is the tradition of treating every individual with consideration and respect and recognizing personal achievements."[8]

The insistence on valuing persons as important in their own right—not seeing them merely as cogs in an impersonal production machine—echoes again an important insight by Immanuel Kant. When we analyze further the demands of the categorical imperative—which says that we should be able to universalize our principle of action without contradiction—this moral principle leads us quickly to the principle of treating people with respect. After all, this is the way we want to be treated—with respect—and to be valued as individuals, not as means for the self-aggrandizement of another. Universalizing the principle of respect means, according to Kant, treating others as ends in themselves, not as means only.

KANT ON TREATING PEOPLE AS ENDS IN THEMSELVES

Now suppose that something exists which in itself has absolute worth as an end in itself and which could provide the basis for definite laws. . . .

   Now I say that human beings, and in general all rational beings, are ends-in-themselves and are not to be used at the pleasure of this or that individual. Like all rational beings, they must always be treated and given consideration as ends. Non-rational natural entities that exist independently of human will have only relative worth as means and are consequently called *things*. In contrast, rational beings are called *persons* since their nature already indicates that they are ends-in-themselves—that is, beings which ought not to be used merely as a means. This consequently limits all arbitrary treatment of them and presents them as subject to respect. Persons, therefore, are not merely subjective ends to be treated like things but rather have worth for us. . . .

   If there is a highest moral principle—from the human perspective a categorical imperative—it must be derived from what is necessarily an end for everyone because it is an end-in-itself forming an objective volitional principle conceived as a general moral law. The basis for this principle is that rational nature exists as an end-in-itself. This is how persons necessarily conceive their own existence, and all other rational beings conceive their existence on the same rational basis making it valid also for me; thus it is at the same time an objective principle. . . . The practical imperative will therefore be as follows: *Never treat human beings, whether in your own person or in the person of any others, merely as a means, but always simultaneously as an end.*

   Source: Immanuel Kant, *Grundlegung zur Metaphysik der Sitten* (Foundations of the Metaphysics of Morals), trans. David Stewart from the German using the Prussian Academy texts. Darmstadt: Wissen-Schaftliche Buchgesellschaft, 1968, bd. 6, pp. 59–61.

Respect a Key

To understand Kant's point fully, we must first look at what is meant by saying that we treat someone as a means only. The classic example of this attitude is found in the work of the American management consultant Frederick Winslow Taylor. In his book, *The Principles of Scientific Management,* Taylor lays the foundations of modern, assembly-line production techniques. The noted writer on business ethics Kenneth Goodpaster observes that because Taylor "considered human individuality cumbersome, he shaped a standardized work system that made employees replaceable, like the parts of a machine." Taylor's approach, according to Goodpaster, assigned thinking to managers and acting to workers. "This eliminated work done by rule of thumb or learned through the apprenticeship system. Management selected and trained workers, and all tasks were standardized. Under Taylor's system, labor required little skill and was, therefore, cheap."[9]

The alternative to considering workers as just another (replaceable) variable in the manufacturing process requires that workers be looked upon as more than a mere means to production. Treating workers as part of the management team, not just as replaceable cogs in the production machine, seems to be the norm at Japanese manufacturing plants in the United States. The *New York Times* describes the Toyota plant in Georgetown, Kentucky, as a showcase factory. In contrast to older American manufacturing approaches, where each worker has one or two repetitive tasks to perform in the assembly process, Toyota enlists workers in making decisions that in most other manufacturing plants would be made by managers.

Encouraged by management through bonus awards and being given more control over their own production work, assembly-line workers contribute to what is described as a "lean production" environment. Workers in such an environment "learn numerous jobs and shoulder broader responsibility, including maintenance, inspection and machine setup."[10] Worker involvement in production decisions includes having authority to stop the production line in order to fix mistakes, being rewarded for suggestions that improve production techniques, and even introducing new manufacturing processes. According to *New York Times* writer Doron Levin, Toyota has discovered that when allowed to participate in the decisions that shape the workplace, "a smaller number of workers, each capable of doing several jobs, can manufacture automobiles with less inventory, less investment, and fewer mistakes."[11] Such lessons are not being lost on at least some of American manufacturers. According to another *New York Times* report, some American automobile manufacturers are adopting a "friendlier approach towards workers, customers, suppliers and dealers."[12]

Employment at Will

A view that regards employees as just another variable in the production process is allied with an employment doctrine called "employment at will." According to this view, workers may be fired for any reason, or for no reason at all, at the pleasure of the employer. Likewise, employees can quit for any reason at all. Twenty states continue to recognize the employment at will doctrine, although they recognize exceptions to extreme forms of the doctrine. Some states have enacted statutes that restrict employers' right to dismiss employees. Typical of such statutes are protection for whistle-blowers; prohibition against age discrimination or discrimination based on race, sex, or national origin; the nonretaliation provisions of workers' compensation laws and minimum wage laws; and laws that prohibit employers from discharging employees for serving on jury duty, for taking a reasonable amount of time to vote on election day, or as a result of withholding orders placed on wages.[13]

Added to state statutes is federal legislation that also limits employers' ability to terminate employees:

National Labor Relations Act
Title VII of the Civil Rights Act of 1964 and 1991
Nonretaliation provisions of
    Fair Labor Standards Act
    Age Discrimination in Employment Act
    Rehabilitation Act of 1973
Immigration Reform and Control Act of 1986
Occupational Safety and Health Act of 1970
Employee Retirement Income Security Act
Employee Polygraph Protection Act of 1988
Privacy Act/Freedom of Information Act
Fair Employment Liability Act
Americans with Disabilities Act of 1990

There is also an increasing body of case law wherein the courts have limited the grounds on which termination can be based. For example, some courts have overturned dismissals resulting from negligent or intentional infliction of serious emotional distress, defamation, invasion of privacy, assault and battery, or false imprisonment or false arrest.

Public policy shifts in attitudes toward employment at will reflect deontological concerns of fairness; it is not fair to dismiss an employee because of age, for reporting wrongdoing, for exercising the right to vote in an election, or because the person has been falsely arrested or imprisoned. When an employer dismisses a worker, it must not be on grounds of gender, race, national origin, or other irrelevant factors.

Affirmative Action

The flip side of restrictions on employment at will is the view that companies should not be allowed to exclude individuals from consideration for employment because of such irrelevant factors as gender, race, national origin, or a disability that would not prevent them from accomplishing the job. Affirmative action policies not only prevent employers from using such irrelevant criteria in making hiring decisions, they also work to bring into the work force individuals from groups historically underrepresented. Probably no feature of contemporary social policy is more controversial than affirmative action, because preferential hiring practices raise charges of reverse discrimination and the specter of quotas imposed either from within a company or from without.

Affirmative action can mean different things to different people, but it basically comes down to the efforts of employers not to exclude individuals from their work force because of irrelevant criteria. Often the problem is not that companies deliberately exclude certain classes of people (though sometimes they do that, too) but, rather, that individuals making the hiring decisions tend to hire the same kind of people they see around them. If we surround ourselves only with people from a certain race or sex—white males, for example—we tend to think of only those persons as qualified for the jobs we offer. By deliberately excluding certain groups from employment, we have created an injustice against that group, an injustice that can only be addressed by *compensatory* action—that is, we compensate for past wrongs by making a special effort to hire persons from the groups discriminated against. Opponents of the compensatory justice approach argue that the individuals discriminated against are not the same individuals now being compensated for the past wrong. A further argument against the compensatory justice approach is that making a preferential decision to hire a person from a class previously discriminated against is to commit another unjust act of discrimination: if a company has a history of hiring only white males, then for it to make a commitment to hire minority females is to discriminate unjustly against white males who are also qualified for the position.

A counter to this objection is an appeal to something like Rawls's second principle of justice: in a fair society positions to which are attached unequal rewards should be open to all, and a pattern of hiring that excludes certain classes of people is evidence in itself that hiring practices are unfair. Or if all females in an organization receive wages 30 percent lower than males doing comparable work, this is prima facie evidence of wage discrimination on gender grounds. To redress the imbalance in hiring or in wages requires positive steps to correct the situation. The ethical principle appealed to here can be seen as a fairly straightforward Kantian one: if you were a member of the excluded class, or if you were paid less than your coworkers simply because of your gender or race, this would not be a principle with which you would agree. Therefore, a principle of action (a maxim) that tries to universalize discriminatory conduct based on irrelevant criteria would not be maximized.

Qualifications for a position are not irrelevant criteria, and it is hard to argue against the view that the best qualified person should receive the position regardless of race, gender, or national origin. A more subtle form of bias can creep in here, however. Requiring certain kinds of tests may disqualify those individuals from social groups unfamiliar with testing procedures. Or a company may look for only women to fill certain kinds of jobs and only men to fill others, thus failing to consider a woman seriously for a role traditionally viewed as a male position. Even educational requirements not necessary for the job can serve as a form of discriminatory hiring.

There are also utilitarian arguments for affirmative action in hiring and promoting individuals within an organization. One could argue that a society becomes unstable when sizable numbers of its people are systematically excluded from access to the most desirable jobs. We could also argue that a company severely limits its ability to compete when it draws its talent from a limited range of people and excludes over half of the work force (women and minorities). It also risks losing the competitive edge that comes from diversity of outlook.

Levi Strauss & Co. went from being a company that employed mostly white females in its production facilities to a firm whose work force now is 56 percent minorities. The population of the executive suites also has changed; 14 percent of its executive officers are nonwhite and 30 percent female, and the company is working hard to increase the number of women and minorities in top management positions. In its commitment to minority representation in the ranks of management, Levi Strauss since 1984 has increased minority managers to 32 percent.[14] Its diverse work force has contributed to the company's competitive ability, according to company managers. Its billion-dollar-a-year Dockers line was suggested by an Argentine employee,

---

A Case in Point . . .

The Saturn Corporation is General Motors' effort to develop a new style of manufacturing that exhibits different attitudes toward production workers than are the norm in the American auto industry. The quality of the product is high, and customer satisfaction ratings are greater than for any other automobile manufactured in the United States. The main problem Saturn dealers have is keeping enough stock on hand to meet consumer demand. *Business Week* credits Saturn's quality ratings as being the result of new labor agreements that give all Saturn workers—blue- and white-collar—authority to make management decisions in order to improve quality of the product.

At Saturn's Spring Hill, Tennessee, plant, workers assume many roles previously reserved to management. Production is organized into teams that plan their work and are even given responsibility for ordering many of the tools and parts needed for their jobs, thereby bypassing bureaucratic purchasing systems that add both costs and delay. Absenteeism is low, averaging 2.5 percent, in contrast to a rate between 10 and 14 percent at other GM plants. Coupled with no-layoff guarantees, employees are empowered to make decisions that would make Frederick Winslow Taylor roll over in his grave. At Saturn each worker team has authority to manage its own budget and has control over inventory and hiring decisions without supervision from top management.

Treating workers as ends and not as means only is not only good ethics but also good business for the Saturn Corporation.

Sources: BW, Aug. 17, 1992; BW, Reinventing America 1992; NYT, Oct. 23, 1992.

---

and the company recognizes that its ability to be a vibrant company depends on an influx of persons and ideas. *Business Week* observed that "as the U.S. labor force becomes increasingly diverse, companies that want to hire the best people must be open to that diversity."[15] The commitment of Levi Strauss to positive conditions for its workers even extends to the company's factories located outside the United States. The *Wall Street Journal,* in a front-page article highlighting the ethical commitments of the company, reported that Levi Strauss in 1992 "became the first multinational to adopt a wide-ranging set of guidelines for its hired factories, covering the treatment of workers and the environmental impact of production. Levi even promised to inspect the factories regularly and cancel contracts with those that violated the rules."[16]

To summarize, arguments for affirmative action are the following:

1 Affirmative action can be seen as compensatory justice to correct past wrongful discrimination.

2 Fair hiring practices require us to make sure that favored positions are open to all, regardless of race, gender, or class.

3 Discriminatory hiring practices create instability both in a society and in a company that practices them.

4 Developing a diverse work force aids a company's creativity and competitiveness.

Broadly speaking, the first two arguments are deontological and the last two are utilitarian. This list shows again how both consequentialists and deontologists can agree about courses of action while disagreeing on the grounds for such action. In the case of hiring practices, both lines of moral reasoning point to the importance of creating a diverse work force, and it is in the confluence of these two moral demands that much of the current discussion of this issue is couched. However, perhaps the most compelling motivation for encouraging diversity in the workplace are the forces of the marketplace itself.

Workforce 2000

Although the point has already been made, its importance demands that it be repeated: no company can be successful if it refuses to consider for employment half of the population on the grounds of irrelevant criteria unrelated to whether these individuals are qualified for the job. Yet this is precisely what a company does if it keeps women off its work force. Similarly, a company's management may be crippled if it arbitrarily limits its management team to one gender and race. Yet that is precisely what a company does that allows the glass ceiling to remain in place. The phrase "glass ceiling" refers to the invisible barriers that seem to keep women in some companies from rising above a certain level in management.

But let's suppose a company further narrows its hiring field only to those workers who look just like its present work force. Subtle patterns can produce such homogeneity: hiring family members of present employees, looking only to traditional sources of labor supply for new employees, or requiring entry-level qualifications that exclude certain segments of the potential work force. Further, consider the effects on this company's hiring policy if its traditional source of labor were shrinking. It would find itself less able to hire the workers it needed to compete effectively in the twenty-first century.

These are the conclusions of a government study entitled *Workforce 2000*. Using demographic data from the census and other government studies, the report describes the work force that businesses will encounter by the year 2000. These data are not projections, because the workers who will be in the work force in the year 2000 have already been born. Here are some of the document's conclusions:

- Only 15 percent of new entrants to the labor force . . . will be native white males, compared to 47 percent in that category today.
- The average age of the population and the workforce will rise, and the pool of young workers entering the labor market will shrink.
- Non-whites will make up 29 percent of the new entrants into the labor force between now and the year 2000, twice their current share of the workforce.
- In combination, these demographic changes will mean that the new workers entering the workforce between now and the year 2000 will be much different from those who people it today. Non-whites, women, and immigrants will make up more than five-sixths of the net additions to the workforce between now and the year 2000, though they make up only about half of it today.
- By the year 2000, approximately 47 percent of the workforce will be women, and 61 percent of women will be at work. Women will comprise about three fifths of the new entrants into the labor force between 1985 and 2000.[17]

These demographic realities also point to important public policy issues, the most important of which is educational programs that will prepare all citizens for the jobs of the twenty-first century. Again, a utilitarian standard would argue for public policies that seek to open up equal opportunities for all citizens as the surest way of providing stability in society. Without equality of opportunity, and social policies that make response to those opportunities possible, the result will be an unstable society fractured by inner turmoil and unrest.

CONTEMPORARY APPLICATIONS

Kant argues that the proper approach to the study of ethics is, first, to understand the fundamental principles of morals. That is, Kant's approach is not to examine various actual cases of conduct (that would be best left to anthropology, he argues) but, rather, to ask the questions, What is a moral action? How are we to define it? How are we to recognize it? How does reason function when it is used to make moral judgments (Kant uses the term "practical" to refer to moral judgments; the term is derived from the Greek word for action)? After we understand the fundamental principles of morals or ethics, we can then proceed to analyze real-world cases and apply the principles to new situations. Several contemporary management issues are made clearer by examining them in the light of the principle of respect and autonomy that Kant espouses.

Employees and Quality

Among the concerns expressed most often by contemporary managers is the quest for quality in all operations of a company, a concern known under various names but commonly called quality assurance programs, continuous improvement programs, or total quality management. One of the strategies in this pursuit of quality is to rely more on the creative talents of employees and less on management techniques that, like those of Frederick Winslow Taylor, treat workers as interchangeable ingredients in the manufacturing and service processes. The problem with lack of quality, so the management theory has it, is not with people but with processes. A *Business Week* report on the quality imperative noted that "empowering workers" may be the best strategy for achieving quality "because it's the employees themselves who generally find the best solution." This means getting rid of the attitude that "harks back to the time of Henry Ford and the productivity theories of Frederick Winslow Taylor. . . . Most U.S. companies are still struggling to leave this structure behind."[18]

In the rhetoric about the need for "reinventing the corporation," which calls for, among other things, rethinking the way the company does business and getting back to core competencies, a familiar refrain is the importance of unleashing the creative talents of a company's employees. A discovery made by managers who focus on processes rather than on the company's internal structure is that "self-managed teams throw more challenge and meaning into employment" and "today's best managers, the theory goes, must step back to allow their workers to assume alternating roles as leaders in teams."[19] None of this would have surprised Kant, for treating people as a means only is a perfect description of Taylor's management theories that treated workers as things, replaceable cogs in the industrial machine. To treat individuals as ends includes taking their own interests seriously; treating them with respect also means taking their ideas and insights seriously as well.

"In TQM [total quality management]," one writer observed, "85 percent of the problems that arise in the course of work are attributable to the organization's systems, just 15 percent to the shortcomings of individual employees. The manager's job, then, is to improve constantly the work systems of the organization, to drive out blaming and fear, to remove obstacles in the system that prevent persons or teams from doing their best work."[20]

A Harassment-Free Workplace

In 1977, the courts included sexual harassment as a violation of workers' rights under Title VII. This decision brought about increased protection to those being harassed and also led to wider discussion of the issue of harassment. Originally sexual harassment was defined as quid pro quo, the implicit—or often explicit—offer to exchange certain job benefits (better assignments, promotions, raises) for sexual favors. The concept was broadened from this somewhat narrow definition to include *hostile environment,* which is defined as a workplace where unwanted comments, touching, offensive sexual references, language, and even outright sexual intimidation have the effect of "transforming the office into a remake of *Animal House,* " to use the salient description of *Fortune* magazine.[21]

The issue here can be understood as a variant on Kant's theme of treating persons as means only. The individual who is the target of unwelcome sexual advances is being treated as an object, as a means for the gratification of the harasser. The way the issue is frequently framed is that women (and it is most often women) are being treated as sex objects. The issue becomes one of power, the abuse of superior station and authority to take advantage of those subordinate in the chain of command. Certainly the harasser could not legitimately claim to be treating the harassed as an end in itself, a person worthy of respect and dignity. The definition of sexual harassment formulated by the Equal Employment Opportunities Commission makes this abundantly clear:

> Unwelcome sexual advances, requests for sexual favors or other verbal or physical conduct of a sexual nature constitute sexual harassment when (1)

submission of such conduct is made either implicitly or explicitly a term or condition of an individual's employment, (2) submission to or rejecting such conduct by an individual is used as the basis for employment decisions affecting such individual, or (3) such conduct has the purpose or effect of creating an intimidating, hostile, or offensive working environment.[22]

It is not difficult also to formulate a utilitarian argument—certainly in the sense of rule utilitarianism—against people as objects by harassing them sexually. The success of a business organization depends on the morale of its employees. The greatest good for the greatest number of persons—stockholders (in terms of profitability of the company), customers (in terms of customer satisfaction), and employees (in terms of high morale and productivity)—will result if the company provides a harassment-free workplace. The absence of harassment does not guarantee higher productivity, profitability, or morale, but its presence is certainly detrimental to these objectives. Of course, it is possible to argue that an occasional act of harassment would not affect these objectives and that the utilitarian standard really does not address an occasional or isolated case. It is just such counterarguments that led to rule utilitarianism: the rules against harassment are defensible on utilitarian grounds, and therefore one cannot use utilitarian arguments to defend exceptions to those rules.

It is also clear that such conduct is prohibited by deontological standards. As was encountered earlier, not only is there a Kantian appeal for the treatment of individuals with respect, it is also the case that the first formulation of the categorical imperative prohibits such action. The one doing the harassing could not make the principle of action a universal law, for the harasser would not want to be the recipient of such actions, and, likewise, the principle could not be made universal because the actions are unwelcome.

An article on harassment in the workplace featured in *Fortune* reported that of "executives at 600 major U.S. companies . . . about half planned to increase the amount of sexual harassment training they give managers and employers." The article went on to note that "a dozen or so big corporations have already built shining reputations among consultants and researchers for the quality, creativity, and overall earnestness of their training programs."[23] This report, along with others frequently appearing in national media, makes clear that more and more businesses are discovering that one key to productivity is to treat their employees with dignity. Not only is such corporate behavior good for business, it is also the right thing to do.

Making Diversity Work

Throughout this book the argument has been advanced through a variety of ways that ethics is not just an expensive veneer for a company's activities but is essential for the long-term success of a business operation. The general form of this argument is that human society can only function within a framework of mutual respect and that it is better both for individuals and for the collective affairs of a society for there to be an acceptance of ethical principles to regulate behavior. Whether it be the principle of fairness, the search for the greatest good for the greatest number of persons, or the development of a cultural ideal that reinforces virtuous acts, ethical systems all coalesce in the view that human life is better when lived with a moral point of view.

Business publications as well as the popular news media contain frequent reports of corporate commitment to values in the workplace. A *Fortune* magazine report reveals that some CEOs are beginning to embrace diversity as a strategy for being competitive in a global economy.[24] Customers are diverse, and unless the work force is also diverse, a firm may find its products appealing only to a subset of the general population. IBM's CEO Louis V. Gerstner, Jr., remarks that "our marketplace is made up of all races, religions, and sexual orientations, and therefore it is vital to our success that our work force also be diverse."[25] According to Ernest H. Drew, the CEO of Hoechst Celanses, the solutions found by heterogeneous management are broader than those of groups composed of a single race. Formerly the company thought of diversity only in terms of the number of women and minorities. Current thinking is that it needs "diversity at every level of the company where decisions are made," according to Drew.[26] A similar point of view is expressed by Robert D. Haas, CEO of Levi Strauss, whose values-driven management style includes a commitment to broadening its work force at all levels to include those historically excluded. According to Haas, "We are not doing this because it makes us feel good—although it does. . . . We are doing this because we believe in the interconnection between liberating the talents of our people and business success."[27]

DISCUSSION STARTERS

1 Make a list of specific business practices that treat people as means only. Say how you would change those practices so as to treat people with respect.
2 Frame a Kantian argument in support of the Saturn Corporation's attitude toward its work force. Now form a utilitarian argument for the same thing.

3 Sexual harassment is usually understood as a misuse of one's power to inflict unwelcome sexual attention on subordinates. Does this mean that those with less power cannot sexually harass those to whom they report? Specifically, can students sexually harass professors? Is it possible for secretaries to sexually harass their boss? Why or why not?

4 *Workforce 2000* was the government's attempt to alert business leaders to the changing demographics of the work force. Does the data presented by this report provide any guidance for companies seeking to do the morally right thing? Why or why not?

5 Do you think that the employment at will doctrine should be restricted even more than it already has? Or do you think that this doctrine should be expanded and that some of its limitations be removed? Give reasons for your answer.

NOTES

1 CD, Oct. 19, 1992, "Body Shop Reshaping the Workplace." An article highly critical of The Body Shop appeared in the September/October 1994 issue of *Business Ethics*. Among other things the article charged that the company sells products that are contaminated and that its charitable contributions and values-oriented management style fall short of its claims. Gordon Roddick, chairman of The Body Shop, supplied a ten-page rebuttal to the article in which he charges the article's author, Jon Entine, with failing "to observe the normal standards of journalism." Roddick says that the author did not interview company officials before writing his story and that the piece relies heavily on "disgruntled former employees or franchisees, current competitors, or disappointed bidders for our business." He further offers to send anyone who is interested a point-by-point refutation of the charges made in the article.

2 *Computer World,* Oct. 22, 1990, p. 67.

3 CD, June 29, 1992, "Satisfied Employees Bottom Line at Steelmaker."

4 BW, Nov. 11, 1991, p. 22.

5 Lester Thurow, *Head to Head: The Coming Economic Battle Among Japan, Europe and America* (New York: Morrow, 1992), p. 54.

6 Thomas J. Peters and Robert H. Waterman, Jr., *In Search of Excellence: Lessons from America's Best-Run Companies* (New York: Harper & Row, 1982), p. 39.

7 CD, Oct. 19, 1992.

8 Peters and Waterman, *In Search of Excellence,* p. 244.

9 Kenneth E. Goodpaster, "Note on the Corporation as a Moral Environment," in *Ethics in Practice: Managing the Moral Corporation,* eds. Kenneth R. Andrews and Donald K. David (Boston: Harvard Business School Press, 1989), p. 90.

10 Doron P. Levin, "Toyota Plant in Kentucky Is Font of Ideas for U.S.," NYT, May 5, 1992.

11 Ibid.
12 Adam Bryant, "New Attitude, Not New Boss, the Key, G.M. Watchers Say," NYT, Oct. 23, 1992.
13 Thanks to Ann Stewart for the legal research in this section on Ohio and federal law.
14 BW, Aug. 1, 1994, p. 49.
15 *Business Week,* "Reinventing America," 1992, p. 72, supplied both this quotation and the information about Levi Strauss and Company.
16 WSJ, July 28, 1994, p. 1.
17 *Workforce 2000,* pp. xiii, xix, xx, 85.
18 "Questing for the Best," BW Bonus Issue, "The Quality Imperative," Oct. 25, 1991, p. 16.
19 "Management's New Gurus," BW, Aug. 31, 1992, p. 46.
20 Ted Marchese, "TQM: A Time for Ideas.," *Change,* May/June, 1993, p. 13.
21 Anne B. Fisher, "Sexual Harassment: What to Do," FOR, Aug. 23, 1993, p. 84.
22 EEOC Interpretative Guidelines on Discrimination Because of Sex under Title VII, 29 C.F.R. 1604.11 (1984).
23 Fisher, "Sexual Harassment," pp. 86–87.
24 FORT, Aug. 8, 1994, pp. 78–86.
25 Ibid., p. 79.
26 Ibid.
27 "Managing by Values," BW, Aug. 1, 1994, pp. 46–47.

CASE STUDY

As we have discussed in previous chapters, the companies that continue to prosper year after year, through business booms as well as business recessions, are those guided by principles of conduct that rise above the expediency of the moment. The case that follows provides an interesting Canadian corollary to the U.S. government document *Workforce 2000*. We can argue that work force equity is the right thing to do on moral grounds; complementing this ethical argument is evidence that it is also the necessary business strategy. As you read the following analysis, ask yourself whether the coinciding of moral and business interests strengthens the case for moral business behavior or whether it is irrelevant to such behavior.

Excerpted from an article by Michele S. Darling in *Canadian Public Administration/Administration Publique du Canada*, 34, no. 1 (Spring/Printemps), pp. 57–61. Reprinted with permission of The Institute of Public Administration of Canada.

EMPLOYMENT EQUITY: A Sound Business Strategy for The 1990s

The ethics of managing a diverse workforce is really about how to learn to appreciate, acknowledge, respect, accommodate and integrate divergent opinions about what is right and wrong in the context of the workplace. . . . In my view, accommodating differences isn't just an issue of moral obligation; *it is a matter of urgent business necessity.* . . .

THE CHALLENGES

Canada's population is changing dramatically and will continue to change over the next decade. The changes fall under three broad headings: demographics, immigration and education.

Demographics

There are three significant and enduring demographic trends: a declining birthrate, an aging population, and urbanization.

As a result of Canada's declining birthrate, its population will grow only very slowly over the next few decades. Statistics Canada estimates a slowdown in growth, probably to zero by 2006, followed by a population decline a few years later. In fact, it is estimated that by the year 2031 the Canadian population will have returned to its 1992 level. Let's have a more detailed look at this trend.

An extremely important consequence of the continuation of the current low fertility rate is the aging trend in Canada's population, already evident in the current demographic structure and becoming even more pronounced in most future scenarios. The young and elderly age groups are moving in opposite directions; at one end of the age spectrum the population is shrinking, while at the other end it is growing rapidly. In the 1981 Census, young people (0–17) made up 28 per cent of the population and elderly people 10 per cent. By 2006 young people will account for 19 per cent and the elderly 15 per cent. By 2031, if this trend continues, elderly people will be 27 percent of the population compared with only 15 per cent for young people. In effect, the traditional population pyramid will be turned on its head by the year 2031.

The phenomenon of urbanization in Canada has been well documented. Canada's largest cities have become major population centers.

The population growth has created a wide range of challenges for urban dwellers.

Immigration

The ethno-cultural make-up of Canada is also changing, and is likely to change even more dramatically if politicians decide to offset the declining population patterns through increased immigration. Our immigration policy has already undergone significant change since the 1950s. Other western countries are experiencing the same population trends (low fertility, aging population) as we are. As a result, they are no longer as good a source of immigrants as they were in the past. Third World countries, most notably in Asia, are experiencing a population explosion and are, therefore, a good source from which to draw. It is estimated that by the year 2006, 149,000 members of visible minority groups will immigrate to Canada each year. Some people have argued that this is mainly Ontario's "challenge," because there is a perception that visible minorities come to Ontario in proportionately much larger numbers than to any other province. This is a misconception. The fact is that British Columbia's visible minority population is the largest, followed by Ontario, Manitoba and Saskatchewan. Among Canadian cities, however, Toronto has the largest population of visible minorities.

It is estimated that by the year 2036, approximately 20 per cent of Canada's population will be composed of visible minorities, and 40 per cent will have been born outside of Canada. Some people resent our immigration policy, arguing that immigrants "take away jobs from Canadians" and do not make a contribution to Canadian society. The fact is that Canada desperately needs immigrants to maintain even current levels of economic growth.

If the current demographic trends continue, the profile of the human resources that we will be managing by the year 2000 will be older and more culturally and linguistically diverse. Canadian businesses will be managing a far more multicultural workplace than ever before.

Education

In the emerging global economy, with its focus on information and knowledge, education is the essential raw material. As we move from an industrial to a service-based economy, economic wealth is no longer so much in the ground as it is in people's minds—in their training, education and ability to understand and respond to the forces driving the intensification of competition. Our school systems must produce people with creativity, vision, professional expertise, and understanding of the competitive challenges to be faced when our future growth and prosperity depend on Canada's ability to compete and win in world markets. In an era when the world competes on the bases of new knowledge and new technology, education must be at the leading edge of a nation's investment in its people. . . .

EMPLOYMENT EQUITY AS PART OF THE SOLUTION

. . . Most organizations today are pyramidal structures with many layers of supervision and management. Heavy reliance is placed on the bottom levels of the organization to carry out the more routinized, less responsible work activities. These entry-level positions are quite abundant in most companies, and we have relied on young people to fill these positions. If we superimpose the population pyramid of the year 2000 onto the typical organizational pyramid, several problems become evident. The most obvious problem is that the pyramid has holes at the bottom. These holes are called skills shortages and, as noted above, most organizations are now feeling the effects of these shortages.

This problem is occurring at a time when certain skilled groups and individuals within our society are experiencing high levels of unemployment or under-utilization. In particular, four groups of people referred to as the designated groups—women, visible minorities, persons with disabilities and aboriginal peoples—experience higher levels of unemployment and underemployment than do their white male counterparts. For example, although women now comprise approximately 46 per cent of labour force, they continue to be occupationally segregated into a few job categories, the bulk of which are comparatively poorly paid. This is, of course, one of the problems that employment equity and pay equity set out to rectify.

To this point, I have not referred to such topics as discrimination and historical injustices done to these designated groups . . . I have chosen . . . to argue that our workforce is changing; that employers will need to tap into previously excluded, forgotten, or under-utilized pools of skilled workers; and that to do this we will need to accommodate differences to ensure successful and long-term integration of these workers into our workforces. *This is the objective of employment equity.*

The process of pursuing and achieving employment equity is not an easy one; indeed, it can be quite painful because it requires all of us to confront the validity of strongly held traditions and beliefs about ourselves and others. It requires sensitivity, openness, flexibility, innovation, teamwork and collaboration—qualities that are not only important to achieving employment equity, but that also form the core competencies for successful managers of the future.

Business and Society

Anita Roddick, O.B.E.

Founder and Chief Executive
The Body Shop International

"Ethics in business is not just obedience to rules; it is about reputation, your good name, how you feel about yourself. Being ethical also means doing the best for the greatest number of people. Your employees become the guardians of your company's ethics. They are your guarantee that ethics are infused into your company's genetic make-up. I have never forgotten that it is the head that protects the ethics, but the heart is what is human. The head can preserve morality, but the heart understands—at least, that has been The Body Shop's experience."

Today we hear terrifying reports about the thinning of the ozone layer, acid rain that destroys the life-supporting capability of our lakes, the deforestation of vast sections of the planet, the turning of fertile lands into desert that makes more and more of the planet uninhabitable, the threat of the greenhouse effect that could warm the atmosphere to a dangerous extent, and the regurgitation of garbage by the seas that have been turned into dumping grounds. How did things get so bad? Why do we have such a callous attitude toward our world? To what extent is this an issue for business ethics?

In answering these questions we must first look at society's attitudes toward the natural environment before we examine specific business practices. This is because businesses operate within a framework of general attitudes shared by society, and until we understand these attitudes we will not be able to prescribe changes for the better. When a way of looking at the world becomes so embedded in a culture that it is unquestioned, it is difficult for someone growing up in that culture to view the world in any different way. An American high school student, for example, cannot even imagine the Native American attitude of respect toward nature or Mother Earth. If we have the attitude that we can do pretty much whatever we want with our natural environment, it is difficult to imagine how anybody could ever have worshiped nature or have had an attitude of awe and respect in the face of the forces of nature. It is, perhaps, even more difficult to envision an attitude toward nature that does not see it as just another commodity to be used, even *used up*.

THE NATURAL ENVIRONMENT

In the current discussion about the environment, businesses are frequently portrayed as having an especially callous attitude toward the natural environment. Is this because economic activity is, by its very nature, at odds with preservation of the environment, or is something more basic involved? The answer of yes to the first question is detailed with sympathy by John McPhee, who reports the following conversation between Charles Park, a mining engineer who believes that both the country's economic well-being and its affluent lifestyle depend on mining metals wherever they are found, and David Brower, who champions restraint in exploitation of the few remaining wilderness areas. The specific issue of dispute between them is whether a wilderness area should be opened up for mining. Here is Brower arguing that preservation of the wilderness is preferable:

> Wilderness was originally a nice place to go, but that is not what wilderness is for. Wilderness is the bank for the genetic variability of the earth. We're wiping out that reserve at a frightening rate. . . . Now that we know that we ourselves are on a spaceship, we have to get into our heads a concept of limits. Some things must stop or the world will become repugnant. There are limits everywhere, whether we are dealing with an island, a river, a mountain, with people, or with air. Living diversity is the thing we're preserving.[1]

In responding to Brower's comments, Park catalogues some of the items drawn from mining that are necessary for a modern house:

> Dave's electrical system is copper, probably from Bingham Canyon. He couldn't turn on a light or make ice without it. The nails that hold the place together come from the Mesabi Range. His downspouts are covered with zinc that was probably taken out of the ground in Canada. The tungsten in his light bulbs may have been mined in Bishop, California. The chrome on his refrigerator door probably came from Rhodesia or Turkey. His television set almost certainly contains cobalt from the Congo. He uses aluminum from Jamaica, maybe Surinam; silver from Mexico or Peru. . . . Our whole economy—our way of doing things, most of what we have, even our culture—rests on these things.

Park's view represents the other pole in this debate.

> People have a tendency to get a little bit emotional about preservation of the environment, I'm afraid. . . . While I love the out-of-doors, I have no use for wilderness. We need to lumber, we need to mine. They [preservationists] don't realize the contribution that minerals and metals make to their lives. You can't live without industry.[2]

This debate comes down to deciding on the proper role of human beings in nature. The word *ecology* has come to be used to refer to this discussion, but ecology itself refers to the relationship between any living thing and its environment. What these issues address is *human ecology,* the interrelationship between human beings and their natural environment. How to balance the equation—humans first, nature second, or nature first, humans second—forms the core of the debate. Until we have some sense of the balance of these two, there will not be much guidance for business. The question still remains what influences in the intellectual history of the West have produced the prevailing attitudes toward nature.

The Roots of a Tradition

What is the source of our contemporary attitudes toward the natural environment? Some critics point an accusing finger at the biblical tradition which presents human beings not as just a part of nature but as a special creation placed within nature and given a dominant place there. This situation is one in which nature is prepared first for human use, as a resource to support human activity. It is this sense of our preeminence that, according to the social critic Lynn White, is responsible in large measure for the insensitive attitude we have toward our natural environment. White created a stir when he accused the Judeo-Christian beliefs concerning the relation between human beings and nature as being responsible for the ecological crisis. In defense of his controversial claim, White cited the oldest of all Jewish stories found in the opening pages of Genesis. After having creating male and female, God says to them, "Be fruitful and multiply, and fill the earth and subdue it; and have dominion over the fish of the sea and over the birds of the air and over every living thing that moves upon the earth."[3] The key words here are *dominion* and *subdue*. Humanity is said to have dominion over the earth and its plants and animals, and is told to subdue it. Here White sees the mandate for a view of nature as a resource to be exploited and that exalts human beings as the dominant feature in creation.

There are, however, other biblical authorities who argue against White's interpretation. A major objection is that White's claim rests on a somewhat dubious reading of the passage. One can just as easily read this story as giving humanity responsibility and stewardship over the earth, not carte blanche to exploit it. Even if one rejects the more extreme aspect of White's claim, however, we are still left with the view that what a society thinks about itself has direct implications for its attitude toward the natural environment. As White puts it, "What people do about their ecology depends on what they think about themselves in relation to things around them. Human ecology is deeply conditioned by beliefs about our nature and destiny—that is, by religion. To Western eyes this is very evident in, say, India or Ceylon. It is equally true of ourselves and of our medieval ancestors."[4]

According to White, not only does the biblical tradition place human beings squarely at the center of creation, with nature as a resource to be exploited; it takes the further step of eliminating nature as an object of worship (as it was with many ancient peoples). In the Bible, God is sacred, nature is not. To worship nature is an abomination. The theologian Harvey Cox refers to this as the desacralization of nature, a process that began hundreds of years before such ancient Greek thinkers as Democritus and Leucippus had described all reality in terms of little bits of stuff, atoms, moving around in the void. This change of view in which the natural world is seen as other than sacred is the secular turn, and the seeds of the secularization of nature are found in the biblical tradition itself. "Presecular man lives in an enchanted forest," Cox observes. "Its glens and groves swarm with spirits. Its rocks and streams are alive with friendly or fiendish demons."[5] As long as such a view of reality persists, technological progress will be impeded. One does not mine coal from the magic mountain or intrude upon the spirits of the forest by harvesting timber.

The biblical doctrine of creation, Cox says, presents a radically secular view of the world that must have seemed to those presecular persons who first heard it as atheistic propaganda in that it denied the divine status of nature. The Law of Moses, that moral, civil, and religious code that is the basis for Jewish civilization, insisted at the beginning that nature was not an object of worship. Neither is there anything within nature that should be worshiped. As White points out, in the great creation accounts that begin the Torah, God creates the world, places human beings in it "to subdue the earth," and gives them freedom to find their way in the world, so long as they don't try to usurp God's place, to "become gods," as the wily serpent tempts them to do. In the garden of Eden, the first couple cannot resist the temptation, and the result is that they are driven from the garden to make their way in a world now filled with hardship and pain. But— and here is an important point—the basic command to subdue the earth is unchanged. The earth is for human use; it is never, never to be worshiped. God is sacred, the earth is not. For Jews and Christians there are no spirits in the woods, the streams, or the mountains. Nature is a creation of God but is not God, and that is the end of the matter.

The Modern Turn

The seventeenth century looms in Western intellectual history as a pivotal age, a time frame that Alfred North Whitehead calls "the century of genius." Not only did the thinkers of that century consider themselves as moderns, they also laid the foundations of physical science that remain important to this day. Here is just a partial list of some of the great thinkers of this period: William Harvey (1578–1657), Isaac Newton (1642–1727), Galileo Galilei (1564–1650), Johannes Kepler (1571–1630), Christiaan Huygens (1629–1695), René Descartes (1596–1650), Gottfried Leibniz (1646–1716), Francis Bacon (1561–1626), Thomas Hobbes (1588–1679), Baruch Spinoza (1632–1677). Not only was this a century of great accomplishments in theoretical understanding, it was also a time when the power to observe was greatly increased. Developed during the 1600s were the telescope and microscope; researchers studied planetary motion, and investigators increased their understanding of the behavior of gases, the circulation of the blood, and the fundamentals of mechanics. Also occurring was the development of calculus and analytical geometry. Important also were the changes in attitude that accompanied the development of these new tools. Chief among them was the emergence of an attitude that Whitehead claims was lacking in the ancients—the desire to ask questions about nature through experimentation.

When looking for a single individual who perhaps best exhibits this new experimental attitude, the name that stands out is that of Francis Bacon. Whitehead cites Bacon's attention to the experimental method as revealed in his "attention to 'irreducible and stubborn facts.'"[6] An example of Bacon's dedication to experimentation is the fact that he died of bronchitis contracted while performing an experiment involving the stuffing of snow into a chicken to determine whether cold could preserve meat.

Note that the notion of experiment is more than just gathering information. An experiment is, by its modern definition, the gathering of data according to a plan or, to put it differently, getting answers to questions that the experimenter asks about nature and natural processes. Immanuel Kant, whose ethical writings we have already encountered, characterizes the role of reason in scientific discovery as reasoning according to a plan devised by the human mind. Citing the discoveries of several important researchers, Kant claims, "They learned that reason has insight only into that which it produces after a plan of its own, and that it must not allow itself to be kept, as it were, in nature's leading-strings . . . not . . . in the character of a pupil who listens to everything that the teacher chooses to say, but of an appointed judge who compels the witnesses to answer questions which he himself has formulated."[7] Notice the metaphors Kant uses. We approach nature as a judge—or to change the metaphor to reflect the differences in our judicial system from the one Kant was familiar with—we approach nature as a prosecuting attorney demanding that nature answer our questions.

This is a different way of looking at the world; the mind is not just a passive receiver of impressions gained through the senses but an active participant in the process of discovery. Kant expresses well the modern shift that emphasizes the active participation of human reason in the search for understanding of nature and natural processes. We see this clearly in the writings of the seventeenth-century thinker Francis Bacon. In his work *The Great Instauration,* Bacon proposes to rebuild the sciences on a firmer foundation than the ancients had. The present "fabric of human reason which we employ in the inquisition of nature," he observes, "is badly put together and built up, and like some magnificent structure without any foundation." Note Bacon's use of a judicial metaphor similar to Kant's—the *inquisition* of nature. Bacon proposes to change our approach to discovering "the remoter and more hidden parts of nature" and through this new approach to establish "for ever a true and lawful marriage between the empirical and rational faculty, the unkind and ill-starred divorce and separation of which has thrown into confusion all the affairs of the human family."[8]

Knowledge as Power

Behind all this brave talk about discovering nature's secrets is a desire to do something more than just learn about nature. The hidden agenda—and sometimes it is not even hidden—is the desire to take control of nature and natural processes. Control, not mere knowledge, was one of the concerns of the seventeenth-century thinkers, and this factor, perhaps more than any other, distinguished them from the thinkers of antiquity. Why do we want to understand things better? For Francis Bacon the answer is clear: to be able to exert our power over the physical environment. Nowhere does this come out more clearly than in his first book of aphorisms, no. iii: "Human knowledge and human power meet in one; for where the cause is not known the effect cannot be produced. Nature to be commanded must be obeyed; and that which in contemplation is as the cause is in operation as the rule."

Knowledge is power. This was Bacon's fundamental motivation. Knowledge acquisition is aided by the combination of the experimental and rational, the empirical and contemplative aspects of our nature. Unlike the empirical ants, which only gather data, and unlike the rational spiders, which only build airy theoretical structures, the true scien-

A Case in Point . . .

The water in Sugar Run, a creek in southern Ohio, looks more like yesterday's coffee than a country stream that used to provide fishing opportunities to the local residents. The reason: Southern Ohio Coal Company, a subsidiary of American Electric Power, needed to remove a billion gallons of water that somehow flowed from a sealed wall in an abandoned section of a coal mine into a working section. If the water were not pumped out, the 230 under-ground workers would lose their jobs, perhaps even face the possibility that the entire mining operation would have to close down. If that happened, 800 jobs would go with it. The rusty colored water discharging into Sugar Run and other creeks—Leading Creek and Parker Run—contained massive amounts of iron oxide, fatal to fish because it coats their gills. A spokesman for Southern Ohio Coal acknowledged that the pumping would kill the fish in the creeks, but he claimed there would be no long-term ecological effects. "We can mitigate the short-term effects, but we couldn't bring back the jobs if the water re-mained in the mine," he said.

Some local residents expressed willingness to trade pollution for jobs, but the U.S. Environmental Protection Agency (EPA) disagreed and ordered the pumping stopped. A federal judge intervened and issued a ten-day restraining order against the EPA so the pumping could continue—though the company said it needed at least thirty days to complete the pumping. The EPA went back to court seeking to have the restraining order overturned. Several resi-dents in the area expressed concern that heavy rains would cause flooding, and the overflow would dump pollutants on their fields. American Electric Power authorities promised to stop the pumping if the threat of flooding occurred but also admitted that all aquatic life in two of the creeks had been destroyed. The governor of Ohio intervened with federal authorities and called the pumping the "right thing in regard to the jobs and the right thing in regard to the environment."

Sources: CD, Aug. 8, 1993; *Athens* (Ohio) *Messenger,* Aug. 7, 8, 9 26, 27, 28, 29, 1993.

tist, the *knower* (which is what the term "scientist"means), combines the best of both. The goal of knowledge is power and control.

THE ETHICAL QUANDARY

Let's be careful here. What is wrong with the desire to have power over the forces of nature? It is easy to make superficial judgments about our predecessors when we live in a world in which we have so much control over our physical environment. Think for just a moment of the things we have that the seventeenth century did not: sanitation, anesthesia, electricity for light and power, antibiotics, vaccines, polymers. This partial list focuses on the things that have improved the quality of human life. Whereas smallpox ravaged the population then, it has now been eradicated totally. The last person to have smallpox was Maow Maalin, a Kenyan.[9] Think of other diseases that have been controlled: polio, influenza, diptheria, tetanus, measles, just to name a few. Automobiles and cheap fuel have overcome regional barriers. Polymers made from plentiful raw materials have made inexpensive clothing and housewares available to millions. Consider also computers, lasers, satellite communications, CD players, shuttle boosters, jet aircraft. Which would you undo if you could?

The answer most of us would give would probably be: none of it. We want it all, but only the good part. We want cheap and available electricity without the problems of air pollution or radioactive waste. We want relatively inexpensive transportation but without urban sprawl and blight or hydrocarbon buildup in the atmosphere. We want inexpensive and durable products made from polymers, but not the problem of disposing of nonbiodegradable wastes.

There are those, to be sure, who long for the simple life, who, like Thoreau, wish to turn back the clock to a simpler, more pastoral life. The attractions of living alone in the woods in a shack made by hand, freed from dependence on larger society, are largely illusory. But, like all utopian visions, it does embody a truth that can serve as a corrective to an overdependence on technology. That truth is that the worth of life does not depend on the abundance of things with which we surround ourselves or the technology that makes them possible. We find ourselves in a dialectical tension. At one pole lies an excessive dependence on a technological vision of the world; at the other lies an excessive desire for total independence from technology. As Aristotle discovered, the rational approach lies in discovering the mean between the two. But how to find that mean is not easy.

BUSINESS AND THE ENVIRONMENT

The issues are so formidable that no single business or industry can attack them alone. Consider the following questions:

Is it reasonable to expect a single business (or business sector) to put itself at a competitive disadvantage by following ecologically sound practices?

Is lower economic growth, with attendant loss of jobs, a desirable social goal?

How do we decide what level of economic growth and pollution is acceptable? How do we enforce these restraints?

Should we cut back on this generation's use of resources so that there will be resources for future generations? To what ethical principles would you appeal to support this claim?

Is it fair to attempt to slow the industrialization of third-world nations so we will not add to the ecological crisis?

The Rio Summit on the environment, held in 1992, attempted to deal with just such questions. Technically known as the United Nations Conference on Environment and Development, the conference tried to produce consensus—unsuccessfully, it turned out—on steps to be taken worldwide to reduce the harmful effects on the environment produced by modern industrialized civilization. The challenges are enormous, as *Business Week* pointed out:

> In only 20 years, global population has leaped 66%, to 5.3 billion, while world economic output has nearly doubled. In vast areas, the decline of nature is disturbingly evident. The Baltic Sea is dying from sewage and other pollution. Every year, 25 billion tons of topsoil are lost. In places such as Mexico City and Eastern Europe, millions breathe toxic air. China soon will have cut all its harvestable forests. The ozone layer is thinning, the globe may be warming, and more devastation lies in store.[10]

As the Rio conference showed, rational solutions to the problems of living with environmental fragility are beyond the capabilities of a single industry, or even a single country, and requires concerted worldwide action. The situation Hobbes describes as the state of nature, the warfare of all against all, is an appropriate way of thinking about the predicted ecological crisis in which human life will be "poor, nasty, brutish, and short," though not solitary, with the predicted doubling of the world's population by the year 2030.[11] Here are some of the responses to these problems that reflect an ethical awareness of humankind's collective responsibility.

Market Forces and Free Resources

One approach to the issues of environmental responsibility is to attempt to bring market forces to bear on businesses for their use of air and water, which traditionally have been treated as free resources. No one owns the air or the rivers and oceans. Hence business generally does not have to pay for its use of air and water to carry away industrial by-products. Certainly the costs of air and water pollution are real, but these costs—called "externalities" by economists—are not borne by the users of the products and services of the polluting industries. They are paid by those who suffer health costs associated with breathing toxic air and drinking impure water, and these are usually the poorest in society. Eventually the costs of pollution are paid by taxpayers, not necessarily the customers of the firms causing the pollution, at a cost estimated to be as much as $750 billion.[12]

The Superfund law in the United States requires the government to seek reimbursement for the cleanup from the original polluters, but this effort has become mired in litigation, with more money being spent on legal costs than on cleanup costs. There are advocates of an alternative that would require all companies, whether they polluted or not, to participate in a no-fault system that would help pay for the cleanup. The EPA has also issued rules shielding banks that merely hold mortgages on property from financial liability for cleaning up polluted land they own and that would also put caps on the amount small municipalities must pay for removing wastes from publicly owned land. Defenders of the process of attempting to place the financial burden of the cleanup on the biggest polluters say it is changing business behavior. The head of the EPA claims, "Superfund's environmental liability scheme has brought a new environmental ethic to America."[13]

A similar strategy is being used by the U.S. government for industries that generate air pollution. Those industries that reduce their level of pollution below government limits get credits for this reduction, which they, in turn, can sell to firms that have not yet reached government-prescribed levels. The strategy here is to encourage companies to reduce pollution below legal levels by making this reduction a salable commodity.[14] While angering some conservationists, this approach does have the effect of lowering the overall amount of pollution, though its use has been less than was originally anticipated.[15]

Often cited in defense of the use of the free market to reduce negative effects on the environment is the claim that the free market is the fairest system available for allocating a society's goods and services. Notice that this claim is not that it is the fairest conceivable but the fairest available system. Therefore any activity that makes the market less free, or gives a producer an advantage based on an unfair use of the market, is an interference with the market mechanisms and should be rejected on ethical grounds. By passing some manufacturing costs (that is, the expense of dealing with pollution) onto others, a polluting company is able to underprice its product. Such a company gains an unfair advantage over a firm that does not pollute and therefore produces the product at a greater cost.

A Philosophical Change

Because a large part of the blame for environmental insensitivity can be placed on a culture's worldview, a shift in the public's attitude will be required if business and industry are to change their practices. Already we see examples of companies advertising their commitments to environmental responsibility. A company specializing in the management of waste advertises itself as helping the environment.[16] Oil companies urge the recycling of used oil for commercial purposes.[17] This "green marketing" strategy, so-called because it is tied to the claim that the company is environmentally friendly and helps preserve the greenness of the planet, is found increasingly in the marketing plans of corporations. It can backfire, though, as it did in the case of a manufacturer of plastic trash bags that claimed the bags were biodegradable, though fine print on the packaging indicated that in order to decompose, the bags had to be exposed to the elements, which most are not when deposited in landfills. Faced with opposition from the Environmental Defense Fund, organized consumer boycotts, and pressure from the Federal Trade Commission, the manufacturer dropped the claim.[18]

More than just a change in marketing strategies is needed, however. The philosophical tradition in the West has not been friendly to the environment. The brief survey at the beginning of this chapter is just a sampling of the Western attitudes that emphasize the human over the natural, that place human beings in a privileged position over the natural environment. The ancient biblical texts saw nature as a resource. The seventeenth-century philosophers saw nature as something to be conquered. The eighteenth-century philosophers continued this tradition by seeing the control of nature as the pathway to power. The nineteenth and twentieth centuries treated nature as a commercial commodity, to be used up with little thought given to future consequences or to the question of whether the present generation has an obligation to future generations. These attitudes are not so prevalent in Eastern thought, where nature and the humans are seen in a more reciprocal relationship, and the desired goal is to find balance and harmony between the two.

Drawing on these resources, the contemporary Jewish philosopher Martin Buber offers a new way of thinking about the relationship between humans and their natural environment. In a probing study of human relationships, Buber applies the terms "I" and "Thou" to describe a relationship of mutuality and trust. The term "thou" is derived from older English usage where it served as a familiar personal pronoun, used only with family or close friends. Contemporary German and French preserve such distinctions in pronoun usage "Sie" and "vous" (for formal usage) and "Du" and "tu" (for informal usage). Entitled *Ich und Du,* Buber's book explores in almost poetic language what it means to relate to another person as a Thou rather than an It. When we relate to another person as a Thou, we open ourselves up for a relationship, an interactive mutuality in which there is both give and take. To relate to someone as an It is to debase a personal relationship, to treat a person as a thing, which destroys any possibility of a relationship that reinforces and enlarges one's humanity.

BUBER ON NATURE

The first question may be formulated with some precision as follows: If—as the book says—we can stand in the *I-Thou* relationship not merely with other men, but also with beings and things which come to meet us in nature, what is it that makes the real difference between the two relationships? Or, more closely, if the *I-Thou* relationship requires a mutual action which in fact embraces both the *I* and the *Thou,* how may the relation to something in nature be understood as such a relationship? More precisely still, if we are to assume that we are granted a kind of mutuality by beings and things in nature as well, which we meet as our *Thou,* what is then the character of this reciprocity and what justification have we for using this fundamental concept in order to describe it? . . . It is part of our concept of a plant that it cannot react to our action towards it: it cannot "respond." Yet this does not mean that here we are given simply no reciprocity at all. The deed or attitude of an individual being is certainly not to be found here, but there is a reciprocity of the being itself, a reciprocity which is nothing but being in its course *(seiend).* That living wholeness and unity of the tree, which denies itself to the sharpest glance of the mere investigator and discloses itself to the glance of one who says *Thou,* is there when he, the sayer of *Thou,* is there: it is he who vouchsafes to the tree that it manifest this unity and wholeness; and now the tree which is in being manifests them.

Source: Martin Buber, *I and Thou,* Ronald Gregor Smith (New York: Charles Scribner's Sons, 1958), pp. 124–126.

Buber extends his analysis to new ways of thinking about nature. We can look at the natural environment as only a resource, an *It* to be used for commercial gain, or we can relate to the natural environment as a resource that we use but toward which we also must exercise care and responsible stewardship.[19] The essence of the I-Thou relationship is one of mutuality, a two-way interaction involving respect and concern. At first glance, the natural environment does not appear to provide the kind of mutuality that comes from a relationship with another human being. After more careful consideration we see, however, that we live on the most intimate terms with the natural world—whether it be the fertility of the soil that provides food, the minerals from the earth that provide resources for our civilization, or the air that we breathe that supports life. We depend on the natural environment for our very sustenance. To deny this dependence is to treat nature as an It. And we will continue in this mode of thinking at our peril.

Buber's view of nature recognizes our mutual dependence on nature for our very survival. The continued existence of nature, in turn, depends upon our willingness to treat it in a way that does not destroy it.

It is important to note that social attitudes do change. Witness the dramatic change in public attitudes toward smoking and toward driving while intoxicated. When social attitudes change, the behavior of our institutions, both business and government, change as well. As the Rio conference shows, we can no longer ignore what we are doing to the natural environment, the effects of which on ecology, *human ecology*, pose one of humanity's greatest challenges. Thinking "green," and marketing "green" must come to be recognized by consumers as attitudes essential to human survival.

Recognizing the importance of safeguarding the environment, a coalition of organizations named CERES—Coalition of Environmentally Responsible Economies—formulated the Ceres Principles to which over sixty-five corporations have subscribed, including the Sun Company, an oil refining and marketing company and the first Fortune 500 company to accept the principles. The International Chamber of Commerce has also issued "The Business Charter for Sustainable Development," which declares, "There is widespread recognition today that environmental protection must be among the highest priorities of every business."

Protection of the environment is only one of the societal obligations of corporate management, hence the notion of "stakeholders" has entered the vocabulary of business ethics. As a contemporary writer in the field has noted, "Employees, customers, suppliers, creditors, governments, the local community, and the general public are also affected seriously by the activities of the corporation. Executives must not only help their corporations make money for the stockholders but must also . . . help produce products at a reasonable market price, ensure adequate working conditions for employees, operate under prevailing government restrictions, deal equitably with creditors and suppliers, minimize potential harmful impact on the local community, and do many other things."[20] Given our dependence upon a livable environment, we are all stakeholders of companies whose activities affect that environment.

THE CERES PRINCIPLES (FORMERLY THE VALDEZ PRINCIPLES)

Introduction

By adopting these Principles, we publicly affirm our belief that corporations have a responsibility for the environment, and must conduct all aspects of their business as responsible stewards of the environment by operating in a manner that protects the Earth. We believe that corporations must not compromise the ability of future generations to sustain themselves.

We will update our practices constantly in light of advances in technology and new understandings in health and environmental science. In collaboration with CERES, we will promote a dynamic process to ensure that the Principles are interpreted in a way that accommodates changing technologies and environmental realities. We intend to make consistent, measurable progress in implementing these Principles and to apply them to all aspects of our operations throughout the world.

Protection of the Biosphere
We will reduce and make continual progress toward eliminating the release of any substance that may cause environmental damage to the air, water, or the earth or its inhabitants. We will safeguard all habitats affected by our operations and will protect open spaces and wilderness, while preserving biodiversity.

Sustainable Use of Natural Resources
We will make sustainable use of renewable natural resources, such as water, soils and forests. We will conserve nonrenewable natural resources through efficient use and careful planning.

Reduction and Disposal of Wastes
We will reduce and where possible eliminate waste through source reduction and recycling. All waste will be handled and disposed of through safe and responsible methods.

Energy Conservation
We will conserve energy and improve the energy efficiency of our internal operations and of the goods and services we sell. We will make every effort to use environmentally safe and sustainable energy sources.

Risk Reduction
We will strive to minimize the environmental, health and safety risks to our employees and the communities in which we operate through safe technologies, facilities and operating procedures, and by being prepared for emergencies.

Safe Products and Services
We will reduce and where possible eliminate the use, manufacture or sale of products and services that cause environmental damage or health or safety hazards. We will inform our customers of the environmental impacts of our products or services and try to correct unsafe use.

Environmental Restoration
We will promptly and responsibly correct conditions we have caused that endanger health, safety or the environment. To the extent feasible, we will redress injuries we have caused to persons or damage we have caused to the environment and will restore the environment.

Informing the Public
We will inform in a timely manner everyone who may be affected by conditions caused by our company that might endanger health, safety or the environment. We will regularly seek advice and counsel through dialogue with persons in communities near our facilities. We will not take any action against employees for reporting dangerous incidents or conditions to management or to appropriate authorities.

Management Commitment
We will implement these Principles and sustain a process that ensures that the Board of Directors and Chief Executive Officer are fully informed about pertinent environmental issues and are fully responsible for environmental policy. In selecting our Board of Directors, we will consider demonstrated environmental commitment as a factor.

Audits and Reports
We will conduct an annual self-evaluation of our progress in implementing these Principles. We will support the timely creation of generally accepted environmental audit procedures. We will annually complete the CERES Report, which will be made available to the public.

Disclaimer

These Principles establish an environmental ethic with criteria by which investors and others can assess the environmental performance of companies. Companies that sign these Principles pledge to go voluntarily beyond the requirements of the law. These Principles are not intended to create new legal liabilities, expand existing rights or obligations, waive legal defenses, or otherwise affect the legal position of any signatory company, and are not intended to be used against a signatory in any legal proceeding for any purpose.

This amended version of the CERES Principles was adopted by the CERES Board of Directors on April 28, 1992.

Reprinted with permission of CERES, 711 Atlantic Ave., Boston, MA 02111

DISCUSSION STARTERS

1 Some would argue that the change in cultural attitudes that resulted in modern business activity also produced a callous attitude toward the natural environment. Do you agree that these are linked? Why or why not?
2 Why are the forces of the free market alone not very effective in curbing industrial pollution?
3 What incentives do businesses have for adopting the CERES principles or something like them? What incentives *should* they have?
4 Is it in the interests of consumers for companies to "go green" in their business decisions? Defend your answer.
5 Using Buber's categories, does thinking of nature as a Thou rather than an It provide a useful way of thinking about the interactions between humans and the natural environment? Explain

NOTES

1 John McPhee, *Encounters with the Archdruid* (New York: Noonday Press, 1971), pp. 61, 62–63.
2 Ibid., pp. 48–49, 67.
3 Genesis 1:28, New Revised Standard Version.
4 Lynn White, Jr., "The Historical Roots of Our Ecologic Crisis," in *Dynamo and Virgin Reconsidered: Machina ex Deo* (Cambridge, MA: MIT Press, 1981), p. 84.
5 Harvey Cox, *The Secular City* (New York: Macmillan, 1965), p. 21.
6 Alfred North Whitehead, *Science in the Modern World* (New York: Free Press, 1953), p. 42.
7 Immanuel Kant, *Critique of Pure Reason,* trans. Norman Kemp Smith (New York: Macmillan, 1961), p. 20.
8 Francis Bacon, *The Great Instauration,* in *The English Philosophers from Bacon to Mill,* ed. Edwin A. Burtt (New York: Modern Library, 1939), p. 12.
9 See "Smallpox—Epitaph for a Killer," *National Geographic,* Dec. 1978, pp. 797–805.
10 BW, May 11, 1991, p. 67.
11 Ibid.
12 BW, May 11, 1992, p. 32.
13 BW, May 11, 1992, p. 33.
14 *Time,* Feb. 12, 1990, p. 67; WSJ, Apr. 14, 1992, p. A1.
15 NYT, May 12, 1992.
16 BW, Sept. 13, 1992, inside back cover.
17 BW, May 11, 1992, p. 33.
18 *Advertising Age,* Apr. 1, 1991.
19 Buber appeals to Heraclitus, Taoism, and the Upanishads in weaving together a way of looking at nature, which he refers to as "what is com-

mon to all" in his book *The Knowledge of Man* (New York: Harper Torch-
books, 1964).
20 Joseph R. Desjardins and John J. McCall, *Contemporary Issues in Business
Ethics* (Belmont, CA: Wadsworth, 1990), p. 34.

CASE STUDY

The reports given in the following excerpt from a book on corporate
behavior belie the claim that social responsibility is incompatible with
the bottom line. As social policy more and more emphasizes the importance of environmental responsibility and social concerns, corporate
behavior likewise is beginning to reflect these values. Since news
reports seem to concentrate on unethical business behavior, reports on
responsible business behavior are needed to dispel the notion that
social responsibility and business success are incompatible.

COMPANIES WITH A CONSCIENCE

From Chicago's Stony Island Avenue, about nine miles south of the
city's fabled Loop, you can see both the peril of urban America in the
1990s—and the promise of a new kind of American company.

On one side of the wide asphalt strip is Woodlawn, a section filled
with burned-out buildings, debris-strewn lots, graffiti-scarred walls,
and general despair.

On the other is South Shore, a section brimming with rehabilitated
apartments, neat single-family homes, clean streets, and hope.

Stony Island physically separates these two adjoining neighborhoods
in the heart of America's third-largest city—but in reality they are worlds
apart. The difference between them is the Shorebank Corporation.

Formed in 1973, when Woodlawn and South Shore were equally
experiencing early stages of urban decline, Shorebank is an unusual
kind of community development organization. With a bank at its
core—and a group of non-bankers at its helm—it is a multifaceted def-
initely-for-profit business created specifically to bolster the fortunes of
South Shore.

From *Companies with a Conscience* by Mary Scott and Howard Rothman. Copyright © 1992 by Mary Scott and Howard Rothman. Published by arrangement with
Carol Publishing Group. A Birch Lane Press Book.

By most measures—and particularly in contrast to the deterioration that ultimately destroyed Woodlawn—it is a remarkable success. Indeed, after the Los Angeles riots last spring, Shorebank was often cited as *the* model for small-business development and residential rehabilitation.

"People always ask me if that is risky," says Joan Shapiro, a senior vice-president at Shorebank's South Shore Bank. "But where have the losses in this industry been in the last 10 years? Not at a bank like South Shore. Our loan losses in 1991 were a little over 6/10ths of 1%, the year before that they were 46/100ths of 1%, and the year before that 42/100ths of 1%. Who has really taken the risks?"

No wonder we found Shorebank, a financial institution, among more nationally familiar names like Ben & Jerry's (ice cream), Patagonia (clothing), Smith & Hawken (mail order), and Celestial Seasoning (herbal teas) when we set out to track leading examples of the new kind of socially responsible company that has surfaced in America.

They are driven by what Ben and Jerry call "caring capitalism"—an uncanny flair for business and an uncommon commitment to people. From visionary company founders like Yvon Chouinard of Patagonia to dedicated second-generation managers like Ms. Shapiro of Shorebank, the people who run these organizations combine a social worker's sympathies with an entrepreneur's instincts, an inventor's street smarts with an MBA's business savvy. They are interesting *to,* and interested *in,* those around them. And, fortunately for the rest of us, they are becoming the role models for successful corporate leadership in the '90s.

It was early in 1991 when we as writers began talking about the way corporate America seemed to be resetting its moral compass. We marveled at how the greed-is-good, house-of-cards economic engineering of the '80s was no longer in favor. And how the Michael Milkens, Charles Keatings, and Gordon Dekkos of the world—real-life Wall Street Money Men and cinematic West Coast power brokers alike—were suddenly and decisively out of fashion.

"The '80s were about style and life style," says clothing designer and entrepreneur Susie Tompkins of Esprit de Corp, headquartered in San Francisco. "The '90s are about soul-searching . . . about encouraging volunteerism. Before, we gave our employees French lessons, sent them on river trips—all of those personal things. Now, we're giving them character-building opportunities." To support employees' volunteer work, Esprit allows up to 10 hours per month of paid leave, to be matched by a similar amount of the employee's own time.

We saw evidence of the new-found ethical standard everywhere. Companies like Apple Computer and Wal-Mart were actively encouraging their employees and customers to recycle. Campbell Soup and H. J. Heinz were among those offering on-site day-care programs. Avon Products and General Mills were developing policies to help female and minority workers. Coca-Cola and 3M were investing heavily in community outreach efforts. Even General Motors released a packet of information called "General Motors and the Environment."

But we remained skeptical until we learned more. What we eventually found was a still small—but steadily growing—network of companies with a conscience. We decided to explore these companies as subjects for a book.

The giants got the publicity, but we quickly discovered that smaller, often unknown companies really were the leaders in this nascent movement toward corporate responsibility. What's more, we discovered that many of these small- and mid-sized firms were actually making a regular and substantial profit.

We noted the mushrooming number of business schools requiring classes on environmental or ethical issues for the MBA degree. And we watched as companies like IBM began supporting major conferences on business ethics for their peers across the U.S.

"We're not trying to get people to stop consuming, we're trying to get them to cut back and consume better," says founder Chouinard of the Patagonia company.

Ms. Tompkins of Esprit de Corp recalls rewriting the company's mission statement: "We hired facilitators and we went over and over what we wanted to say." Finally the collective group of employees came up with three simple lines: "Be informed. Be involved. Make a difference."

Involving employees and decentralizing responsibility are tenets of the companies with a conscience. Alfalfa's Inc. of Denver, Colorado, is so successful (500 employees, $30 million gross in 1991) it had to decentralize by adding to its chain of natural-foods groceries.

"It has not been easy," admits Kashmir-born, London-educated Sahid M. Hassan, the firm's co-founder and CEO. "When I go into a store, I look at every shelf and every can and every display and every interaction, and I have an idea of how every one of those things should be to be perfect. It's not easy for me to acknowledge that I wouldn't do it the way that it's been done, but now it's essentially someone else's store. And if I want them to take complete pride in it, and to treat it like their own store, it isn't going to work if I constantly butt in."

To involve employees the management of Birkenstock Footprint Sandals Inc., a California-based wholesaler, shares projected sales and profits figures with everyone in the company. "Everyone feels that we are in on what was always a big secret," says Suzanne in the payroll department. "Once we learn what the company-wide goals are, each department works on its action plan on how to achieve those projections."

In addition, Birkenstock believes in paying for productivity. "We look at our location, our industry, and our position," says vice-president Mary Jones. "If there is a job we feel is especially important to us, then we will provide extra compensation." Among those positions considered essential is that of warehouse shipping clerk, and Birkenstock pays above the industry norm for it. "They're our vital link between the company and the customer," Jones explains.

Here are a few case histories of organizations with corporate and social responsibility:

America Works Inc.

Dawn, a native of New York's South Bronx, had never been to Wall Street. A single mother to a three-year old son, she was living at her mother's apartment and relying solely on public assistance. When she went to interview for a secretarial position with a prestigious Wall Street law firm, she didn't know what to expect.

"I was scared," she says. "I had graduated from high school and a business trade school, but when I had my son, I couldn't keep up the job. Then, when I was ready, I couldn't find one. I was depressed and anxious."

Then Dawn learned about America Works Inc., a different kind of employment agency. After being placed on a three-month waiting list, she went through its one-week pre-employment session and three-to-five-week business lab. With the company's help, she eventually landed a job as assistant to a lawyer specializing in immigration law.

America Works, with offices in Hartford and Manhattan, takes in $4 million annually by finding jobs in the private sector for more than 550 welfare recipients each year. Once a match is made, the newly hired employee works on a trial basis for four months. America Works pays a modest hourly wage while billing the employer a somewhat higher figure—depending on the wage for that particular position—to cover wages, benefits, and monitoring expenses. Typically, the cost to employers is about $1 an hour less than ordinary payroll costs. The employee receives reduced welfare benefits.

If the tryout proves successful, the employee then goes on the company's payroll at its going rate, and the welfare payments stop. If the employee stays on the job for a year, the employer can qualify for a federal tax credit amounting to more than $1,000. And each time an America Works client is fully weaned from welfare, the company charges the state—$4,000 in Connecticut, $5,300 in New York. To illustrate, a recent New York audit found that 80% of the employees are with the same companies after $2\frac{1}{2}$ years.

"For $5,300 we guarantee the state doesn't have to pay $24,000 [the estimated cost of keeping a mother and two children on welfare]," says Peter Cove, founder of the company. He started it in 1985 and now runs it with his wife, sociologist Lee Bowes, who serves as CEO.

A veteran of several nonprofit efforts for the disadvantaged, Cove says: "I learned that . . . helping to provide a job is perhaps the central and most important thing I or society could do for a person. I also learned that the majority of people on public assistance would rather be working. And that's what America Works is all about."

Smith & Hawken

From a line of clothing made from cotton unpolluted by pesticides and processing chemicals to a brand of organic coffee grown and harvested by a collective of Mexican farmers, the Smith & Hawken mail-order firm practices what it preaches in a recent Christmas catalog:

"Because gifts we have long taken for granted—air, water, soil, natural and human diversity—are now endangered and need our attention, we try to create products that are restorative, natural, and beneficial to our society on many levels."

Founded in 1979 by Dave Smith and Paul Hawken (founder of the Erewhon natural-foods company in Boston in the 1960s), it now employs about 275 people in a series of old buildings in Santa Rosa and Mill Valley, California. Its products include recycled wrapping paper created by schoolchildren and packaged by disabled workers; silk socks made by former coca farmers in the Colombian Andes; clothing with buttons made of tagua nuts harvested from the Ecuadoran rain forest without destroying the trees; and shirts, jeans, and jackets to be colored with natural indigo dyes instead of toxic aniline substitutes. A portion of pre-tax profits goes to environmental causes.

Newman's Own Inc.

These days movie stars are often as well known for their off-screen antics as their on-screen performances. One of the most famous, Paul Newman, is unique because his private-life fame comes partially from racing cars—and partially from his establishment of a multimillion-dollar food company. And partially because Newman's Own Foods—founded in 1982 by the author and his friend, writer A. E. Hotchner—gives away 100% of its pre-tax profits. The private company based in Westport, Connecticut, has donated $48 million to hundreds of charities—while selling more than $60 million in salad dressing, popcorn, lemonade, pasta sauces, and salsa in 1991 alone.

The two friends invested $40,000 to set up the company, with Newman as president, Hotchner as vice-president and treasurer, and the latter's wife, Ursula Hotchner, as second vice-president. To economize they furnished their offices with Newman's poolside furniture and a ping-pong table. Many of these furnishings are still used today.

Instead of spending hundreds of thousands of dollars on test-marketing and research—which is customary in the food business—Newman invited friends over for a tasting. Today the company remains lean. Only 10 employees work in the unpretentious headquarters. Goods are produced in 14 North American factories. The company keeps tight control over quality.

Each year Newman and the Hotchners go through thousands of grant requests and, according to Hotchner, "simply give to the neediest." Such recipients include a nun in Florida, who ran a school for the children of migrant farm workers. When her schoolbus broke down, she wrote Newman a letter and soon received a $26,000 check for a new one.

Aspen Skiing Company

Aspen may be best known as the ski resort for the rich and famous, but for more than a decade the former mining town in the heart of the Colorado Rockies has also been at the cutting edge of the environmental movement.

The commitment began in the late '70s, when Aspen Skiing—which operates the ski runs at Aspen Mountain as well as at nearby Buttermilk and Snowmass—started its free bus system for both employees and guests. This removed a large number of cars from the town's narrow streets throughout the winter, greatly diminishing automobile-generated air pollution.

During 1989–90 Aspen became the first ski area in the U.S. to initiate an on-mountain recycling program, which created a system for handling all the glass, aluminum, and cardboard that was discarded at its 11 mountainside restaurants.

The program was expanded to recycling motor oil, computer and typewriter ribbons, and plastic toner containers, and purchase of a variety of recycled products such as paper for trail maps, brochures, business cards, letterheads, toilet paper, paper towels, and copy-machine paper.

In 1991 the company installed energy-efficient lighting and water-efficient bath fixtures at its base area and hotels. It also began working with the Pitkin County Water Recovery Center on an experimental program to compost all waste from the mountain eateries—which quickly cut Aspen Skiing's refuse collection so dramatically that now less than 10% of it goes into the county landfill.

. . . As the '90s wear on, it becomes increasingly apparent that business in general can no longer function, and no longer be judged solely on the basis of nets and grosses. A positive impact on employees, customers, and the community at large has assumed an equal or even greater significance in the overall picture. Today's bottom line encompasses more than just dollars and cents, and corporations of all sizes and philosophical orientations are beginning to recognize this.

PART THREE

ACTING ETHICALLY IN A BUSINESS ENVIRONMENT

"Have you noticed ethics creeping into some of these deals lately?"

Why Bad Things Are Done by Good People

CHAPTER OUTLINE

Robert A. Kierlin
President
Fastenal Company

"Ethical practices are nothing more than the appreciation of how humanity is special. If we respect human life for what it is and can be, we will understand how acting unethically debases everything that makes humans unique."

When we open the newspaper and read about a Wall Street dealer who trades on inside information, a milk company executive who rigs a bid, an accountant who falsifies a balance sheet, an operating engineer who approves a faulty product design, we immediately ask ourselves what kind of person would do something like that. If we were to ask these persons about their ethics, their answer would most probably be that they consider themselves ethical, and the chances are high that their associates would agree with them. Most persons who act unethically in a corporate setting care for their children, are kind to their coworkers, contribute to local charities, and don't kick their dogs or cheat on their golf scores. Why do otherwise good people behave unethically in their business affairs or, as the title of this chapter asks, why are bad things done by good people?

BAD BEHAVIOR AND SELF-UNDERSTANDING

Before proceeding, it is important to acknowledge the inherent difficulty in using the term "good" in the context we have set for it here. The ancient Greek philosopher Plato devoted considerable effort to analyzing what the term "good" means, and what at first might seem to be a somewhat easy inquiry is soon revealed to be a major philosophical mystery. Pursuit of the good is the ultimate challenge for all philosophy, according to Plato, and the idea of Good defies complete understanding (hence the use of the capital G to name it). The Good is to knowing what the sun is to seeing, according to one of Plato's more powerful metaphors, and catching a glimpse of the Good is almost akin to a mystical experience. Plato's student Aristotle also considered the concept of the good a pivotal issue for philosophy, but in his own somewhat more worldly approach, Aristotle pointed out that there are many goods, each appropriate to the particular thing on which it is predicated. For human beings, as we saw in Chapter 2, goodness consists in the exercise of our rational faculties and the development of that which is most human in our nature. The good life, by extension, is that manner of life that leads to the achievement of well-being, and well-being or the good life has many facets. There is, however, no sense in which individuals can be said to be living a good life if in some areas they seek to be good but in other areas abandon that quest. It is in the Aristotelian sense that we are using the term "good" here. A good person is one who seeks goodness in all areas of life, and this for Aristotle means a life ruled by reason and guided by moderation.

A Case in Point . . .

The former number two person at the Pentagon, Paul Thayer, was sentenced to four years in prison and fined $5,000 for lying to the Securities and Exchange Commission in an insider-trading case. He also agreed to pay a $550,000 fine to the SEC to settle a civil suit. The Anheuser-Busch Company, for which he served as director, sued him for giving inside information to friends about the company's plans to acquire a Dallas Company, Campbell Taggart, Inc. The suit alleged that Anheuser-Busch paid $80 million more for Campbell Taggart stock than it should have due to Thayer's activities. At his sentencing, Thayer told the judge, "It is an understatement to say I am sorry and very remorseful for violating the law. I have destroyed a life of achievement. The last two years have been a living nightmare. I don't like myself as much as I used to."

Sources: *Chicago Tribune*, Apr. 28, 1985, May 9, 1985; FOR, June 10, 1985; FORB Aug. 10, 1987.

An Existentialist Analysis

To understand such conduct better, we turn to a philosopher from the twentieth century, Jean-Paul Sartre. One of a group of philosophers loosely grouped as existentialists, Sartre emphasizes the total freedom of the individual. Coupled with such total freedom is total responsibility. In especially vivid language, Sartre says that human beings are "condemned to be free." Most of us experience such freedom, he thought, as a terrible burden, and we devise numerous ways to escape from it. We play roles. We submerge ourselves in a larger group. We put responsibility—and blame—onto someone else; we say "they" made me do it. We treat ourselves as impersonal entities who are merely being swept along by forces over which we have no control.

Sartre refuses to tolerate any of these excuses. He was one of the few thinkers of his era gladly to accept the label of existentialist, and for him *existence* is the particular property of human beings. Things—rocks, trees, manufactured objects—just *are*. They are the sum total of their essential nature and will never be more than this essence. But human beings *exist*. Although in English the terms "to be" and "to exist" do not seem to be widely different, Sartre, following the German philosopher Martin Heidegger, takes the meaning of the term "exist" from its Greek roots, which emphasize the open-endedness of human life. To be human means to be open to possibilities, and—here is the important point—*we choose which of these possibilities we will be*. But, you might say, I do not choose everything. I did not choose to be born, for example. Even here Sartre does not let you off the hook. Your being in the world as an existing individual is a fact with which you have to come to terms. "I am ashamed of being born or I am astonished at it or I rejoice over it, or in attempting to get rid of my life I affirm that I live and I assume this life is bad. Thus in a certain sense I *choose* being born."[1]

Now all this may strike you as merely a lot of wordplay, simply a clever way of talking. But the important point Sartre is insisting on is the total freedom of the individual. To be human is to exist in a field of open possibilities, and we are free to choose among these possibilities. To attempt to get rid of the burden of this freedom by passing responsibility on to someone else (we really can't do this, Sartre argues, but we try anyway) he calls *bad faith*. It is a kind of lying, not to someone else but to ourselves. And here is what makes bad faith so intriguing: the one doing the lying and the one lied to are *one and the same*. If you think about it for a moment, you'll realize that self-deception or bad faith, or whatever you choose to call it, is quite a feat. We know we are lying, but we convince ourselves that we are not.

The threat of bad faith is everywhere. Some instances of bad faith are significant, and some are trivial. An example Sartre gives is taking on a role or playing a part. Sartre's description of this example in the extract reprinted in this chapter is that of a waiter playing a role so completely that his own individuality is subsumed in that of being a waiter. By playing roles, people retreat from freedom. They do not have to confront the morality of their choices if they believe that their actions are forced on them by forces or persons outside of their control. "It's only business," can be one excuse that we use to deflect responsibility away from ourselves and onto others, to the "game" of business, or to expected patterns of behavior that we feel we cannot control. Sartre's response to this is that we are always in control. When we do something that we feel is expected of us but that we know is wrong, we try to escape responsibility by blaming others. This, however, is simply another instance of bad faith.

Patterns of Bad Faith

The opposite of bad faith is good faith, and although Sartre promises many times in his writings to do a comparable analysis of good faith, he never got around to it.[2] The notion of bad faith stands as a warning to us not to retreat from responsibility by patterns of self-deception, for that is what bad faith is. The major task of a course in business ethics should be to make us aware of what these patterns are by looking at behavior in which they emerge. Just as Sartre's example of the waiter shows us patterned behavior that removed the waiter from full awareness of his actions, it is easy to be led into patterns of behavior by slogans that we use to deceive ourselves. Whenever these or similar phrases are being thrown about, you may be encountering examples of bad faith. It is possible that your associates are attempting to excuse their behavior by retreating to patterned behavior. The list of rationalizing slogans given here is not complete—it could be extended by many other examples—but it is sufficient to alert us to the dangers of such ways of thinking.

1 Nobody is going to be hurt. This is perhaps one of the most widely used of all rationalizations. Time and time again persons whose activities are illegal use it to justify themselves. This rationale was appealed to by a person found guilty of misusing stocks placed in his care. His justification was that the money he was going to make would benefit those who owned the stocks as well as himself. This, of course, would happen if all went as planned. If the financial scheme for which

---

SARTRE ON BAD FAITH

Let us consider this waiter in the cafe. His movement is quick and forward, a little too precise, a little too rapid. He comes toward the patrons with a step a little too quick. He bends forward a little too eagerly; his voice, his eyes express an interest a little too solicitous for the order of the customer. Finally there he returns, trying to imitate in his walk the inflexible stiffness of some kind of automaton while carrying his tray with the recklessness of a tight-rope walker by putting it in a perpetually unstable, perpetually broken equilibrium which he perpetually reestablishes by a light movement of the arm and hand. All his behavior seems to us a game. He applies himself to chaining his movements as if they were mechanisms, the one regulating the other; his gestures and even his voice seem to be mechanisms; he gives himself the quickness and pitiless rapidity of things. He is playing, he is amusing himself. But what is he playing? We need not watch long before we can explain it: he is playing at being a waiter in a cafe.

Source: Jean-Paul Sartre, *Being and Nothingness* (New York: Philosophical Library, 1956), p. 59.

the stocks were being used went awry, then many people would have been hurt, some disastrously.[3]

2 We were just trying to keep the industry healthy. This justification was used by an electric company executive whose firm was implicated in price-fixing activities. The company was one of four dominating the heavy equipment market. The executive was echoing management's concern that, without some kind of agreement among the companies, they would all be ruined by "cutthroat competition."[4] If one accepts the free market, with all its imperfections, as the fairest known way of distributing a society's goods and services, then attempts to manipulate that market unfairly are unethical, no matter how noble the purpose. The executive in question admitted that such rationalizations were attempts to salve his conscience. Another rationalization used to justify price-fixing was, "We were just trying to make a decent return on our stockholders' investment."

3 This is the way this street (or this business, or this industry) works. This rationalization came from a person implicated in an insider-trading deal. Like all patterns of bad faith, this one is partially true. The knowledge of business and industry trends is a stock trader's strength, and there is often a fine line between knowledge that is publicly available and that which is limited to a few insiders. Securities trading laws prohibit trading on knowledge that is not publicly available, for such activities would undercut public confidence in the market. The long-term effect of loss of confidence in the market would be harmful to all interests, so using good utilitarian justification, laws are written to prohibit insiders from taking advantage. The laws prohibiting such activities are not precise, again to encourage caution on the part of traders. Clearly, crossing the line, however, is both illegal and unethical; thus a pattern of bad faith like the one described was necessary for the trader to convince himself that his activity was acceptable. There are other variations on this, such as "If you don't think this is common practice, you aren't in the real world."

4 If I don't do this, somebody else will. This slogan has taken on something of the status of a classic. Not only does it enable the person contemplating the action to shift responsibility onto someone else, it is also a way of refusing to face the moral dimensions of the action. If an action is truly unethical, it does not matter whether someone else will do it or not. A good way of spotting a fallacious mode of reasoning is to apply the same pattern of thought to a known case of immoral behavior. Who would say any of the following? "If I don't commit this murder, someone else will." "If I don't rob this store, someone else will."

5 Nobody will ever find out. This one should really be a bell ringer. Whenever you hear this, run for cover immediately. As we saw in Chapter 4, one of Kant's tests for the morality of a principle of action is whether or not it could be made a universal law. Universalizing a principle implies that it become common practice. If it could not— either because universalizing the behavior would be self-contradictory or would find us willing to do different things, depending on which side of the issue we are on—then the action cannot be an ethical one. By saying that our behavior will remain secret, we are admitting that the practice could not become a universalized pattern for action, a dead giveaway of the inherent unethical nature of the contemplated conduct. A less formal test of whether an action is or is not moral would be to ask yourself how it would look reported on the front page of the local newspaper.

6 The prices were fair; we didn't gouge anyone. Said by someone accused of rigging bids to inflate prices artificially, the justification offered was a classic example of the fallacy known as begging the question. Begging the question occurs whenever a person assumes what the argument attempts to prove. The person setting up this defense assumed that the price was fair even though the market had not determined that it was. In a market economy, a fair price is the price a free market establishes. Manipulating the market in order to achieve a different price from what the free market would have generated cannot therefore determine a fair price. The individual in this case presumed to know what a fair price was and then offered the product to the marketplace at that price.

7 In other countries this practice would not be illegal. To repeat a point made earlier, these patterns of bad faith would not work if they were totally untrue. It is entirely true that laws differ from country to country. Some of these differences reflect dissimilar cultural patterns. Other differences may be due to the fact that the country in question has not made certain kinds of unethical behavior illegal. Just because a country's laws do not prohibit a given activity is no guarantee at all that the behavior is ethically acceptable. If a business practice is illegal in a given country, the presumption is that it is unethical to engage in that activity. There is, of course, justification for civil disobedience, but that is not the practice usually being defended by this pattern of bad faith. The converse of this statement, however, is not true. Just because

---

A Case in Point . . .

Doug Adams, who pled guilty to fraud charges in 1987, said in an article under his own byline, "I always feel sick when I look back at my criminal actions and try to figure out why. How could I knowingly come to violate my personal moral beliefs, convictions I had believed in through my childhood and most of my adult life?" His own introspective answer to this question involved two principles. The first was not to believe the old cliché, often promoted by coaches to sports teams, that "winning isn't the only thing; it is everything." According to Adams, this led him to fear failure. "Instead of being able to stop and examine a mistake, my solution was to try to rebound using any means possible." A second principle he suggests is to be wary if you find yourself thriving on closed-door meetings. "If your decisions aren't something you would be proud to have announced publicly," Adams said, "watch out—you're headed for trouble. If you have any doubts, share them honestly with people you respect and get their reactions."

Source: Management Accounting, June 1990, pp. 43–46.

---

the laws of a country do not prohibit an activity does not mean that it is ethical to engage in that activity. For example, some U.S. pharmaceutical companies have been criticized as acting unethically when they sold drugs that were banned in the United States in third-world countries.

8 We were following the spirit, not the letter, of the law. This slogan is particularly deceptive because it seems so high-minded. Its power consists in its ability to convince us that we really are acting from higher motives rather than base ones. The spirit/letter distinction is a good one, but when applied in a legitimate sense, the people invoking the principle do not usually benefit by the action being defended. When we appeal to this formula to bestow a benefit upon ourselves, we are likely to be engaging in self-deception.

9 They have plenty of money; they can afford it. This excuse is the pettiest of them all. Used by people contemplating some kind of fraud, it is self-justification based on resentment. Unpacked, the argument goes something like this: they have plenty of money (probably gained unethically), so when I cheat them I am only giving them a taste of their own medicine. This is a favorite of those who rig government bids or send inflated estimates for auto repair jobs to insurance companies. No one would accept the attempt to justify a burglary by saying the victims had plenty of money and the robber did not really take much.

10 The market is not free, so there is no reason for us to act as though it is. A favorite of insider traders and price fixers, this rationalization appeals to the belief that nothing in this world is perfect. A perfectly free market is a philosophical ideal, and like all such ideals cannot be fully realized in an imperfect world. It is also the case that social policy restrains the market in many ways for the sake of the common good (regulated utilities, licensing requirements for entry into a profession, government subsidies for selected industries, and so forth). When social policy restrains the freedom of the market, it does so for the sake of a common good; when an individual attempts to restrain the market, it is usually for the sake of private benefit. Thus the two cases are not parallel at all, and this slogan is just another example of self-deception.

As a collection of rationalizing slogans that hide examples of bad faith, this list is far from complete, but it is a good starting point. Here are some questions to ask yourself to discover possible patterns of bad faith: Am I willing to take full responsibility for my action, or am I pushing this responsibility off on someone else? Do I attempt to justify my action by appealing to a role I am expected to play—a role as employee, manager, a player in the business "game," a justification that keeps me from having to face up to the fact that it is *my* action, not that of someone else? Is my action something that I would be willing to have known publicly, or would I prefer that it remain secret?

The Power of Abstraction

Part of the power of the kind of self-deception we have been analyzing is that it puts distance between us and the action we are performing. This strategy allows us to avoid thinking about the fact that we are freely choosing to act in this way, whether we admit it or not. Another distancing technique that is at the root of many of our ethical difficulties is that of *abstraction*. The power of abstraction, according to another twentieth-century existential thinker, Gabriel Marcel, is at the root of war, for "it is only through organized lying that we can hope to make war acceptable to those who must wage or suffer it."[5] The practice of business is different from waging war, although sometimes the metaphors used in business discourse are warlike: "we've got a real battle on our hands facing up to foreign competition," or "our market share is under attack," or "we're going to introduce this product with a blitz campaign." Marcel's point, though, is just as applicable to business activity as to any other human endeavor in which we deal with people. The more we remove ourselves from having to regard other persons as human beings like ourselves, the more we will be willing to do outrageous things to them. To kill other persons, even in wartime, requires that we think of them as an abstraction—the enemy, the fascists, the gooks, or whatever. Notice how abstractions enter into the vocabulary of business and how different it is to think of customers as persons or merely as an impersonal market. Here is one way of listing an ascending hierarchy of abstractions: clients, customers, consumers, the market. Similarly we can speak of the work force as associates, staff, employees, workers, labor.

In the Honda automobile plant at Marysville, Ohio, and in the Toyota plant at Georgetown, Kentucky, the term "associates" is used to refer to those working in the plants. A *New York Times* article highlighting the production techniques at the Georgetown plant reported, "'Here it's more like a family,' said Diana Hobbs, 40 years old, of rural Hardin County, Kentucky, who assembles brakes. 'Supervisors listen to you and everyone works together.'"[6] Critics of these industrial plants say that such talk is just a clever way of undermining employee resolve to unionize. The point is, however, the more abstract the terminology we use in referring to a group of persons, the more willing we will be to act unethically toward them.

The sense of powerlessness many people feel in large corporate structures is another example of the power of abstraction. The less control people have over their lives, the less responsibility they feel for their actions. In spite of Sartre's claim that we are totally free and therefore totally responsible, people who perceive themselves as powerless have a diminished sense of accountability. As one contemporary writer in business ethics put it, "Employees of large-scale organizations follow bureaucratic rules that link their activities together to achieve corporate outcomes of which the employee may not even be aware. The engineers in one department may build a component with certain weaknesses, for example, not knowing that another department plans to use that component in a product that these weaknesses will render dangerous. Or employees may feel pressured to conform to company rules with whose corporate outcomes they may not agree but which they feel they are not in a position to change."[7]

GABRIEL MARCEL ON ABSTRACTION

There are a number of urgently relevant observations that force themselves on us here. The most important of them seems to me to be the following: as soon as people (*people*, that is to say, the State or a political party or a faction or a religious sect, or what it may be) claim of me that I commit myself to a warlike action against other human beings, . . . it is very necessary that I lose all awareness of the individual reality of the being whom I may be led to destroy. In order to transform him into a mere impersonal target, it is absolutely necessary to convert him into an abstraction: *the* Communist, *the* Anti-Fascist, *the* Fascist, and so on. . . . It is from this point of view that we ought to consider the sinister use that has been made of the ideas of "the masses" in the modern world. "The masses"—this seems to me the most typical, the most significant example of an abstraction which remains an abstraction even after it has become real: has become real, I mean, in the pragmatic sense of becoming a force, a power. Such realized abstractions are in some sense pre-ordained for the purposes of war: that is to say, quite simply, for the purposes of human inter-destructiveness.

Source: Gabriel Marcel, *Man Against Mass Society* (Chicago: Henry Regnery, 1962), pp. 157–159.

Bureaucracy and Depersonalization

Closely associated with the notion of abstraction that Gabriel Marcel describes with such power is depersonalization, the loss of both a sense of authority and responsibility. Depersonalization is a hazard for any organization but especially so for a bureaucracy. A bureaucracy, according to the dictionary definition, is administration through bureaus and departments. Yet the term has ceased to be merely descriptive and has taken on a negative, pejorative connotation. This is due to the tendency of bureaucratic types of organization to reduce the individual's sense of worth and power, a tendency toward *depersonalization,* to use Marcel's term.

In no uncertain terms Marcel says, "Bureaucracy is evil, and it is essentially a metaphysical evil."[8] "Metaphysical" in this context means it is fundamentally evil. This may seem to be a harsh judgment, but it is one that Marcel was driven to by the events he witnessed in Europe during the middle of the century in which faceless bureaucrats unleashed unspeakable horrors on the world and justified their actions by saying they were just following orders or that they were powerless to resist because they were just cogs in a machine. "Has, in fact, the employee who is a tiny cog in a great administrative machine normally the sense of serving a cause, a suprapersonal principle?" Marcel asks. "The answer to this question," he says, "can only be a negative one. Apart from some exceptional cases . . . we cannot seriously maintain that such an employee has a consciousness of serving, in the precise and noble sense of the word: by that I mean above all that he can hardly know what the honour of serving is."[9] The answer to this problem, as Marcel sees it, is to infuse an administrative organization with values, with ethical principles. "The real problem is that of knowing to what degree an administrative machine can be informed with spiritual values; and it is very hard not to feel very pessimistic when dealing with this problem."[10]

This pessimism is shared by others. In his article "Moral Mazes," which is another "best-seller" from *Harvard Business Review,* Robert Jackall describes how bureaucracy erodes moral values. It "breaks apart substance from appearances, action from responsibility," he says. And "because moral choices are inextricably tied to personal fates, bureaucracy erodes internal and even external standards of morality, not only in matters of individual success and failure but also in all the issues that managers face in their daily work." Pessimism occurs as the result of the particular pressures posed by bureaucracy. Jackall's description of this process can be read as an explanation of the process of depersonalization that Marcel deplores. The problem with a bureaucracy, as Jackall sees it, is that "what matters in the bureaucratic world is not what a person is but how closely his many personae mesh with the organizational ideal; not his willingness to stand by his actions but his agility in avoiding blame; not what he believes or says but how well he has mastered the ideologies that serve his corporation; not what he stands for but whom he stands with in the labyrinths of his organization."[11]

Business leaders are beginning to see the wisdom of Marcel's concerns and the need to counteract the depersonalization that is an occupational hazard of modern corporate life. The reasons? A discovery of the close relation between ethical corporate behavior and the bottom line. To be successful in a global environment, corporations must compete for the long term, building on relations of trust and responsibility. As a *Fortune* magazine feature on ethics observed, "Successful enterprises are inevitably based on a network of trust binding management, employees, shareholders, lenders, suppliers, and customers—akin to the network that Japanese calls keiretsu. When companies slip into shoddy practices, these crucial relationships start to deteriorate."[12] Echoing this thought is Daniel M. Galbreath, chairman and chief executive office of the Galbreath Company, a Columbus, Ohio, development firm, who insists that good ethics are important to his company. "We have to be beyond reproach," for "without our name or without our word, we're just another developer fighting to survive."[13]

ENCOURAGING MORAL BEHAVIOR

If tendencies toward bad faith, abstraction, and depersonalization are hazards of modern corporate life, then counteracting these pressures becomes imperative for those managing business enterprises. There is no rigid formula for how to do it, but here are some strategies that seem to pay off.

Make Employees Moral Guardians

If employees feel depersonalized by their position in an organization, businesses can counteract this sense of powerlessness by empowering associates to take responsibility for their company's moral values. Some businesses set up special offices—ombudsmen, ethics officers, ethics advisory committees—to receive employee reports of possible ethical problems in the organization.[14] The advertising firm N. W. Ayer, based in New York but with offices all over the world, encourages its staff to help the company maintain its high standards. It continually screens its television advertisements in specially designed rooms and distributes comment cards on which employees can note any problems they perceive with the advertisements. A committee is then required to deal with each comment. *Fortune* reports that "more and more companies are appointing full-time ethics officers, generally on the corporate vice-presidential level, who report directly to the chairman of an ethics committee of top officers. One of the most effective tools these ethics specialists employ is a hot line through which workers on all levels can register complaints or ask about questionable behavior."[15]

Reward Ethical Behavior

Stanley C. Pace, chairman of the board and CEO of General Dynamics Corporation, reports that his company responded to criticisms about Defense Department procurement procedures by establishing an elaborate in-house system of moral accountability. All employees are responsible for ensuring that the company's ethical standards are followed. One way the company encourages this sense of employee responsibility is by rewarding ethical behavior. According to Pace, "General Dynamics provides continuing counsel on company rules and regulations to any employee who seeks it and recognizes employees who make an exemplary effort to implement and uphold the standards."[16]

Establish Role Models

When Salomon Brothers was rocked by allegations of trying to manipulate the Treasury securities market, the company sent a message of commitment to reform to the government and the financial community by the appointment, even though temporary, of Warren E. Buffett as chief executive officer. Buffett, a midwesterner, according to the *New York Daily News,* "buys suits off the rack and has a modest home in Omaha, Nebraska," and is described as "a very ethical man, often putting the interest of his clients above his own personal gains."[17] A company's values are reflected in its culture, and its role models may include the founders of the firm whose exemplary conduct still guides the company's attitudes. Leon L. Bean's personal example of giving refunds to customers who purchased his boots stands as an icon in the company's culture and its advertisements. *Fortune* quoted one manager whose advice is, "Senior management has got to find a way to create heroes, people who serve the company's competitive values—and also its social and ethical values."[18]

Good people will be less tempted to do bad things when companies encourage them to feel responsible for their actions. It requires work and attention, from the CEO to the packer on the loading dock, but it can be done, as an increasing number of companies are discovering.

DISCUSSION STARTERS

1 Do you agree with Sartre that we experience our freedom as a burden from which we try to escape? Can you think of nonbusiness examples of how we try to excuse our behavior by putting the responsibility for it on someone else?

2 Cite some examples from your own experience of patterns of bad faith. Do you think that becoming aware of such patterns will reduce their effectiveness as excuses for wrong behavior? Why or why not?

3 Discuss how *abstraction,* as Marcel uses the term, makes us less sensitive to the ethical dimensions of our conduct. Give some nonbusiness examples of abstraction at work in human relationships.

4 If bureaucracies blunt our ethical sensitivities, how can they be reformed to encourage a stronger commitment to ethical behavior?

5 As the CEO of a firm, what procedures would you put in place (in addition to those discussed in this chapter) to encourage those working for your company to be morally responsible? As a middle manager, what procedures would you institute?

NOTES

1 Jean-Paul Sartre, *Being and Nothingness* (New York: Philosophical Library, 1956), p. 556.

2 The posthumously published writings of Jean-Paul Sartre, *Notebooks for an Ethics,* trans. David Pellauer (Chicago: University of Chicago Press, 1992), deal with some of the problems of bad faith that were first described in *Being and Nothingness.*

3 This is an actual experience related by one of my students to a class in business ethics. In his settlement with the SEC, he was prevented from continuing his career as an equities salesman.

4 This example is from Manuel G. Velasquez, *Business Ethics: Concepts and Cases,* 3rd ed. (Englewood Cliffs, NJ: Prentice-Hall, 1992), pp. 204–205.

5 Gabriel Marcel, *Man Against Mass Society* (Chicago: Henry Regnery, 1962), p. 154.

6 NYT, May 5, 1992.

7 Velasquez, *Business Ethics,* p. 43.

8 Marcel, *Man Against Mass Society,* p. 200.

9 Ibid., p. 202.

10 Ibid., p. 204.

11 Robert Jackall, "Moral Mazes: Bureaucracy and Managerial Work," *Ethics in Practice: Managing the Moral Corporation,* eds. Kenneth R. Andrews and Donald K. David (Boston: Harvard Business School Press, 1989), pp. 182–183.

12 Kenneth Labich, "The New Crisis in Business Ethics," *Fortune,* Apr. 20, 1992.

13 CD, Mar. 18, 1992.

14 BW, Sept. 23, 1991, p. 65.

15 FORT, Apr. 20, 1992, p. 176.

16 Stanley C. Pace, "The CEO's Page: The Business of Ethics," *Graduating Engineer,* Mar. 1989, p. 47.

17 *New York Daily News,* Aug. 17, 1991.

18 FORT, Apr. 20, 1992, p. 176.

CASE STUDY

One of the functions of the moral point of view is to override the demands of self-interest. Self-interest, however, is a powerful impetus to conduct, and the ways people deal with it can provide further examples of bad faith. The case that follows shows how easy it is to convince oneself that self-interest has not been a factor in one's decisions.

COMMISSIONS ON SALES AT BROCK MASON BROKERAGE

James Tithe is manager of a large branch office of a major midwestern brokerage firm, Brock Mason Farre Titmouse. He now manages 40 brokers in his office. Mr. Tithe used to work for E. F. Hutton as a broker and assistant manager, but when that firm merged with Shearson-Lehman/American Express, he disliked his new manager and left for Brock Mason. He knew the new firm to be aggressive and interested primarily in limited partnerships and fully margined common stock. He liked the new challenge. At Hutton his clients had been predominantly interested in unit investment trusts and municipal bonds, which he found boring and routine forms of investment. He also knew that commissions are higher on the array of products he was hired to sell at Brock Mason.

Although bored at Hutton, James had been comfortable with the complete discretion the firm gave him to recommend a range of investments to his clients. He had been free to consult at length with his clients, and then free to sell what seemed most appropriate in light of their objectives. Hutton of course skillfully taught its brokers to be salespersons, to avoid lengthy phone calls, and to flatter clients who prided themselves on making their own decisions; but the firm also did not discourage the broker from recommending a wide variety of products including U.S. government bills, notes, and bonds, which averaged only a $75 commission on a $10,000 bond.

This same array of conventional investment possibilities with small commissions is still available to him and to his brokers at Brock Mason, but the firm has an explicit strategy of trying to sell limited partnerships first and fully margined common stock second. The reason for this strat-

This case was prepared by Tom L. Beauchamp. Not to be duplicated without permission of the holder of the copyright, © 1993 Tom L. Beauchamp. Used by permission.

egy at the brokerage house is that commissions on a $10,000 investment in a limited partnership run from $600 to $1,000, and commissions on a $10,000 investment in fully margined common stock average $450.

James has been bothered for some time by two facts: The first fact is that the largest commissions in the brokerage industry are paid on the riskier and more complicated forms of investment. In theory, the reason is that these investments are more difficult to sell to clients. Real estate and oil and gas drilling partnerships, for example, typically return between 4 percent and 8 percent to sellers—although lately most have been arranged to return the full 8 percent. Some partnerships return more than 8 percent, because they rebate management fees to any securities firm that acts as a participant in the partnership.

The second fact is that James trains brokers to make recommendations to clients based on the level of commission returned to the broker and the firm. He is therefore training his brokers to sell the riskier and more complicated forms of investment. Although Brock Mason, like all brokerage firms, advertises a full range of products and free financial planning by experts, all salespersons dislike financial planning per se because it takes a large amount of time and carries zero commission.

James has long appreciated that there is an inherent conflict of interest in the brokerage world: The broker is presumed to have a fiduciary responsibility to make recommendations based on the financial best interest of the client; but the broker is also a salesperson who makes a living by selling securities and who is obligated to attempt to maximize profits for the brokerage house. The more trades made, the better it is for the broker; although this rule seldom works to the advantage of the client. Commissions are thus an ever-present temptation in the way of presenting alternatives or making an entirely objective recommendation.

Brock Mason does have a house mutual fund that is a less risky form of investment—the Brock Mason Equity-Income Fund. But the return to brokers and to the firm is again substantial. The National Association of Securities Dealers (NASD) allows a firm to charge up to an 8.5 percent commission or load on a mutual fund, and Brock Mason charges the full 8.5 percent. As an extra incentive, an additional percentage of the commission on an initial investment is returned to a broker if he or she can convince the client to automatically reinvest the dividends rather than have them sent by mail. Brock Mason also offers a fully paid vacation in Hawaii for the five brokers who annually sell the largest number of shares.

The firm has devised the following piggyback strategy: Brokers, as we have seen, are trained to sell limited partnerships first and fully margined stock accounts second. In the latter accounts an investor is allowed to purchase stock valued at up to twice the amount of money actually deposited in the account. The "extra" money is a loan from the brokerage firm. Twice the normal stock entails twice the normal commission on the amount of money in the account. In addition, sales-persons are given a small percentage of the interest earned on the loan made to the client.

Brock Mason, like most brokerage firms, is now suffering because a stock market slump has caused business to fall off sharply. Business has been off 24 percent, and Brock Mason is encountering difficulty paying for the sophisticated electronic equipment that sits on each broker's desk. James's superiors are pressuring him to persuade his brokers to aggressively market limited partnerships as a solid form of investment during a period of instability in stocks.

Last year the average annual commission brought into a firm by a broker in the U.S. brokerage industry was $249,500. Each broker personally takes home between 25 percent and 50 percent of this amount, depending on the person's contract and seniority. James's take-home earnings last year amounted to $198,000, 35 percent more than he had ever earned at Hutton. A friend of his began his own financial planning firm last year and retains 100 percent of his commissions, netting him $275,000 in his first year. His friend rejected the idea that he charge a flat fee or a percentage of profits in lieu of commissions for his recommendations and services. In his judgment, flat fees would have cost him more than 30 percent of his earnings.

Securities firms are required by law to disclose all commissions to clients. However, James and his brokers are aware that limited part-nerships and mutual funds are usually easier to sell than straight stock and bond purchases, because the statistics on fees are buried beneath an enormous pile of information in a prospectus that most clients do not read prior to a purchase. Most clients do not obtain the prospectus until after the purchase, and there is no report of a dollar figure for the commission. Brokers are not required to disclose commissions orally to clients and rarely do; moreover, it is well known that clients virtually never ask what the commission is. James has been instructed to tell his brokers to avoid all mention of commissions unless the subject is explicitly raised by the client.

The Securities and Exchange Commissions (SEC) does not set ceil-ings on commissions and does not require a broker to receive a written consent from a client prior to purchase. The SEC does occasionally determine that a markup is so high at a brokerage house that the commission amounts to fraud. It is here that James has drawn his personal "moral line," as he calls it. He has tentatively decided that he will market any product that has passed SEC and NASD requirements. Only if the SEC is considering a judgment that a markup is fraudulent will he discourage his brokers from marketing it.

But James also wonders about the prudence and completeness of these personal guidelines. He has been around long enough to see some very unfortunate circumstances—they are *unfortunate* but not *unfair,* in his judgment—in which unwary clients bought unsuitable products from brokers and had to live with the consequences. Recently one of his brokers had steered a 55-year-old unemployed widow with a total account of $380,000 (inherited upon the death of her husband) into the following diversification: 25 percent in limited partnerships, 25 percent in dividend-paying but margined stocks, 25 percent in corporate bonds yielding 9.8 percent, and 25 percent in the mutual fund. But the woman had not appreciated at the time of purchase how low the dividends on the stocks and the mutual fund would be. She now has far less annual income than she needs. Because she cannot sell the limited partnerships, she must now sell the stock at a loss and purchase a high dividend-paying instrument.

James and the woman's broker have been modestly shaken by this client's vigorous protest and display of anger. James decided as a result to take the case to the weekly staff meeting held on Wednesday mornings, which all brokers attend. There was a lively discussion of the best form of diversification and return for the widow. But James's attempt to introduce and discuss the problem of conflict of interest during this session fell completely flat. His brokers were not interested and could not see the problem. They argued that the brokerage industry is a free-market arrangement between a broker and a client, who always knows that fees are charged. Disclosure rules, they maintained, are well established, even if particular percentages or fees are sometimes hidden in the fine print. They viewed themselves as honest salespersons making a living through a forthright and fair system.

James walked away from this meeting thinking that neither the widow nor the broker had been prudent in making decisions that met her specific needs, but again he viewed the outcome as unfortunate rather than unfair. He had to agree with his brokers. No client, after all, is forced either to deal with the firm or to make any purchase.

Company Loyalty and Whistle-Blowing

Howard E. Nolan
Executive Vice President and
Chief Executive Officer
Moody/Nolan LTD, Inc.

"A company's business ethics are its self-established standards for its relationships with employees, customers, and the community as a whole. It is the fabric, describing the integrity and values of a business, as exhibited by its leadership and its employees. Moreover, good business ethics lead to improved products and services, improved employee performance and greater customer loyalty. The continued well-being of a business depends upon strong respect and support for its products and services by its employees and customers. Loyalty is the glue which binds these separate constituents to a business. Good ethics is the source and catalyst for this loyalty."

Chapter 6 explored the obligations of companies to their employees. We now turn to the obligations of employees to their employers and to the difficult issue of when employees have a loyalty greater than that which they owe the companies that employ them—a loyalty to society, to their profession, or even to their own conscience.

When an employee publicly exposes an employer's misconduct, that act is called "whistle-blowing." The metaphor is drawn from the world of sports and refers to when a referee announces a foul by blowing a whistle, stopping play, and assessing a penalty. Similarly, an employee who reports fraud, waste, or an employer's illegal activities not only brings the reported behavior to a stop but also causes the company to be penalized by regulatory agencies or the courts or be subject to other government action. When to engage in such behavior, and the consequences that follow from it, are essential topics in any consideration of business ethics. First, however, let's take a closer look at the nature of whistle-blowing itself.

UNDERSTANDING SOME TERMS

Whistle-Blowing Defined

Some writers in business ethics see whistle-blowing as any act of reporting corporate wrongdoing, regardless of the position of the one doing the reporting. This definition, therefore, could include acts of public reporting by journalists, public interest groups, even a single individual who becomes aware of activity that is either harmful, illegal, or both.[1] Most interpreters of business ethics, however, explicitly avoid such a broad definition, mainly because it blurs the distinction between the acts of a person outside a business organization and one inside it.

The fact that a person is a part of a business organization and has duties to that business, and that the business, in turn, has a right to expect loyalty from its employees, is what makes whistle-blowing such a difficult ethical decision. For example, if you live near a steel plant and become aware of the fact that it is violating emissions standards (let's say, by way of illustration, that the paint starts coming off your car because of the plant's emissions), your reporting the plant to the Environmental Protection Agency is not fraught with much moral ambiguity. On the other hand, if you are the plant's environmental safety officer, and in the course of your job it comes to your attention that the plant is deliberately violating EPA emissions standards, then you face an ethical problem. Should you report this act to the EPA, or should you work within the business system? If you report the violation to your immediate supervisor, has that fulfilled your ethical obligation? What if the supervisor ignores the report? Should you attempt to go over your supervisor's head, to your boss's boss, knowing that this sort of behavior is frowned upon by the company? Should you take your suspicions to a professional organization, such as a local engineering society? To a news reporter? To a regulatory agency? To a political leader?

There is still a more fundamental question: When is it ethically acceptable to violate the principle of loyalty to your employer?

Further complicating the individual's decision whether or not to become a whistle-blower is the fact that not all allegations made by whistle-blowers are correct. To engage in whistle-blowing is to be labeled a troublemaker, for sometimes whistle-blowers make unsubstantiated accusations in an effort to retaliate against an employer for real or imagined grievances. If patriotism is the last refuge of a scoundrel, as Samuel Johnson said, then whistle-blowing can be the last refuge of a malcontent. What better way to cause a business organization an immense amount of discomfort than to make allegations of wrongdoing, especially when the whistle-blower can claim moral superiority and is often protected by state and federal law that prevents retaliation. Given the nature of some state statutes, the employer will then have to spend considerable amounts of money and staff time proving the charges are false. The laws designed to protect whistle-blowing can be criticized as encouraging frivolous retaliatory actions by unhappy employees. Critics have also charged that protective legislation undermines the loyalty that a business organization must expect if it is to function.

It is important to note that the consensus of contemporary moral philosophers is that whistle-blowing should be defined as the action of a person within an organization, for it is only in this context that the full moral complexity of the act becomes apparent.[2] A definition that incorporates much of the moral ambiguity involved is that "whistle-blowing is the voluntary release of nonpublic information, as a moral protest, by a member or former member of an organization outside the normal channels of communication to an appropriate audience about illegal and/or immoral conduct in the organization or conduct in the organization that is opposed in some significant way to the public interest."[3]

Given the moral ambiguity of whistle-blowing, it is not easy for an employee to reach the decision to engage in this ultimate act of disloyalty to an employer, and the grounds for justifying whistle-blowing are likewise clouded with conflicting considerations.

F. H. BRADLEY: MY STATION AND ITS DUTIES

What is it then that I am to realize? We have said it in "my station and its duties". To know what a man is (as we have seen) you must not take him in isolation. He is one of a people, he was born in a family, he lives in a certain society, in a certain state. What he has to do depends on what his place is, what his function is, and that all comes from his station. . . . We must content ourselves by pointing out that there are such facts as the family, then in a middle position a man's own profession and society, and, over all, the larger community of the state. Leaving out of sight the question of a society wider than the state, we must say that a man's life with its moral duties is in the main filled up by his station in that system of wholes which the state is, and that this, partly by its laws and institutions, and still more by its spirit, gives him the life which he does live and ought to live. . . . In short, man is a social being; he is real only because he is social, and can realize himself only because it is as social that he realizes himself. The mere individual is a delusion of theory; and the attempt to realize it in practice is the starvation and mutilation of human nature, with total sterility or the production of monstrosities. . . .

   The point here is that you can not have the moral world unless it is willed; that to be willed it must be willed by persons; and that these persons not only have the moral world as the content of their wills, but also must in some way be aware of themselves as willing this content. . . . We must never let this out of our sight, that, where the moral world exists, you have and you must have these two sides; neither will stand apart from the other; moral institutions are carcasses without personal morality, and personal morality apart from moral institutions is an unreality, a soul without a body.

   Source: F. H. Bradley, *Ethical Studies.* First published in 1876. Second edition 1927. (Oxford: Clarendon Press, 1876, 1927); excerpts from Chapter 5, "My Station and Its Duties."

Loyalty, Honesty, and Fidelity

Before proceeding, we should define some additional terms. One concept important for discussing an employee's obligations to the employer is that of *loyalty.* Closely associated with loyalty in recent discussion are two other terms: *honesty* and *fidelity.* In a document prepared for the American Philosophical Association's Committee for Education in Business Ethics, the noted American philosopher Kurt Baier defined fidelity as an agent's willingness to promote the interests of someone ahead of the interests of others due to the agent's obligation to that someone. To put it in more specific terms, an employee (the agent of a business concern) incurs an obligation to the employer by accepting employment. The relation between employer and employee can be thought of as a contractual one: in return for the agent's labor, creativity, and time, the employer gives payment (wages and benefits).

By taking the employer's money, the employee has incurred an obligation that includes giving full effort to the job and being honest in all dealings with the firm (not to lie, steal, or cheat). Failure to carry through on this incurred obligation would be an example of lack of fidelity. An additional obligation of an employee is to put the interests of the employer's business above that of other agencies or firms. Failure to do so would be an example of failing in loyalty.

Some observers of the American business scene have noted the remarkable *lack* of loyalty felt by most employees to their firm (and often reciprocated by a similar lack of loyalty by the organization to its employees). According to Lester Thurow, this is one of the major contrasts between American management styles and those of America's principal economic rivals, Japan and Germany. "In both Germany and Japan," he notes, "job switching is a far less prevalent phenomenon than it is in the United States or Great Britain. Labor-force turnover is bad in communitarian capitalism, since no one will plant apple trees (make sacrifices for the good of the company) if they do not expect to be around when the apples are harvested."[4] In a company wherein management and labor are both bound by ties of loyalty—to the success of the business enterprise and to each other—the issue of whistle-blowing would take on a different dimension than it does when an employee feels no particular loyalty to an employer.

Moral decisions would be easier if we were bound by ties of loyalty to only one person or organization. But life is not that simple. We do have an incurred obligation of loyalty to an employer, but we also have obligations to others—to our family, friends, coworkers, to the government, and to society as a whole. It is not always easy to know where our obligation to one person or group ends and where our obligation to another person or organization begins. The difficulty of dealing with this issue is partly what makes the decision to blow the whistle so difficult. Because whistle-blowing raises the issue of choosing among competing loyalties, we need to investigate further the grounds for one's loyalty to an employer.

DUTIES TO AN EMPLOYER

By freely accepting employment, we incur both responsibilities and duties. We obligate ourselves to work for the employer, to deliver our best, both in terms of time and talent, and to put the interest of the employer above that of other business firms. As articulated by two con-

---

BAIER ON HONESTY, FIDELITY, LOYALTY

Honesty is the virtue of straightforwardness and trustworthiness in dealing with others. . . . Honesty refers to the element of straightforwardness in trustworthiness, fidelity to the element of reliability. As philosophers have recently used the term, "fidelity" refers to the virtue of always keeping one's word or vows, of doing what one has committed oneself to doing by one's promises, undertakings, or contracts. A person who gives a false promise is dishonest, but a person who breaks a promise honestly given, when the keeping of it is unexpectedly onerous or costly is not dishonest, but lacking in fidelity. . . .

Honesty, fidelity, doing one's fair share, are thought of as virtues. All three refer to manners of dealing with others. All three are aspects of trustworthiness, the virtue one looks for in others when one has dealing with them. Honesty refers to the willingness not to misrepresent things for one's purposes; fidelity refers to reliability in discharging assumed obligations even under difficult conditions, and doing one's fair share refers to the willingness to make a fair contribution to the maintenance of a cooperative enterprise from which one does and wants to profit. . . .

Loyalty is closely related to fidelity: Jones's loyalty to X is his readiness to promote the concerns and interests of X (whether a person or institution) ahead of those of other claimants, in the belief that Jones, through association with X, has become subject to legitimate claims on him by X going beyond the obligations he has assumed.

Source: Report of the Committee for Education in Business Ethics (Newark, DE: American Philosophical Association, 1979), pp. 34–35.

---

temporary philosophers, Norman Bowie and Ronald Duska, "Each job carries with it a responsibility or obligation to do what the job or role demands. This is because there is either an explicit contract with a very complete description of the job and its obligations, or there is a less formal agreement, where the agent or the employee agrees to do what is in the best interest of the principal."[5]

My Station and Its Duties

We can enlarge on this specific point by using the language of the philosopher F. H. Bradley, who argues that each of us has a "station" in life that brings with it duties and obligations. To be the parent of a child means that one has certain obligations to the life under one's care. To be a student in a class means that one has taken on certain obligations; and the teacher, by virtue of that individual's station in life, also has certain duties—namely, to present material accurately and without bias, to evaluate students' work consistently and fairly, and to be available to assist students in the pursuit of their studies. Bradley's analysis of "my station and its duties" is tempered in large part by a metaphysical view popular during the nineteenth century that saw all persons in their relation to a larger, even cosmic, whole. Known as "idealism," Bradley's metaphysical views have fewer supporters today than they did during his lifetime, but his basic insight still has value even though his metaphysical position is open to debate.

Bradley continues in the tradition of Aristotle, who thought that to be fully human means that we must have meaningful relationships with others. As we saw in Chapter 2, Aristotle's insistence on human relationships had many facets: friends, family, the larger society, the state (or in his time the city, the *polis*) all provided a basis for meaningful relationships. Bradley's analysis of the notion of one's station and its duties can help us understand that each of us may have a different set of duties, depending on our station. If you are not a parent, then you do not have a parent's obligations. If you are a student, your duties are different from those of a recent graduate with a new job in corporate headquarters. To apply Bradley's point, the wholes of which we are a part (a business organization, a family, a state) have no moral values apart from the individual values of those persons in the organization. This led Bradley to use the metaphor of soul and body to compare the relation of the individual to the whole; individuals constitute the souls of the organization, and institutions, he says "are carcasses without personal morality."

Ought Implies Can

The notion of "my station and its duties" points to another important moral principle: one is *morally* responsible only for that which one can do. If I pass by a lake and see someone drowning, I am not morally obligated to jump in the water and try to save the person if I cannot swim. A lifeguard assigned to this lake, on the other hand, has a moral responsibility to do precisely that by virtue of the position as guard, and failure to do so would be a serious failure in duty. Even if I cannot swim, though, there are many things I can do, such as calling for help, throwing the drowning person something that will float, calling the lifeguard back from a rest break, or whatever is within my power. The general principle we appeal to here, again to quote Bowie and Duska, is that "ought implies can." Here is how they put it: "It is a funda-

A Case in Point . . .

In July 1992, an employee of a defense contractor was awarded $7.5 million for informing the government of his company's fraudulent billings on Pentagon contracts in the 1980s. This was the largest settlement to date under the 1986 False Claims Act, which provides whistle-blowers up to 25 percent of any amount recovered by the government as a result of their disclosures. At about the same time General Electric Company settled a Justice Department suit arising out of allegations that it defrauded the Pentagon and the Israeli Defense Department in a sale of jet engines. GE was fined $9.5 million and agreed to settle a related civil case for $59.5 million, making the cost of the total settlement $69 million. Executives of the company alleged that the whistle-blower did not bring his accusations to management, as company policy requires, and in fact delayed for several years bringing the problems to anyone's attention, thereby allowing the situation to worsen. The whistle-blower denies the company's claim, insisting that he attempted to alert GE officials of the improprieties but that the company hushed up the inquiry under pressure from a Pentagon official. Critics of the False Claims Act say that it encourages unwarranted suits by "gold-digging or disgruntled employees." Defenders of the law claim it is necessary to protect whistle-blowers from reprisals and to encourage persons to come forward with knowledge of wrongdoing. Cases like these provide additional evidence for the conclusion that in whistle-blowing, we encounter vividly the difficulties of sorting out conflicting loyalties.

Sources: NYT, July 15, 1991, July 23, 1992; CD, July 23, 1992.

mental principle of ethics that 'ought' implies 'can.' That expression means that you can only be held morally responsible for events that are within your power."[6]

Do No Harm

Closely allied with the "ought-implies-can" principle is the sense that moral responsibility also includes efforts to avoid problems that a reasonable person could foresee. This leads to the principle that we have a moral obligation to avoid harm. If a company makes a product with known defects, society reacts with a sense of moral outrage at a company's failure to prevent deaths that were foreseeable and avoidable.

These two principles, then, "ought implies can" and "do no harm," provide at least a basic framework for a discussion of whistle-blowing.

With the realization that whistle-blowing violates the principle of loyalty to an employer, the pressing question is, Under what circumstances does the obligation to blow the whistle take precedence over the principle of loyalty to an employer? Here, again, we can see the difficulty of knowing precisely which of two conflicting moral principles takes precedence in our decision making. The two principles are loyalty to an employer and the duty to avoid harm. Further complicating a decision about whistle-blowing is the role of self-interest.

SELF-INTEREST AND WHISTLE-BLOWING

Philosophers from Immanuel Kant in the seventeenth century to Kurt Baier in the twentieth have argued that self-interest is not a moral basis for action and that a moral point of view should provide a way of overcoming the demands of self-interest. When Kant discussed this point he concluded that when self-interest enters into our thinking, we just cannot know for sure whether our action is moral.[7] It may well be that an action can be both in our self-interest and the ethically correct thing to do, but self-interest clouds the decision to such an extent that we can never know for sure if our action was prompted by a sense of duty or an inclination toward self-interest. Kurt Baier puts it even more strongly when he observes that a moral point of view is precisely that required to override the self-interest that can lead, as Hobbes so eloquently showed, to continual warfare of all against all. "The universal supremacy of the rules of self-interest," Baier observes, "must lead to what Hobbes called the state of nature. At the same time, it will be clear to everyone that universal obedience to certain rules overriding self-interest would produce a state of affairs which serves everyone's interest much better than his unaided pursuit of it in a state where everyone does the same. Moral rules are universal rules designed to override those of self-interest when following the latter is harmful to others."[8]

The Costs of Whistle-Blowing

If one followed only the principle of self-interest, one would never become a whistle-blower, for the costs can include loss of employment, loss of the esteem of coworkers, and even a decline in one's emotional and physical health. Laws such as the False Claims Act, however, are intended to provide a powerful incentive to the whistle-blower and to compensate for some of the harm he or she undergoes. In a 1987 study, researchers found that "as a group, the whistle blowers were moderately religious. They tended to assume the best could be achieved by following universal moral codes, which guided their judgments."[9] The study also found that whistle-blowers paid a high price for their actions. "One out of every five of those in the survey reported they were without a job, and 25 percent mentioned increased financial burdens on the family as the most negative result of their action. Fifty-four percent of the whistle blowers said they were harassed by peers at work."[10] Other reports confirm the high emotional and professional toll on whistle-blowers: "Whistle blowers almost inevitably pay a heavy price. With few exceptions, they are driven out of not just their jobs, but their professions too," according to the conclusions reached by a study of whistle-blowers by a team of sociologists.[11]

A 1989 federal law was designed to protect whistle-blowers working for the government or on government contracts, but even this protection does not remove the personal cost associated with whistle-blowing. Articles in *Federal Times,* an independent newspaper circulated among government employees, warns of the possible costs of whistle-blowing, describing it as "confronting a non-nurturing system" and warning that "whistle blowers say agencies usually respond to their concerns with indifference, intransigence and cruelty," adding that "often, it's a losing battle and the whistle blower ends up harming himself in the race for truth."[12] The same publication offered advice on how to report wrongdoing but included the caveat, "It is not easy to be a whistle blower."[13]

Protection for Whistle-Blowers

Many states have also enacted laws to protect whistle-blowers from retaliation,[14] but none offers the incentives to reporting wrongdoing as are embodied in the federal False Claims Act. The act offers a reward to the person reporting fraud or abuse amounting to 25 percent of the amount recovered by the government as a result of the information received. This reward constitutes a powerful appeal to self-interest in its own right. But here again we see that self-interest is not a moral guide, and when self-interest is a possible motive it is difficult for an individual whistle-blower to know whether the act of reporting wrongdoing results from genuine moral concern or greed. Prior to the passage of the False Claims Act, which encourages whistle-blowing, the grounds of self-interest would work against whistle-blowing; now the grounds have shifted somewhat, toward encouraging whistle-blowing with the expectation of huge returns to the whistle-blower. If we are to move beyond self-interest to a more moral basis for deciding when to become a whistle-blower, we need additional guidance.

Working against whistle-blowing is not only the loyalty one feels to the company and, perhaps more important, to one's fellow workers but also the general stigma attached to being a troublemaker and undermining the viability of the organization. Sissela Bok, a writer on ethical issues, notes that "there comes a level of internal prying and mutual suspicion at which no institution can function." She goes on to point out that "the disappointed, the incompetent, the malicious, and the paranoid all too often leap to accusations in public. Worst of all, ideological persecution throughout the world traditionally relies on insiders willing to inform on the colleagues or even on their family members."[15] The tradition of solidarity with one's associates, the known ostracism that will result from whistle-blowing, the loss not only of esteem but even of livelihood—all these are powerful pressures that work against the obligation to become a whistle-blower. At some point, however, loyalty to the greater society overrides loyalty to the company and is more important than one's job and the esteem of fellow workers. It is important to probe some of the possible bases for reaching this decision.

SURVEYING THE OPTIONS

Here William James can be a guide. A noted American philosopher who was also a pioneer in the development of psychology as an academic discipline (he established the first psychological laboratory at Harvard), James spent considerable effort in examining the bases upon which we make decisions. A scientist with the empiricist's dedication to brute fact, James was unfaltering in his insistence that we should base our actions on the best possible information we can assemble. In two areas of human endeavor, however—religion and ethics—we frequently must act without full information and cannot base our decisions on empirical data. In his famous essay, "The Will to Believe," James probed the logic that underlies difficult choices when we cannot be guided by empirical fact. "*Moral* questions," he pointed out, "immediately present themselves as questions whose solution cannot wait for sensible proof." The reason for this, according to James, is that "a

JAMES ON MAKING DIFFICULT DECISIONS

Let us give the name of *hypothesis* to anything that may be proposed to our belief; and just as the electricians speak of live and dead wires, let us speak of any hypothesis as either *live* or *dead*. A live hypothesis is one which appeals as a real possibility to him to whom it is proposed. . . . The maximum of liveness in an hypothesis means willingness to act irrevocably. . . .

Next, let us call the decision between two hypotheses an *option*. Options may be of several kinds. They may be—1, *living* or *dead;* 2, *forced* or *avoidable;* 3, *momentous* or *trivial;* and for our purposes we may call an option a *genuine* option when it is of the forced, living and momentous kind.

A living option is one in which both hypotheses are live ones. . . .

Next, if I say to you: "Choose between going out with your umbrella or without it," I do not offer you a genuine option, for it is not forced. You can easily avoid it by not going out at all. Similarly, if I say "Either love me or hate me," "Either call my theory true or call it false," your option is avoidable. You may remain indifferent to me, neither loving nor hating, and you may decline to offer any judgment as to my theory. But if I say "Either accept this truth or go without it," I put you on a forced option, for there is no standing place outside of the alternative. Every dilemma based on a complete logical disjunction, with no possibility of not choosing, is an option of this forced kind. . . .

Finally . . . he who refuses to embrace a unique opportunity loses the prize as surely as if he tried and failed. Per contra, the option is trivial when the opportunity is not unique, when the stake is insignificant, or when the decision is reversible if it later prove unwise.

Source: William James, "The Will to Believe," in *Writings 1878–1899* (New York: Library of America, 1992), pp. 457–458.

moral question is a question not of what sensibly exists, but of what is good, or would be good, if it did exist."[16] In practice, this means that we rarely will be able to know fully the outcome of our actions (another reason utilitarian considerations are often difficult), and the difficulty of ascertaining which among competing values claims our first allegiance further complicates our decision.

When facing difficult decisions, James says, we should first be clear on what our options really are; he used the term "hypothesis," as he was concerned in his essay on analyzing belief, but because the will to believe culminates in the act of belief, we can use the term "option" for this earlier stage of deliberation. Live options are those that we could reasonably be expected to do. Here again we encounter the principle "ought implies can." If we are unable to do something (it would be a dead option, in James's terms), then we have no moral duty to attempt to do it. If faced with a live option, the next question is whether it is *forced* or *avoidable*. An option is forced only if it is the only choice available. If other possible courses of action are open, then a particular choice is avoidable.

Persons within a business organization who know about illegal or harmful activity have several options before considering the possibility of blowing the whistle: they can attempt to bring corrective action from within the company, change employers, even threaten to blow the whistle. If the option is forced, the next question to ask is whether it is *momentous* or *trivial*. To be momentous involves three things: *the situation is unique, the stakes are significant,* and *the decision is irreversible.* If, for example, human life is in danger, the issue becomes significant, and failure to take action may produce an irreversible result.

THE WHISTLE-BLOWER'S QUESTIONS

Like most ethical issues, knowing whether or not to blow the whistle or when to report unethical behavior will be an imprecise decision, but using James's analysis as a guide, we can focus our thinking on several important questions.

1 **What can I do?** First, one should analyze the range of possibilities. Given my station and its duties, what are my duties to the company? Implicit in this criterion is the need to have accurate and dependable information, and part of the anguish of the whistle-blower is wondering whether the information available is accurate. In a case that received a great deal of attention, engineers working on the Bay Area Rapid Transit System (BART) were concerned about possible safety problems connected with the somewhat experimental control scheme designed into the system. In what they intended as a private initiative, three engineers informed a local political leader of their concern and were shocked to discover that their private communication was released to local newspapers. In the aftermath of this affair, the three engineers lost their jobs, and the verdict is still out on whether or not their information was reliable (since they were not specifically responsible for safety concerns) or whether there was ever a safety problem.[17]

2 **Am I forced to blow the whistle?** This picks up on James's second level of decision. Are there alternatives to blowing the whistle? This could include working within a company's existing structure. Some companies have internal grievance mechanisms through which an

employee can report concerns about corporate conduct. In a case involving overcharges by General Electric on Defense Department contracts, company officials charged that the whistle-blower failed to utilize all existing internal mechanisms and in fact delayed reporting his concerns to anyone, thereby allowing the situation to worsen. If one's immediate superiors are unresponsive, other options would include going over their heads to others in the organization who might be responsive to the concerns.

3 Are the issues momentous? There is a difference between informing on a trivial action of an employer and reporting to a supervisor a design flaw that will likely result in the loss of life. When the issues are momentous, involving possible health hazards or loss of life, the decision to blow the whistle appears to those who have done it to have been the right thing. In a study of whistle-blowers, two researchers found that whistle-blowers, though suffering major traumas in their lives as a result of their action, were convinced of the moral rightness of their action. The researchers quote a worker in a nuclear plant who said, "This has turned out to be the most frightening thing I have ever done. But it has also been the most satisfying. I think I did the right thing, and I have caused some changes to be made in the plant."[18] A representative of a nonprofit group that helps whistle-blowers reports that "the individuals who keep going are very strong-willed and have seen some serious wrongdoing, and they're not going to roll over until they've felt they fought the battle the best they could."[19] In almost all cases discussed in media reports, the tenacity of the whistle-blower was in direct relation to the seriousness of the wrongdoing.

Bad faith lurks everywhere here. As we saw in Chapter 8, bad faith is a form of self-deception, of lying to oneself. With whistle-blowing we can see how bad faith could be expressed in several ways. A disgruntled employee may use whistle-blowing not as a way to prevent wrongdoing but as a punishment of the employer for grievances either real or imagined. Even if the charges are unfounded, the employer may have to spend significant amounts of money and staff time responding to the charges. Or an employee, knowing of serious wrongdoing in the company or government agency, may decide that this is not an issue to be concerned with inasmuch as it is someone else's responsibility anyway, and to blow the whistle would probably be ineffective and only result in retaliation against the whistle-blower. As William James pointed out, moral decisions are fraught with ambiguity, and it is impossible to present precise standards for judging every ethical act. Moral ambiguity, however, does not mean lack of moral seriousness, and the individual who wrestles with the decision of whether or not to blow the whistle is encountering firsthand both the importance and the challenge of moral reasoning.

DISCUSSION STARTERS

1 On balance, do you think that laws protecting whistle-blowers are a good thing or a bad thing? Could you be an advocate of extending such laws to the private sector? Why or why not?
2 What kinds of corporate behaviors will encourage worker loyalty? Discourage it?
3 If you were CEO of a company, what management strategies would you adopt to eliminate the necessity for whistle-blowing?
4 Compile a list of conditions that would be serious enough to make you become a whistle-blower.
5 How can potential whistle-blowers know they are acting from ethical principle and not from self-interest?

NOTES

1 See Mike W. Martin and Roland Schinzinger, *Ethics in Engineering,* 2nd ed. (New York: McGraw-Hill, 1989), p. 213.
2 See Normal Bowie, *Business Ethics* (Englewood Cliffs, NJ: Prentice-Hall, 1982), p. 142; Manuel G. Velasquez, *Business Ethics: Concepts and Cases,* 3rd ed. (Englewood Cliffs, NJ: Prentice-Hall, 1992), p. 401; Peter A. French, Jeffrey Nesteruk, and David T. Risser, *Corporations in the Moral Community* (New York: Harcourt Brace Jovanovich, 1992), p. 59; Jerry Cederblom and Charles J. Dougherty, *Ethics at Work* (Belmont, CA: Wadsworth, 1990), p. 125.
3 John R. Boatright, *Ethics and the Conduct of Business* (Englewood Cliffs, NJ: Prentice-Hall, 1993), p. 133.
4 Lester Thurow, *Head to Head: The Coming Economic Battle Among Japan, Europe, and America* (New York: Morrow, 1992), p. 33.
5 Norman E. Bowie and Ronald F. Duska, *Business Ethics,* 2nd ed. (Englewood Cliffs, NJ: Prentice-Hall, 1990), p. 8.
6 Ibid., p. 36.
7 Immanuel Kant, *Grounding of the Metaphysics of Morals,* trans. James W. Ellington (Indianapolis: Hackett), p. 7.
8 Kurt Baier, *The Moral Point of View: A Rational Basis of Ethics* (New York: Random House, 1965), p. 146.
9 Clyde H. Farnsworth, "Survey of Whistle Blowers Finds Retaliation but Few Regrets," NYT Feb. 22, 1987.

10 Ibid.

11 N. R. Kleinfield, "The Whistle Blowers' Morning After," NYT, Nov. 9, 1986.

12 Rodrigo Lazo, "Why Blow the Whistle?" *Federal Times,* Apr. 20, 1992.

13 Med Walker, "Tips on How to Blow the Whistle," *Federal Times,* Apr. 13, 1992.

14 Ohio's is found at ORC 124.34.1 and is typical of those passed in other states.

15 Sissela Bok, "Whistleblowing and Professional Responsibility," *New York University Education Quarterly* 11 (Summer 1980), cited in Thomas Donaldson and Patricia H. Werhane, *Ethical Issues in Business: A Philosophical Approach,* 4th ed. (Englewood Cliffs, NJ: Prentice-Hall, 1993), pp. 321–322.

16 William James, "The Will to Believe," in *Writings 1878–1899* (New York: Library of America, 1992), p. 472.

17 Martin and Schinzinger, in *Ethics in Engineering,* discuss the case and conclude that the engineers' concerns were well founded. A book-length discussion of this case by Robert M. Anderson and others, *Divided Loyalties* (West Lafayette, IN: Purdue University Press, 1980), concluded that there was no real safety problem. Even after the fact, expert opinion is divided on whether the whistle-blowers' concerns were legitimate. Under the best of circumstances, the information on which whistle-blowers act may be ambiguous.

18 Farnsworth, "Survey of Whistle Blowers."

19 Lazo, "Why Blow the Whistle?" p. 10.

CASE STUDY

This case study explores a situation in which one can examine the issues raised by whistle-blowing. The DC-10 case is especially instructive because it highlights the difficulty of predicting consequences and the ambiguities faced by a company employee who has to decide whether or not to blow the whistle. The case is well known in the literature and by now has something of the flavor of quarterbacking the game on Monday morning. Given what we now know about how events unfolded because no one blew the whistle, we would no doubt want to say that the engineer described should have taken a different course of action. But as you read the case, put yourself in the position of the company employee and supervisor and ask yourself whether you would have acted differently than did Dan Applegate and at what point you might have taken action.

THE DC-10'S DEFECTIVE DOORS

The Douglas Company had dominated the commercial aviation industry until the Boeing Company captured a significant portion of the jet market with its 707 in the late 1950s. The Douglas Company, keenly aware of new and stiff competition, decided to manufacture a wide-bodied jet that would be attractive in international markets. Management viewed an "airbus" as crucial to long-term economic well-being (although no wide-bodies were actually produced for another ten years).[1]

Douglas was taken over by McDonnell Aircraft in 1967, by which time pressure to produce a wide-bodied jet had intensified. The Boeing Company had already introduced its 747, and neither Douglas nor the Federal Aviation Administration (FAA) wished Boeing to have exclusive control over this aspect of the air travel market. The McDonnell Douglas firm therefore searched for a structural design subcontractor capable of sharing the short-term financial burdens of a wide-bodied jet construction program that would realize long-term profits. General Dynamics' Convair Division was such a subcontractor, with an excellent reputation for structural design. Under the agreement between the two companies, McDonnell Douglas had the primary authority to furnish design criteria and to amend design decisions. Convair's role was to create a design that would satisfy the stipulated criteria.[2]

In August 1968, McDonnell Douglas awarded Convair a contract to build the DC-10 fuselage and doors. The lower cargo doors became the subject of immediate discussion. These doors were to be outward hinging, tension-latch doors, with latches driven by hydraulic cylinders—a design already adequately tested by DC-8 and DC-9 models. In addition, each cargo door was designed to be linked to hydraulically actuated flight controls and was to have a manual locking system designed so that the handle or latch level could not be stowed away unless the door was properly closed and latched. McDonnell Douglas, however, decided to separate the cargo door actuation system from the hydraulically actuated primary flight controls. This maneuver involved using electric actuators to close the cargo doors rather than the hydraulic actuators. Fewer moving parts in the electric actuators presumably made for easier maintenance, and each door would weigh 28 pounds less.

However, the Convair engineers had considered the hydraulic actuators critical to safety. They were not satisfied with these changes, and they remained dissatisfied after the introduction of further modifications. As Convair engineers saw the situation, the two actuator systems would respond very differently to the build-up of forces caused by increasing pressure. If hydraulic latches were improperly secured, they would smoothly slide open when only a small amount of pressure had built up in the cabin. Although the doors would be ripped off their hinges, this would likely occur at a low altitude, so that the shock from decompression would be small enough to land the plane safely. By contrast, if an electric latch failed to catch, it would not gently slide open due to increasing pressure. Rather, it would be abruptly and violently forced open, probably at a higher altitude where rapid decompression would dangerously impair the plane's structure. Convair's Director of Product Engineering F. D. "Dan" Applegate was adamant that a hydraulic system was needed. However, McDonnell Douglas did not yield to Convair's reservations about the DC-10 cargo door design.

Once McDonnell Douglas decided to use an electrical system, the plane required a new and foolproof checking and locking system. In the summer of 1969 McDonnell Douglas asked Convair to draft a Failure Mode and Effects Analysis, or FMEA, for the cargo door system. An FMEA assesses the likelihood and consequences of a specific system. In August 1969 Convair engineers found nine possible failure sequences that could result in destruction of the craft, with loss of human lives. A major problem focused on the warning and locking-pin systems. The door could close and latch, but without being safely locked. The warning indicator lights were prone to failure, in which case a door malfunction could go undetected. The FMEA also concluded that the door design was potentially dangerous and lacked a reliable failsafe locking system. It could open in flight, presenting considerable danger to passengers.[3]

The FAA requires that it be given an FMEA covering all systems critical to safety, but no mention was made of this hazard to the FAA prior to certification of the DC-10 model. McDonnell Douglas maintains that no report was filed because this cargo door design was not implemented until all defects expressed in the FMEA were removed. The FMEA submitted, they contend, was the final FMEA and did not discuss already repaired defects.[4] As lead manufacturer, McDonnell Douglas made itself entirely responsible for certification of the aircraft and, in seeking the certification, held the position that all defects had been removed. By contrast, Convair was not formally responsible because its contract with McDonnell Douglas forbade Convair from reporting directly to the FAA.

During a model test run in May 1970, the DC-10 blew its forward lower cargo door, and the plane's cabin floor collapsed. Since the plane's vital electric and hydraulic subsystems are located under the cabin floor (unlike in the 747, in which they are above the ceiling), the collapse was doubly incapacitating.[5] A McDonnell Douglas spokesperson placed the blame for this particular malfunction on the "human failure" of a mechanic who had incorrectly sealed the door. Although no serious design problems were contemplated, the cargo doors did undergo design modifications purportedly to provide better checks on the locking pins. As modified, the cargo door design was properly certified and authorities at McDonnell Douglas claimed it was safe. Five DC-10s were flight tested for over 1,500 hours prior to certification.

Certification processes are carried out in the name of the FAA, but they actually are often performed by the manufacturers. As a regulatory agency, the FAA is charged with overseeing commercial products and regulating them in the public interest. However, the FAA is often not in an independent position. The FAA appoints designated engineering representatives (DERs) to make inspections at company plants. These are company employees chosen for their experience and integrity who have the dual obligations of loyalty to the company that pays them as design engineers and of faithful performance of inspections to see that the company has complied with federal airworthiness regulations. The manufacturers are in this respect policing themselves, and it is generally acknowledged that conflicts of interest arise in this dual-obligation system.[6]

During the months surrounding November 1970, a number of internal memos were written at both McDonnell Douglas and Convair that cited old and new design problems with the cargo door. New structural proposals were made, but none was implemented. McDonnell Douglas and Convair had disagreements over cost accounting and accountability for remaining design flaws. The FAA finally certified the DC-10 on July 29, 1971, and by late 1971 the plane had received praise for its performance at virtually all levels. Under rigorous conditions it boasted excellent performance ratings. The company vigorously promoted the new aircraft.

But on June 12, 1972, an aft bulk cargo door of a DC-10 in flight from Los Angeles to New York separated from the body of the aircraft at about 11,750 feet over Windsor, Ontario. Rapid cabin decompression occurred as a result, causing structural damage to the cabin floor immediately about the cargo compartment. Though the plane landed safely, nine passengers and two flight attendants were injured. An investigation by the National Transportation Safety Board (NTSB) concluded that the probable cause of the malfunction lay in the cargo doors' latching mechanism and recommended changes in the locking system. The NTSB's specific recommendations were the following:

1 Require a modification to the DC-10 cargo door locking system to make it physically impossible to position the external locking handle and vent door to their normal locked positions unless the locking pins are fully engaged.

2 Require the installation of relief vents between the cabin and aft cargo compartment to minimize the pressure loading on the cabin flooring in the event of sudden depressurization of the compartment.[7]

The FAA administrator, John Shaffer, could have issued an airworthiness directive that required immediate repairs. He elected not to issue the directive, choosing instead an informal agreement with McDonnell Douglas that allowed the company to make the necessary modifications and recommend new procedures to affected airlines. All actions by the company were to be voluntary.

Fifteen days subsequent to the blowout over Windsor (June 27, 1972), Dan Applegate wrote a stern memo to his superior at Convair that expressed his doubts about the entire project and offered some reflections on "future accident liability." The following excerpts from the memo reveal Applegate's anguish and concerns:[8]

The potential for long-term Convair liability on the DC-10 has caused me increasing concern for several reasons.

1 The fundamental safety of the cargo door latching system has been progressively degraded since the program began in 1968.

2 The airplane demonstrated an inherent susceptibility to catastrophic failure when exposed to explosive decompression of the cargo compartment in 1970 ground tests.

3 Douglas has taken an increasingly "hard-line" with regards to the relative division of design responsibility between Douglas and Convair during change cost negotiations.

4 The growing "consumerism" environment indicates increasing Convair exposure to accident liability claims in the years ahead. . . .

In July 1970 DC-10 Number Two was being pressure-tested in the "hangar" by Douglas, on the second shift, without electrical power in the airplane. This meant that the electrically powered cargo door actuators and latch position warning switches were inoperative. The "green" second shift test crew manually cranked the latching system closed but failed to fully engage the latches on the forward door. They also failed to note that the external latch "lock" position indicator showed that the latches were not fully engaged. Subsequently, when the increasing cabin pressure reached about 3 psi (pounds per square inch) the forward door blew open. The resulting explosive decompression failed the cabin floor downward rendering tail controls, plumbing, wiring, etc., which passed through the floor, inoperative. This inherent failure mode is catastrophic, since it results in the loss of control of the horizontal and vertical tail and the aft center engine. We informally studied and discussed with Douglas alternative corrective actions including blow out panels in the cabin floor which would accommodate the "explosive" loss of cargo compartment pressure without loss of tail surface and aft center engine control. It seemed to us then prudent that such a change was indicated since "Murphy's Law" being what it is, cargo doors will come open sometime during the twenty years of use ahead for the DC-10.

Douglas concurrently studied alternative corrective actions, in house, and made a unilateral decision to incorporate vent doors in the cargo doors. This "bandaid fix" not only failed to correct the inherent DC-10 catastrophic failure mode of cabin floor collapse, but the detail design of the vent door change further degraded the safety of the original door latch system by replacing the direct, short-coupled and stiff latch "lock" indicator system with a complex and relatively flexible linkage. (This change was accomplished entirely by Douglas with the exception of the assistance of one Convair engineer who was sent to Long Beach at their request to help their vent door system design team.)

This progressive degradation of the fundamental safety of the cargo door latch system since 1968 has exposed us to increasing liability claims. On June 12, 1972 in Detroit, the cargo door latch electrical actuator system in DC-10 number 5 failed to fully engage the latches of the left rear cargo door and the complex and relatively flexible latch "lock" system failed to make it impossible to close the vent door. When the door blew open before the DC-10 reached 12,000 feet altitude the cabin floor collapsed disabling most of the control to the tail surfaces and aft center engine. It is only chance that the airplane was not lost. Douglas has again studied alternative corrective actions and appears to be applying more "band-aids." So far they have directed to us to install small one-inch diameter, transparent inspection windows through which you can view latch "lock-pin" position, they are revising the rigging instructions to increase "lock-pin" engagement and they plan to reinforce and stiffen the flexible linkage.

It might well be asked why not make the cargo door latch system really "fool-proof" and leave the cabin floor alone. Assuming it is possible to make the latch "fool-proof" this doesn't solve the fundamental deficiency in the airplane. A cargo compartment can experience explosive decompression from a number of causes such as: sabotage, mid-air collision, explosion of combustibles in the compartment and perhaps others, any one of which may result in damage which would not be fatal to the DC-10 were it not for the tendency of the cabin floor to collapse. The responsibility for primary damage from these kinds of causes would clearly not be our responsibility, however, we might very well be held responsible for the secondary damage, that is the floor collapse which could cause the loss of the aircraft. It might be asked why we did not originally detail design the cabin floor to withstand the loads of cargo compartment explosive decompression or design blow out panels in the cabin floors to fail in a safe and predictable way.

I can only say that our contract with Douglas provided that Douglas would furnish all design criteria and loads (which in fact they did) and that we would design to satisfy these design criteria and loads (which in fact we did). There is nothing in our experience history which would have led us to expect that the DC-10 cabin floor would be inherently susceptible to catastrophic failure when exposed to explosive decompression of the cargo compartment, and I must presume that there is nothing in Douglas's experience history which would have led them to expect that the airplane would have this inherent characteristic or they would have provided for this in their loads and criteria which they furnished to us.

My only criticism of Douglas in this regard is that once this inherent weakness was demonstrated by the July 1970 test failure, they did not take immediate steps to correct it. It seems to me inevitable that, in the twenty years ahead of us, DC-10 cargo doors will come open and I would expect this to usually result in the loss of the airplane. [Emphasis added.] This fundamental failure mode has been discussed in the past and is being discussed again in the bowels of both the Douglas and Convair organizations. It appears however that Douglas is waiting and hoping for government direction or regulations in the hope of passing costs on to us or their customers.

If you can judge from Douglas' position during ongoing contract change negotiations they may feel that any liability incurred in the meantime for loss of life, property and equipment may be legally passed on to us.

It is recommended that overtures be made at the highest management level to persuade Douglas to immediately make a decision to incorporate changes in the DC-10 which will correct the fundamental cabin floor catastrophic failure mode. Correction will take a good bit of time, hopefully there is time before the National Transportation Safety Board (NTSB) or the FAA ground the airplane which would have disastrous effects upon sales and production both near and long term. This corrective action becomes more expensive than the cost of damages resulting from the loss of one plane load of people.

F. D. Applegate
Director of Product Engineering

If this memo had reached outside authorities, Applegate might have been able to prevent the events that (to some extent) he correctly foresaw. However, this memo never reached McDonnell Douglas or the FAA. Applegate received a reply to his memo from his immediate supervisor, J. B. Hurt. Both Applegate and Hurt realized that such major safety questions would not be addressed further at McDonnell Douglas. Hurt's reply to Applegate pointed out that if further questions about the plane's design arose, Convair, not McDonnell Douglas, would likely have to bear the costs of necessary modifications. Higher management at Convair subsequently agreed with Hurt that nothing further could realistically be done. Without taking other routes to express his grave misgivings about the DC-10, Applegate filed away his memo, rather than taking his concerns to higher corporate authorities at McDonnell Douglas or to federal agents.

In July 1972, Ship 29 of the DC-10 line was inspected by three different inspectors at McDonnell Douglas's Long Beach plant. All three certified that the ship had been successfully altered to meet FAA specifications. In fact, however, *none* of the recommended cargo door modifications had been implemented. Two years later, Ship 29 came under the ownership of Turkish Airlines. This ship crashed near Paris in 1974, killing all 335 passengers and 11 crew members, the worst single-plane disaster in aviation history. Experts agreed that the immediate cause of the crash was a blowout of the rear cargo door approximately 12 minutes after liftoff. Cargo bay decompression collapsed the cabin floor, thereby severing control cables. Sanford Douglas, President of McDonnell Douglas, alleged that the Turkish airline involved in the crash had attempted to "rework" the door rigging or latching mechanism, was working with an inadequately trained ground crew, and failed to follow specified procedures for proper latching. The Turkish airline denied the charges. Recovery of a flight recorder indicated that there was no explosion, fire, or evident sabotage, and that the cargo door blew because it was not securely sealed.

In 1980 the McDonnell Douglas Corporation issued a special report addressing the public's growing fears about the DC-10's design. The corporation's report aimed to prove "that the DC-10 meets the toughest standards of aerospace technology."[9] The report did not mention the cargo door defects. Although the company eventually corrected the cargo door *locking* systems, the DC-10 still suffered from *hydraulic* failures. On May 25, 1979, an American Airlines DC-10 crashed shortly after takeoff from Chicago's O'Hare Airport, killing 275 in the worst air disaster in U.S. history. Subsequent examination revealed that the plane's left engine had ripped loose, carrying away vital hydraulic lines and control cables. The resulting massive system failures rendered the flight crew unable to land the plane safely.[10] More recently, in July 1989, United Airlines Flight 232 crashed near Sioux City, Iowa, killing 112 of its 296 passengers and crew members. On emergency approach to the Sioux City airport, the pilot informed air traffic controllers that he was confronted with a "complete hydraulic failure."[11] NTSB investigators concluded that an engine explosion severed the plane's hydraulic control cables, rendering the plane unflyable.

The DC-10s hydraulic failures may be due to improper maintenance, or perhaps the model's basic design, inasmuch as design engineers placed the hydraulic lines on the wings' leading edges. By contrast, Boeing designers located the 747's lines on the wings' trailing edges, widely considered to be a less exposed position. However, regardless of the model's history, aviation experts and airline executives give the DC-10 "generally high marks."[12] Air Force crews flying the KC-10, the DC-10's military counterpart, call the model reliable and safe. The military uses KC-10s extensively for resupply missions, including the 1990 Operation Desert Shield in Saudi Arabia. McDonnell Douglas is currently building the MD-11, an updated version of the DC-10.

NOTES

1 This paragraph profited from three unpublished sources: Fay Horton Sawyier, "The Case of the DC-10 and Discussion" (Chicago: Center for the Study of Ethics in the Professions, Illinois Institute of Technology, December 8, 1976), mimeographed, pp. 2–3; correspondence with John T. Sant of the McDonnell Douglas Corporation's Legal Department in St. Louis; and correspondence with Professor Homer Sewell of George Washington University (see his article in note 5).

2 See Paul Eddy, Elaine Potter, and Bruce Page, *Destination Disaster: From the Tri-Motor to the DC-10* (New York: Quadrangle Books, New York

Times Book Co., 1976); John Newhouse, "A Reporter at Large: The Airlines Industry," *New Yorker,* June 21, 1982, pp. 46–93.

3 Eddy, et al., *Destination Disaster;* see also Martin Curd and Larry May, *Professional Responsibility for Harmful Actions* (Dubuque, Iowa: Kendall/Hunt Publishing Co., 1984), pp. 11–21; and Peter French, "What Is Hamlet to McDonnell-Douglas or McDonnell-Douglas to Hamlet: DC-10," *Business and Professional Ethics Journal* 1 (Winter 1982), pp. 1, 5–6.

4 John T. Sant, personal correspondence.

5 See Homer Sewell, "Commentary," *Business and Professional Ethics Journal* 1 (Winter 1982), pp. 17–19.

6 Eddy et al., *Destination Disaster,* pp. 180–81.

7 National Transportation Safety Board, Aircraft Accident Report no. NTSB-AAR-73-2 (February 28, 1973), p. 38.

8 Eddy et al., *Destination Disaster,* pp. 183–85.

9 McDonnell Douglas Corporation, *The DC-10: A Special Report* (Long Beach, Calif.: McDonnell Douglas Corporation, 1980).

10 Newhouse, "A Reporter," p. 89; *New York Times,* June 7, 1979, sec. B, p. 13, and *New York Times,* June 19, 1979, sec D, p. 19; see also "New Testing Methods Could Boost Air Safety," *Science* 205 (July 6, 1979), pp. 29–31.

11 Michael York, "DC-10 Became a Casualty of Its Reputation," *Washington Post,* July 20, 1990.

12 Ibid.

A CORPORATE CODE OF ETHICS

A company's corporate culture can often be found in its statement of corporate responsibility and its corporate code of ethics. The following statement from McGraw-Hill, the publisher of this book, speaks not only to such issues as improper payments, conflicts of interest, and commitments to obey the law, it also encourages employees to report any instances of violation of this code. This code is reprinted here by permission of The McGraw-Hill Companies.

MCGRAW-HILL'S CODE OF BUSINESS ETHICS

McGraw-Hill enjoys a world-wide reputation for integrity and honesty, and for acting in good faith in all its dealings. It is a reputation of which we are proud, for it is our heritage and it reflects our goals and the manner in which we work to achieve them.

Our standards of conduct have been summarized in the paragraphs that follow. Written words alone, however, do not create a moral conscience or lead inevitably to ethical conduct.

The written words, in fact, are nothing more than a reflection of the way we have always done our business. Our reputation for fair dealing was well established long before a written policy was first published. In short, McGraw-Hill is a people-oriented company, and it is the conduct of McGraw-Hill's people that has produced our reputation for integrity and honesty.

What Employees Can Expect of McGraw-Hill You have been employed solely on the basis of McGraw-Hill's estimate of your ability to do your job well. You will not be discriminated against because of race, sex, religion, physical handicap, age, color, sexual orientation, national origin, marital status or veteran's status.

Your future promotion and pay will depend on your demonstrated ability to do superior work, to grow in your job and to accept responsibility. Your salary will reflect the worth of your position in relation to the difficulty and importance of other positions in the company, and will be set at a level that is competitive with compensation paid by other employers.

You can expect courteous and considerate treatment from the company, and guidance and help in learning to do your job well. Through company-sponsored training programs, the sharing of tuition costs, and other means, we will endeavor to provide appropriate opportunities for development that may qualify you for better jobs.

You will, through our Career Opportunities Program, learn of possible job openings throughout the corporation and be able to apply for and receive full consideration for any appropriate position you may be qualified to fill.

Every reasonable effort will be made to provide you a safe and healthy place in which to work. In addition, it is the company's policy to provide a work environment that is free from sexual harassment toward any individual.

The privacy of your personnel and payroll records will be respected, and during your employment you have a right to examine those records yourself.

If you have a problem related to your employment, you may at any time discuss it, in confidence, with your supervisor. If you feel your supervisor hasn't given you an adequate answer, you can ask to have the problem referred to your supervisor's immediate supervisor and also to the Human Resources Department. Through appropriate supervisory channels, you may take a complaint to the highest executive level.

Participation in the company's benefits programs can provide you with financial assistance through medical, disability and life insurance, and with retirement income.

What McGraw-Hill Can Expect of Us as Employees   Of course, the company expects that employees will work diligently and to the best of their abilities. But in addition here are some specific requirements.

Conflicts of Interest   Employees should not engage in any act that might result in a conflict, or the appearance of a conflict, between the individual's self-interest or the interests of another organization, on the one hand, and McGraw-Hill's interest. Each employee should be free from any interest or influence that would make it difficult to give McGraw-Hill the employee's best efforts and undivided attention. Employees may not take for themselves or divert to others any business opportunity in which McGraw-Hill has, or can reasonably be expected to have, an interest.

Outside Employment   There is no objection to employees, on their own time, doing limited amounts of work for other employers so long as such work does not conflict with the employees' obligations to McGraw-Hill. Such a conflict would obviously arise if the outside work consumed so much of an employee's time and energy as to impair his or her ability to do his or her McGraw-Hill job effectively. Also, a conflict of consideration may be accepted by employees or members of their families from any such entities. No gift having more than nominal value and no loan (other than a normal bank loan) may be accepted from any person or firm having current or prospective dealings with the corporation. No employee or member of his or her family should own, directly or indirectly, any interest in a firm that does business with McGraw-Hill, except that this ownership restriction does not apply to the ownership of less than 1 percent of the shares of any public corporation. Nor should such an employee be in a position to receive any benefits from such firm if the employee is in any way involved in decisions for McGraw-Hill regarding that firm or its products.

Government Contracts   Government contracts, whether with federal, state or municipal entities, are subject to complex laws and regulations setting forth the information which must be furnished the government in the course of negotiating a contract or submitting a bid.

Other laws regulate the performance of government contracts, accounting procedures and payment requests in ways different from private commercial contracts. In certain instances, serious violations of government contract laws or regulations may affect McGraw-Hill's ability to do business with the government or even constitute criminal conduct. Employees responsible for government contract work should become familiar with the relevant rules and regulations and should contact the Legal Department with any questions.

Improper Payments to Others   No employee should make, or be involved in any way with making, any improper payment, or offer any improper inducement, to any existing or potential customer or supplier in the form of a bribe, kickback, excessive commission or fee in connection with any McGraw-Hill activity. This prohibition includes, but is not limited to, obtaining business for McGraw-Hill from private businesses or government bodies, in the U.S. and abroad.

Advance Disclosure of Unpublished Information   No employee shall disclose to any person in advance of publication the contents of any McGraw-Hill book, magazine, newsletter, electronic product, securities rating or any other information product or service, produced in any medium, unless appropriate McGraw-Hill management approval is obtained in advance.

Representing McGraw-Hill in Unauthorized Capacity   No employee shall contact any person or entity to seek personal gain or other benefits by claiming the employee represents or is affiliated with McGraw-Hill.

Compliance with Law   All McGraw-Hill employees shall be responsible for conducting their activities on behalf of McGraw-Hill in compliance with applicable laws and regulations. When appropriate, employees should seek advice from McGraw-Hill's Legal Department with respect to questions relating to the application or interpretation of laws and regulations relevant to their respective business activities.

Interpretation of This Code   Employees should seek advice from McGraw-Hill's Legal Department concerning any interpretation of the provisions of this code.

Special Situations   Detailed codes of conduct have been developed by certain McGraw-Hill units to provide guidance in situations that are unique to them.

Reporting Violations of This Code   An employee who observes any conduct by other employees in violation of this code or of any law applicable to McGraw-Hill shares a responsibility to inform his or her supervisor, the head of our Corporate Auditing Department or the Legal Department in confidence.

In General   All employees will be expected to abide by the highest ethical standards and act with complete integrity when dealing on behalf of McGraw-Hill with government agencies, customers, competitors, suppliers, authors, the media, trade associations, fellow employees and the general public.

What the Public has a Right to Expect from McGraw-Hill and Its Staff   Like all other responsible companies, we have an obligation to provide products and services of high quality, to market them fairly, and to conduct our affairs honorably. But our company has some special responsibilities beyond these. One is to be a good citizen in the communities in which we work. We are sensitive to the economic role we play in those communities, and to the standards of service of our broadcasting stations and other community-related functions. The McGraw-Hill Foundation contributes to community as well as to national institutions, and encourages employees to do so by matching their gifts to educational institutions, libraries, public broadcasting and arts and cultural organizations. In addition, all McGraw-Hill employees are encouraged to take an active personal role in organizations dedicated to public service, and the Foundation will back up their participation with appropriate financial contributions to qualified projects and institutions to which they are contributing volunteer services.

There is a further responsibility that comes from our being in the business of communicating information and serving the need for knowledge. No day passes in which there are not millions of persons throughout the world who make some use of McGraw-Hill publications, services and broadcasts. Through these, we have built our major and pervasive impact. And we are trusted. That trust is what imposes on us all a special responsibility to produce the very best and the most completely reliable materials and services we can. That is the basic ethical demand upon us. Nothing must compromise that. All of us should share a sense of that responsibility in all our work.

International Business

CHAPTER OUTLINE

Gary Armstrong
General Manager
S.C. Johnson Europlant B.V

"International business has an extra measure of risk and uncertainty. You want to deal with companies which ensure that their products and services consistently meet your high standards. You want them to deal openly and honestly with you because you don't want any surprises in this market of diverse customs, cultures and languages. These are the successful companies; they replace uncertainty and risk with confidence and trust."

"Corruption's Many Tentacles are Choking India's Growth," announces a *New York Times* headline. Listing bribes, payoffs, and graft as endemic to India's way of doing business, the article claims that such practices are a drag on India's economic progress.[1] A report in *Business Week* examines efforts underway in countries with emerging securities markets to ensure their global competitiveness by stressing to investors the intention of these markets to meet stringent standards of public accountability. "In their zeal to attract foreign investors by demonstrating their markets' safety and soundness, other countries have become more cooperative with the SEC in rooting out fraud and corruption." The article goes on to state that "more than 20 countries, including many in Europe and Latin America, have signed a cross-border SEC initiative to assist one another on securities-enforcement actions."[2]

The practice of international business raises a host of issues, among the most important of which is the need to clarify the proper mode of conduct for business leaders operating in foreign cultures. Put bluntly, is bribery right in India, because it seems to be tolerated, even encouraged there, but wrong in the United States, where it is illegal? Or is it even bribery in some third-world countries to give monetary "gifts" to government representatives for services rendered, even though they are services their position requires them to do? Can companies morally distribute drugs in other countries that have not achieved FDA clearance for distribution in the United States? If a company meets all applicable local laws and standards for conduct, is it to be blamed when an accident occurs, an accident that would not have happened had the company conducted business according to the standards of its own country?

OPPOSING STANDARDS

There are three major responses to questions such as those we have just raised. The first is that the only standards companies are responsible for meeting are those established by the countries in which they do business. This is a version of the old slogan "When in Rome, do as the Romans do." This phrase articulates the claim that there are no cross-cultural standards of conduct, that values are determined by each society or culture for itself, and those of a different society or culture are simply irrelevant. This view has come to be known as "cultural relativism."

A second, opposite point of view is that a company is bound only by those standards of conduct forced on it by its own culture, and that its mode of doing business elsewhere is bound to those standards. If it is illegal to sell products in the home country that have been banned for safety reasons—such as selling a drug with known harmful side effects—then it is improper for the company to sell that drug abroad, even though the risk of side effects is less than the dangers of the disease that the drug could prevent. In its most extreme form, this attitude results in what is known as "ethnocentrism"—the view that the standards of one's own culture are superior to those of other cultures. Not only does ethnocentrism consider cultural standards other than one's own as inferior, it seeks to apply one's own standards to other cultures wherever this is possible. Such attitudes were associated with the colonialism of Western nations.

Midway between these two extremes is the view that there are objective standards of conduct that transcend any particular nation or culture and that the cultural values of both the company's home nation and those of the nation in which the company does business may be ethically lacking. This view is often called "ethical objectivism." Whether there are in fact such standards is an issue of considerable philosophical significance, for until we come to grips with this issue, it is difficult to find moral guidance in the often bewildering world of international business.

THE CHALLENGES OF RELATIVISM

The issue of universal moral standards, whether they exist and, if so, what they are, is as old as Western philosophy itself. Put briefly, ethical relativism is the view that the rightness or wrongness of an action is a function of attitudes taken toward that action by an individual or a group of individuals. Relativism is a variety of a view known as "subjectivism," which holds that there are only subjective standards (dependent on individual or group decisions), not objective standards (whose truth or falsity is independent about what individuals or groups think).

Naive Relativism

Part of the attractiveness of relativism is that it seems so tolerant. You do what you think is right, I do what I think is right; live and let live. Who am I to judge your actions? And by what right do you think you can tell me what I should do? Put in this form, it is an expression of what has been called "naive relativism," the view that right and wrong are relative to each individual. This view is naive because it is uncritical and cannot get us very far in responding to ethical challenges. If true, naive relativism would forever destroy the possibility of resolving moral disagreements, for it would finally come down to the fact that you believe one thing, I believe something else, and that's that. This is precisely what is wrong with naive relativism, for it focuses solely on *belief* and fails to distinguish between the fact that a person believes something and the *content* of that belief.[3] In hardly any field other than ethics would such a view be considered seriously. You believe the big bang theory, I do not. Your belief is right for you, my belief is right for me, and that is the end of the discussion. Clearly this is logically unacceptable, for it gives up the idea that reason will allow us to search for the true account of the origin of the universe.

In another sense, naive relativism brings us back to Hobbes and the state of nature in which each individual determines what is right or wrong, the result of which is the continual warfare of each against all. As was discussed earlier in this book, the way out of this barbarous state, in which life is "solitary, poor, nasty, brutish, and short," is through the adoption of reasonable standards of restraint that limit the claims of each for the good of all. To be a naive relativist, as one writer on ethics put it, is to "give up hope of coping with the world better than we do now" and is to "give up hope of becoming better human beings."[4] Indeed, naive relativists have to give up the notion of becoming better in any sense, for "better" implies a standard against which one measures conduct, judging some actions as more ethical than others. Without a standard—and there would be no independent standard if indeed each human being "was the measure of all things"—there would be no better or worse.

Cultural Relativism

An alternative form of relativism is the view that moral values are determined by the common agreement of a society or culture, and that one culture cannot judge the rightness or wrongness of another culture's value system. This point of view has received powerful support from such social sciences as anthropology, whose study of cultural diversity uses a value-free method of inquiry. It is of interest to philosophers to debate whether in fact there can be a purely value-free inquiry, as even asking questions presumes the kind of responses that will count as answers. But the social sciences, in an effort to provide objectivity and scientific certainty to cross-cultural study, attempt to refrain from making value judgments about the cultures under investigation. This value-free method has led some, but not all, social scientists to take a further step and claim that it is thus illegitimate to make value judgments about the behavior of other peoples, that what those societies consider the right thing to do is right for them and should not be judged by the standards of the society of the investigator. This is another attempt to avoid ethnocentrism.[5]

But this claim needs to be investigated further. Consider the following statements.[6]

1 Different societies make different ethical judgments.
2 Different societies have different ethical standards.
3 Different ethical standards are correct for different societies.

Accepting statements 1 and 2 does not commit us to cultural relativism. Only statement 3 is an expression of a relativist point of view. In order to clarify this claim about cultural relativism, we will examine each of these statements.

Different Societies Make Different Ethical Judgments This statement is certainly true. There is wide variation among countries, cultures, and peoples in the judgments they make about human conduct. But is it valid to argue from this claim to the conclusion that all ethical judgments are relative to an individual culture? Not necessarily. Remember that cultural relativism is the view that what is right or wrong is relative to a culture or society and that there is no basis for saying that one culture's moral judgments are superior to those of another culture. That different cultures make different ethical judgments proves nothing. Let's go back to the example given at the beginning of this chapter. Culture A accepts bribery as a necessary cost of doing business. Culture B rejects bribery as a legitimate business activity and tries to discourage it with severe penalties. A cultural relativist could correctly report that Culture A and Culture B differ on the moral status of bribery. That would be a true statement. But the cultural relativist wants to say more, namely, that bribery is *both* right (in Culture A) and wrong (in Culture B). It is this self-contradictory claim of relativism that leads philosophers to reject it, for it fundamentally is the claim that an action is both right and wrong, a manifold contradiction.

Let's probe this issue a bit further. To give an accurate account of the differences between Culture A and Culture B, we should say that persons in Culture A *believe* that bribery is acceptable, whereas persons in Culture B *believe* that bribery is unacceptable. Again, this is a true statement, but it does not prove that the content of both beliefs is correct. One could argue on empirical grounds that the belief in the acceptability of bribery as a business practice is mistaken: it stifles growth; it makes industries that practice it uncompetitive because they make decisions not on the basis of quality and cost effectiveness but on the basis of who gives the best bribes. We could say that bribery fails on utilitarian principles, for instead of providing for the greatest good for the greatest number, it provides for a good for a limited number while diminishing the good of the greatest number. So we could conclude that whereas persons in Culture A believe that bribery is acceptable (a true statement), the content of that belief is wrong, because it fails to meet a basic utilitarian standard.

Ethical theories aside, there are instances of behavior on the part of cultures that are so monstrous and heinous that they call for near-universal condemnation. Examples could include such actions as government-sanctioned genocide (the Holocaust, the mass murder of Armenians in 1915), torture of political prisoners, rape of civilians by invading armies, the use of famine as a political weapon, medical experimentation on prisoners of war, to name just a few. A cultural relativist, if consistent, cannot retreat to any value judgment about these actions, for the relativist is committed to the principle that we cannot make cross-cultural ethical judgments. But is it really acceptable to say of the Holocaust that because German society at that time allowed for (and legalized) the appropriation of property owned by Jews and provided for their mass extermination that such actions are morally right? Can we really accept the view that when a culture (such as one of those in the Balkans) believes it is acceptable to engage in "ethnic cleansing" that it is therefore right to do so? Relativists might retreat to the view that they personally abhor such actions and would do everything in their power to prevent them, but they cannot force their views on others. This is the strongest condemnation a cultural relativist can logically make, but it does not satisfy our moral judgment that such behavior is fundamentally wrong. Fortunately, most relativists behave better than their philosophy would allow.

There is yet another implication of cultural relativism: a cultural relativist, left with little in the way of reasoned argument against such practices as listed above, has to fall back on some other mode of conflict resolution. Fundamentally this again brings us back to Hobbes's state of nature. Relativism, in all its forms, has been characterized as "an admission that our human reason can no longer be useful" and "represents an admission that we must engage in other forms of human interactions such as deception, physical coercion, even war, rather than try to do the admittedly difficult job of resolving conflicting moral viewpoints."[7]

Different Societies Have Different Ethical Standards This second statement seems to follow logically on the heels of the first, but a little analysis shows that it does not. When analyzing the first statement we had to distinguish between the fact of belief and the content of belief. Similarly, we have to distinguish between *matters of belief* and *matters of attitude.* A belief, as used here, is that to which persons give assent, either correctly or incorrectly. I may believe (incorrectly) that the world is flat and, given this belief, will behave in certain, predictable ways (such as not voyaging too far for fear of falling off the edge of the earth). This is a crude example, but it illustrates the point that what we believe will drastically affect the way we behave. Valid inferences based on mistaken beliefs produce unsound reasoning. When, however, a mistaken belief (that the world is flat) is replaced with a correct belief (that the world is a sphere), the conclusion reached produces changed behavior. Not all beliefs are as easy to change as this one; in fact, it took several millennia to change this one. Consider this list of some other beliefs:

1 A fetus is an immortal soul at the moment of conception.

2 A fetus is nothing but a mass of tissue until capable of independent life.

3 The people living across the river are not really human.

4 If my parents die when in good health, that is the way they will be in the afterlife.

5 Multinational companies are major contributors to third-world poverty in that they are a form of neocolonialism.

6 It is God's will that infidels be exterminated.

7 All forms of capitalistic enterprise result in the exploitation of workers.

8 The only hope for third-world countries to escape from poverty is industrial development provided by multinational corporations.

9 Free trade agreements destroy jobs.
10 Free trade agreements create jobs.

These statements span the gamut of religious beliefs (1, 4, 6) to economic and philosophical beliefs (5, 7, 8, 9, and 10) to what we could call ideological beliefs (2 and 3). Some beliefs can be changed by an appeal to empirical data, such as those that claim that multinational corporations either aid or hinder the escape from poverty by third-world countries. Some beliefs remain to be proved true or false by the unfolding of future events, such as the beliefs about free trade. Religious beliefs are the most difficult to deal with because we often do not know how to determine their truth or falsity; ideological commitments are difficult to disprove because they reflect commitments basic to how we view the world.

The important point is that persons with the same values or attitudes (that is, basic moral values) can act in wildly different ways due to differences in beliefs (that is, what they accept as true). Sometimes this point is obscured by the rhetorical flourishes of public debate, as when prolife advocates accuse prochoice defenders as murderers, and prochoice supporters accuse prolifers as being antifemale. Neither characterization is true, for the fundamental difference between the two groups is one of belief, not of attitude.

Similarly, those who believe that multinational companies operating in third-world countries benefit those countries will behave differently than the critics who believe that the mere presence of multinational companies in third-world countries is exploitative and damaging. Proponents of protectionism accuse advocates of free trade of being against protecting the jobs of workers, whereas free trade advocates accuse their opponents of being against the creation of jobs for workers. Both sides differ in a matter of belief about a future state of affairs, and because it is about the future, deciding which belief is correct is difficult.

There are other ways to understand how people sharing common ethical values (matters of attitude) might behave in different ways. They may face *different circumstances*. The ethicist Richard Brandt illustrates this with a simple example: If one thinks it is wrong for a group of Eskimos to strip a person of "clothing twenty miles from home on January 1 but not wrong for a tribe at the equator," this does not imply cultural relativism. It illustrates, rather, the view "that particular circumstances make a difference to the morality of an act."[8] A country trying to raise itself from poverty might accept lower standards of wages and benefits than would a highly industrialized country. This decision would follow from the fact that the developing country has a lower basis for providing compensation to its workers. When its economic development improves, it will then be able to increase wages and benefits. There are, of course, limits to what is acceptable behavior no matter what the circumstances, and we will return to this point later.

Another reason for different ethical judgments is disagreement on *rules and instances.* To give a nonbusiness example, two cultures, both accepting the value that murder is wrong, may disagree on whether to label as an act of murder such disparate events as capital punishment, abortion, euthanasia, killing in self-defense, and killing in wartime. A company may agree that it is wrong to practice discriminatory hiring practices but disagree with its critics who say that by requiring a level of education not essential for the job the company is discriminating against classes of workers who do not have the stipulated educational requirement.

Still another basis for differences in action for cultures, or individuals for that matter, is disagreement over *values and rankings.* A contemporary difference among cultures is the relative importance given to leisure and that given to the value of working for the company. In France, to deny workers their expected month's vacation would probably cause another revolution, whereas in Japan, workers tend to take very little vacation, valuing instead continual work for their company. In the United States workers treat vacation as a negotiable item and allow for wide differences among companies. It would be unfair, however, to say that France values worker leisure and Japan does not; rather, it is the case that workers in Japan give higher ranking to the value of company loyalty and work, whereas in France workers give high ranking to the value of leisure and recreation.

Different Ethical Standards Are Correct for Different Societies
Here is the issue that is at the heart of the relativist position: the claim that a society's standards of conduct are not only believed by members of that society to be correct, they are in fact correct. Here again we confront the distinction mentioned earlier between the fact of belief and the content of that belief. Put this way, there is a logical contradiction in the relativist position. Let's suppose that Culture A accepts slavery as morally right and Culture B rejects slavery as morally wrong. According to the relativist position, both of the following statements

are true: slavery is morally right and slavery is morally wrong. This, however, cannot logically be accepted, for it is inconsistent to say that a statement and its negation are both true.

But what the relativist means is probably something like this: in Culture A, slavery is morally right *for them;* in Culture B, or in my culture, slavery is thought to be wrong, so slavery is morally wrong *for us.* Put this way, the statement is certainly true, if we mean by it that people in Culture A *believe* that slavery is morally right. Here again we confront the distinction between the fact of belief and the content of that belief. We might even refrain from blaming a person from Society A for this view about slavery while still holding our view that this attitude toward slavery is morally wrong. Part of what bothers some with this interpretation is that it sounds too intolerant of cultural diversity and smacks of ethnocentrism or, even worse, cultural imperialism. But here again the relativist is faced with a logical problem. Why is tolerance an important issue? If Culture A is intolerant and Culture B is tolerant, the relativist has no logical basis to defend tolerance over intolerance, because the essence of the relativist position is that there is no cross-cultural norm by means of which to make ethical judgments about another culture.

BRANDT ON RELATIVISM AND TOLERANCE

The first question we must ask is whether the advocate of tolerance as a creed for relativists is saying that tolerance is only one among "equally valid" conflicting ethical opinions. Does he, that is, say that *intolerance* is equally as valid as tolerance, or not? He could be saying this: "We relativists, for our part, espouse the value of tolerance. But, as scientists, we recognize that intolerance is equally valid." Is relativism with its plea for tolerance only a "point of view," like another culture? Or is tolerance a value securely founded on the methods of science?

Perhaps we do best to answer these questions by considering what relativists can *consistently* say, not what they actually do say. . . . Now, according to this view, the value of intolerance is as justified (or unjustified) as that of tolerance. So why should he advocate it? Certainly there can be no reason in the sense that the correctness of such a position follows from the facts of science; indeed, according to this theory *no* ethical thesis has this status. One who is a relativist might easily as well say, "Since no system is more valid than any other, let each of us advance his own!" So, *intolerance* could be the outcome of relativism.

Source: Richard B. Brandt, *Ethical Theory: The Problems of Normative and Critical Ethics* (Englewood Cliffs, NJ: Prentice-Hall, 1959), p. 289.

THE SEARCH FOR INTERNATIONAL VALUES

To reject cultural relativism is not to ignore the fact that there are vast cultural differences among peoples and nations, and it is not always easy to know when these variations are trivial and when they raise ethical issues. Many differences are part of politeness and good manners: not showing the sole of your shoe to a Malaysian or extending a greeting with your left hand, being prepared to exchange small gifts when doing business with the Japanese, understanding that in some cultures a direct approach is considered ill mannered and that a more indirect approach is preferred, or not offering a business counterpart in a Muslim country an alcoholic drink. Cultural variances can take many forms, such as the mode of dress, the ways families are constituted, diet regulations and restrictions, gender roles, the proper relationship between business and government, and attitudes toward business cooperation. Many such variations are morally neutral and generally reflect differences in history, environmental conditions, and religious and social traditions, and it would be incorrect to assume at the outset that every cultural variation is loaded with ethical significance.

There still remains the question of the proper role of business when faced with these cultural differences. An advertising company doing business in Europe will find itself creating television commercials that incorporate nudity, whereas such commercial messages in the United States would not be acceptable. A difference such as this is a cultural variable, but it is not, strictly speaking, correct to see this as an example of ethical relativism. And here an important distinction must be made between those values that are basic and fundamental and those that reflect the different ways societies and cultures organize themselves. What is also the case is that behind these variations may lie the same ethical value. Another example can be found in the variation of liquor laws of countries and even within a country like the United States from state to state. Behind all these variations is a common value: discouraging the abuse of alcohol and preventing young people from being exposed to it. There are numerous ways to do this, and no one of them is especially better than the other. Similarly, countries may have different standards of modesty, and these standards vary not only from country to country but within a country from decade to decade. The standards for modesty in dress in a Muslim country and those in a West European country will differ, but behind these variances is a similar concern for standards of modesty. Where values shade off from moral significance to mere standards of taste is not always easy to define, but our difficulty with defining this line does not argue against there being one. When we speak of the morality of international business, we are concentrating on the fundamental moral issues and not on standards of taste that reflect cultural variation.

What are some of these basic and fundamental ethical issues? We can start by returning to the issue with which we began this chapter: bribery. United Nations Resolution 3514 condemns bribery, and the writer in business ethics Norman Bowie notes that there is evidence that "bribery—at least of public officials—is prohibited by the laws of practically every nation"[9] and that no state takes the view that there is "nothing wrong with genocide or torture."[10]

Another way of thinking about these fundamental and basic rights is to use something like the Rawls test (see Chapter 4) that will generate the minimal conditions that all disinterested and rational persons would accept if they did not know in which country, developed or undeveloped, they would live. Rawls argues that this approach would place freedom at the top of the list, with other basic rights subordinated to it, for, he concludes, nothing is worth surrendering one's freedom. The business ethicist Thomas Donaldson has suggested a "minimal" list of "international rights" that has been widely reprinted as an example of guidelines for multinational companies. The point of such a list is that no multinational company could reasonably say that it is justified in disallowing these rights in the course of doing business in other countries.[11]

1 The right to freedom of physical movement
2 The right to ownership of property
3 The right to freedom from torture
4 The right to a fair trial
5 The right to nondiscriminatory treatment
6 The right to physical security
7 The right to freedom of speech and association
8 The right to minimal education
9 The right to political participation
10 The right to subsistence

This list is minimal; it is not put forward as the complete list of standards of behavior for multinational companies but as a fundamental point of departure for thinking about international standards of conduct.

Using the Rawls approach can also provide guidance for companies doing business in less developed countries where standards for minimum wages, environmental protection laws, drug approval, public health programs, government regulation, and other similar features of a modern state are less developed than those of the company's home country. Using something like the "veil of ignorance" approach, what minimal standards would you be willing to accept if you did not know whether you would be living in that country? Again, Donaldson suggests that "it makes sense to consider ourselves and our own culture at a level of economic development relatively similar to that of the other country. And, if having done this, we find that *under such hypothetically altered social circumstances* we ourselves would accept the lower standards, then it is permissible to adopt the standards that appear inferior."[12]

These arguments reflect deontological standards that measure the morality of an action by its tendency to reflect behavior that is universalizable and would willingly be accepted by the moral agent were the agent also to be the recipient of the action. (Previous discussion in this book labeled these standards as *universality* and *reversibility*). But utilitarian standards are applicable as well, for businesses, to be successful, require a stable and functional environment in which to operate. A lack of this environment will decrease the economic effectiveness of business activity and reduce the ability of a developing country to provide a better life for its people.

In an article under the headline "The Destructive Costs of Greasing Palms," *Business Week* noted that the worst effect of corruption, and its most destructive consequence, are in developing countries. The article's researchers noted that "in recent years, corruption . . . has affected so many developing and developed nations that a moral revulsion against it has swept politicians out of office in countries from Brazil to Italy to Japan."[13] The *Business Week* report also included efforts being made by the World Bank to assess the costs of bribery and corruption and separate them "from legitimate business costs" and quotes an international economist's statement that "the real cost of corruption lies in the demoralization, cynicism, and enervation of entrepreneurial activity throughout the Third World."[14]

MULTINATIONAL CORPORATE BEHAVIOR

Critics of international business often go beyond specific actions to the deeper issue of multinational corporate behavior itself. According to these critics, multinational corporations, by their very existence, are a form of neocolonialism and a negative factor in third-world countries because they exploit resources for the sake of corporate, not host country, enrichment.

There are several arguments against this claim of ethical impropriety, the first of which is based on an examination of the empirical claim that third-world countries owe their impoverished state to their colonial past and to the continued presence of multinational corporations with their neocolonial attitudes. In a *New Republic* article, Charles Krauthammer examines, and rejects, this explanation, noting that "many of the richest countries in the first world are former colonies" and that "in Asia, those countries that had the most extensive contact with Western ideas, technology, and trade—Malaysia, Singapore, Hong Kong—are among the most advanced." And arguing against the blame for low rates of economic development being laid at the door of multinational companies, Krauthammer notes

> The list of the most rapidly developing third world countries is almost identical with the list of those most heavily penetrated by transnational corporations—Brazil, Mexico, Argentina, Venezuela, Malaysia, Taiwan, South Korea. Conversely, those countries that have had the least colonial experience—Afghanistan, Nepal, and Ethiopia, for example—are among the most backward in the world.[15]

Krauthammer goes on to point out that major causes of much third-world poverty can be identified as overpopulation, politics ("disastrous political decisions and economic models"), dependence on oil, and underdevelopment itself. "The wealth of the West," he says, "derives from its advanced technology, modernized agriculture, and industrial plant. These developments, in turn, rest on certain political institutions, a scientific ethos, and not incidentally, the sacrifices of previous generations of workers."[16]

Other writers discount what has come to be called the "dependency theory," that developing countries are harmed by multinational corporate involvement in their economic growth, citing the diverse causes of development. In the United States, for example, economic development was aided by "a remarkable resource base, a young immigrant population, relatively free and strong social institutions, and an absence of feudal entanglements."[17] They go on to point out that U.S. multinationals face competition abroad from multinationals from other countries—Taiwan, India, Brazil—and note that all multinational companies are becoming "more conscious of social values," which has a variety of causes ranging from "concern for maintaining a good public image, to public pressures, or to a new ethical awareness."[18]

There are times, however, in their rush to economic development, that third-world countries willingly take risks that would be unacceptable in developed countries, and this leads to major problems when companies bring advanced technology in the form of manufacturing processes and developed products to countries that may be ill equipped to use them and lack the trained personnel to ensure worker and user safety. In the much-examined case of the tragedy at Bhopal, India, where in 1984, more than one thousand persons were killed by the leak of toxic gases, responsibility for the event was due to faulty equipment, ignored safety procedures, inadequately trained personnel, and failure to prevent squatters from settling close to the chemical plant itself. Given that operating such plants requires a mastery of technology that may be difficult for countries with an untrained work force and minimal national safeguards, multinational companies will have to accept a more stringent, self-imposed ethical standard than they would adhere to in a more developed country. This claim, however, does not "exonerate local governments from responsibility" for aiding in assuring the welfare of its people.[19] The controversy generated by the conflict between the ethics of the host country and those of the company's home country are addressed in the law passed by the U.S. Congress known as the Foreign Corrupt Practices Act that limits certain kinds of behavior U.S. companies can practice abroad.

A Case in Point . . .

Some physicians in third-world countries were glad to see infant formula available for use by mothers who were sick or undernourished and as an alternative to such traditional substitutes as animal milk or cereal-based foods used in weaning infants. One physician who did not share this view was Dr. Derrick B. Jelliffe, director of the Caribbean Food and Nutrition Institute, who claimed at a 1970 meeting of the United Nations Protein-Calorie Advisory Group (PAG) that there was a direct link between infant mortality in third-world countries and the marketing of infant formula. Dr. Jelliffe's comments unleashed a torrent of criticism of advertising practices for infant formula practiced by multinational corporations. A British publication sponsored by three charity organizations continued the critique in a 1973 article entitled *The Baby Killer* aimed at Nestlé. Later translated into German under the title

Nestlé Kills Babies, the pamphlet generated a counterattack by Nestlé, which sued its publisher, the Third World Working Group (Arbeitsgruppe Dritte Weld—ADW) for libel in a Swiss court, and won. But in announcing the judgment, the judge added, "If the company wishes to avoid the charge of immoral and unethical behavior in the future, it must change its promotional practices." Nestlé's management has stated that these words were used "as the basis for future demands by still other advocacy groups."

Critics charged that companies such as Nestlé encouraged mothers in third-world countries to give up breast-feeding and use infant formula instead, even though breast-feeding is safe and nourishing. Mothers, the critics charged, untrained in the use of such products, often diluted the formula to make it go further; they were forced to mix it with unsanitary water, thereby exposing their infants to disease, and found that their own mother's milk dried up, making them totally dependent on a commercial product that they could not afford. Nestlé countered that it did not advocate its product over breast-feeding and that it offered infant formula as a supplement to, not a substitute for, mother's milk. The company also argued that it had developed a "full-protein" formula offering a margin of safety ensuring the product's nutritional value even when a mother overdiluted it in preparation, and it cited its production of an acidified milk product that is less susceptible to bacterial contamination in tropical areas as a further example of its commitment to infant safety.

The controversy soon spread to the other side of the Atlantic when the Interfaith Center on Corporate Responsibility (ICCR), a coalition of various religious groups, attacked infant formula marketing strategies used in third-world countries. In 1977 a group calling itself INFACT (Infant Formula Action Coalition) called for a consumer boycott of all Nestlé products. Nestlé's U.S. management countered that its U.S. operations did not manufacture or distribute infant formula either domestically or for export, but critics contended that U.S. Nestlé's parent organization did and saw pressure on its U.S. affiliate as a legitimate form of protest.

The consumer boycott continued for seven years, ending in 1984 when Nestlé and INFACT issued a joint statement and Nestlé agreed to accept the 1981 code of the World Health Organization for marketing breast-milk substitutes. In its own report, published in 1985, Nestlé stated that it "does not dismiss constructive criticism out of hand, but it does feel that unsubstantiated reports of corporate misconduct (as well as distortion and oversimplification of the problems) have clouded the issue." A spokesman for INFACT said the organization was committed "to work for strong legislation to see that the international code is implemented with teeth—with sanctions."

Sources: Journal of Commerce, Aug. 7, 1989; *Minneapolis Star and Tribune,* Oct. 5, 1984; *Washington Times,* Jan. 27, 1984; *The Corporate Examiner* (ICCR), Mar. 1977; *The Dilemma of Third World Nutrition: Nestlé and the Role of Infant Formula* (Nestlé Co.), 1985.

The Foreign Corrupt Practices Act

In reaction to scandals involving the paying of bribes to foreign officials by U.S. companies, Congress passed the Foreign Corrupt Practices
Act of 1977. Officially known as Public Law 95-213 [S.305], the act
prohibits publicly traded companies (but not privately held ones) from
making payments to foreign officials, foreign political parties, or individuals running for office to influence government acts or decisions or
to assist in obtaining or retaining business. These provisions were
embodied in the bill due to an SEC report that "indicated that more
than 250 publicly owned U.S. corporations, such as Northrop and
Grumann, had made illegal or questionable payments to foreign (and
domestic) governments."[20]

Some critics of the Foreign Corrupt Practices Act claim that it is an
example of moral imperialism, that it forces on other countries the
morality of the United States and is an example of ethnocentrism. The
counterargument, in the words of two writers in business ethics, is that
the act "did not force other countries or the multinationals of other
countries to follow U.S. morality. It simply required U.S. companies to
follow U.S. moral norms with respect to bribery when doing business
abroad."[21] Noting that "nearly all countries believe that bribery is
wrong," these authors go on to observe that "good reasons often dic-
tate that U.S. companies should adopt U.S. standards rather than those
of host countries."[22]

Sales Abroad of Products Banned at Home

A more difficult analysis awaits us in the examination of behavior of
multinational corporations involved in the international sale of products banned in their home countries, especially the sale of pharmaceutical products that are either unapproved or awaiting approval in the
United States. It does not follow that simply because a pharmaceutical
product is unlicensed for sale in the United States it would be unethical
for the product's manufacturer to offer it for sale in another country.
Getting approval from the Food and Drug Administration for a new
pharmaceutical is lengthy and costly. Many critics charge that the
process is too slow and deprives individuals of drugs whose known side
effects are few and whose therapeutic value is proved. Some drugs, like
U486, a French drug that induces abortion, the so-called "morning-
after pill," is banned from sale in the United States for a variety of reasons, among which is political opposition from groups that reject abor-

tion in any form. Equally critical of U.S. drug approval procedures are advocates of access to experimental drugs for treating AIDS that are unavailable in the United States because of FDA rules.[23] Other drugs remain experimental due to the lack of market potential for drugs to treat a disease affecting only a small number of people. In such cases drug companies judge that the cost of FDA approval is too great to be recouped by the sale of the drug and therefore abandon it as a marketable product. Since drug development in industrialized countries is driven by a drug's market potential, cost-benefits calculations must not only include developmental expense but also the costs of potential litigation and liability risks attached to any new pharmaceutical product.

The question concerning if, and under what circumstances, a company may ethically market drugs unavailable in its own country to persons in other countries that do not have lengthy approval processes is complex. Put another way, the question could be framed as follows: Should other countries be deprived of pharmaceuticals that are unapproved for sale in the United States because of their potential side effects, when these drugs would greatly benefit individuals in countries with medical circumstances different from those in the drug company's home country? Thomas Donaldson argues that this example perfectly fits his model of using a Rawls-type test to choose the best course of action, assuming that circumstances in the home country are dissimilar to those in the host country.[24] In other words, if the drug company's host country were a developing nation with a limited health-care infrastructure, would the drug in question be a boon or bane to the health of the citizenry? Might one be able to argue that refusal to sell such pharmaceutical products abroad because they fail to meet U.S. government standards is itself a form of neocolonial paternalism? The issue is a complicated one, but John Boatright, a writer in business ethics, gives several examples showing that the risks of *not* using such drugs may offset the risks attached to their known harmful side effects:

> In the United States, the risk of prescribing an antidiarrheal drug such as Lomotil to children is not worth taking. But a physician in Central America, where children frequently die of untreated diarrhea, might evaluate the risk differently. Similarly, the effectiveness of Chloromycetin for massive infections might offset the possibility of aplastic anemia in a country where some people would die without the drug. A missionary in Bolivia who spoke with doctors about the extensive use of chloramphenicol (the generic

name for Chloromycetin) reported: "The response was that in the States, because of our better state of general health, we could afford to have the luxury of saving that drug for rare cases. Here, the people's general health is so poor that one must make an all out attack on illness."[25]

Our discussion has focused on the moral ambiguity of some decisions facing companies doing business in multiple cultures and is not intended to provide either a defense or an exoneration of multinational corporate behavior. Certainly there are companies whose behavior is exploitative, and unethical conduct is not the exclusive province of multinational companies but can be found in companies both large and small, domestic and multinational. As is often the case with ethical issues, we find ourselves in a dialectical tension between the twin dangers of a paternalistic, often ethnocentric attitude toward doing business abroad and the opposite but equally real danger of capitulating to local expectations for conduct and justifying unethical corporate behavior by using the defense of cultural relativism. It is important to keep this tension taut by not surrendering to either of the twin poles of this dialectic. In what is becoming increasingly a global economy, multinational corporations will be scrutinized as never before, and high standards of ethical conduct will be required more and more of companies if they are to succeed in the worldwide marketplace.

DISCUSSION STARTERS

1 Choose a country with which you have some familiarity and make a list of cultural differences between it and your own country. Which of these cultural variables reflect a basic ethical difference?

2 Cultural relativism is appealing because it seems to avoid cultural bias, but does it really? Why or why not?

3 Discuss further the claim that the mere fact that different cultures have different ethical values does not, by itself, prove that cultural relativism is true. What evidence would count for cultural relativism?

4 The Foreign Corrupt Practices Act applies only to publicly held U.S. companies. If you were the manager of a privately owned corporation doing business abroad, would you voluntarily follow the FCPA rules? Give reasons for your answer.

5 Consider the following claim: In order for companies to do business successfully in what is increasingly a global economy, they will have to adopt a common set of ethical standards. What arguments would you give to support this view? Against it?

NOTES

1 Edward A. Gargan, "Corruption's Many Tentacles Are Choking India's Growth," NYT, Nov. 10, 1992.
2 "Babysitting the World's Emerging Bourses," BW, Nov. 1, 1993, p. 114.
3 This point is forcibly argued by R. Edward Freeman and Daniel R. Gilbert, Jr., in *Corporate Strategy and the Search for Ethics* (Englewood Cliffs, NJ: Prentice-Hall, 1988), p. 29ff.
4 Ibid., p. 298.
5 A classic statement of the value-free method is found in Ruth Benedict, "Anthropology and the Abnormal," *Journal of General Psychology* 10 (1934), pp. 59–80.
6 A further discussion of issues raised by these statements is found in David Stewart and H. Gene Blocker, *Fundamentals of Philosophy* (New York: Macmillan, 1982), p. 199ff. That discussion includes an analysis of issues in James W. Cornman and Keith Lehrer, *Philosophical Problems and Arguments: An Introduction*, 2nd ed. (New York: Macmillan, 1974).
7 Freeman and Gilbert, *Corporate Strategy and the Search for Ethics*, p. 39.
8 Richard B. Brandt, *Ethical Theory: The Problems of Normative and Critical Ethics* (Englewood Cliffs, NJ: Prentice-Hall, 1959), p. 271.
9 Norman E. Bowie, "Business Ethics and Cultural Relativism," in *Business Ethics: A Philosophical Reader*, ed. Thomas I. White (New York: Macmillan, 1993), pp. 794–795.
10 Ibid., p. 795.
11 Thomas Donaldson, *The Ethics of International Business* (New York: Oxford University Press, 1989), p. 81. Donaldson argues that the floor for all such considerations is universal human rights and appeals to Rawls's second principle of justice. See Thomas Donaldson, "The Ethics of Risk in the Global Economy," in *Business Ethics: A Philosophical Reader*, p. 820.
12 Donaldson, "The Ethics of Risk in the Global Economy," p. 819.
13 "The Destructive Costs of Greasing Palms," BW, Dec. 6, 1993, p. 133.
14 Ibid.
15 Charles Krauthammer, "Rich Nations, Poor Nations," *New Republic*, Apr. 11, 1981, p. 21.
16 Ibid., p. 22.
17 Gerald F. Cavanagh and Arthur F. McGovern, *Ethical Dilemmas in the Modern Corporation* (Englewood Cliffs, NJ: Prentice-Hall, 1988), p. 171.
18 Ibid., p. 191.
19 This point is argued forcibly by Richard DeGeorge, "Ethical Dilemmas for Multinational Enterprise: A Philosophical Overview," *Business Ethics: A Philosophical Reader*, p. 787.

20 Peter A. French, Jeffrey Nesteruk, and David T. Risser, with John M. Abbarno, *Corporations in the Moral Community* (New York: Harcourt Brace Jovanovich, 1992), p. 115.
21 Tom L. Beauchamp and Norman E. Bowie, *Ethical Theory and Business,* 4th ed. (Englewood Cliffs, NJ: Prentice-Hall, 1993), p. 517.
22 Ibid.
23 See Douglas D. Richman, "Public Access to Experimental Drug Therapy: AIDS Raises Yet Another Conflict Between Freedom of the Individual and Welfare of the Individual and the Public," *Journal of Infectious Diseases* 159 (Mar. 1989), pp. 412–415.
24 Donaldson, "The Ethics of Risk in the Global Economy," p. 819.
25 John Boatright, *Ethics and the Conduct of Business* (Englewood Cliffs, NJ: Prentice-Hall, 1993), p. 416.

CASE STUDY

The discussion of cultural variances often seems easier in theory than in real life, particularly when disputes deal not only with differences among cultures but also with a new industry that has not yet established rules for protecting proprietary information and is still struggling to determine what can and cannot be so protected. The case study that follows pits two companies and two cultures in a struggle for a growing market for computer hardware and software.

THE IBM-FUJITSU DISPUTE

In 1982, IBM, the largest computer company in the world, charged Fujitsu, its largest Japanese rival, with creating and selling computer programs that violated IBM's intellectual property rights. After eight months of negotiation, the companies reached a settlement, but it soon unraveled. Critics said the agreement had been poorly drafted.

In 1985, IBM filed a demand for arbitration with the American Arbitration Association (AAA), a private, nonprofit mediation group. Fujitsu agreed to the arrangement. Considering the complexity of the issues, the agreement providing for arbitration was quite short. An arbitrator later commented, "It didn't take long to write down what these two parties agreed on. . . . They have never agreed on anything, other than to agree that the only way to resolve this was to get us to solve it."

The companies disagreed sharply on two matters. One was whether Fujitsu had violated IBM's intellectual property rights in the past. Fujitsu vigorously denied IBM's charges. The other was whether Fujitsu could have access to certain IBM programming materials in future years.

To understand the decisions facing the arbitrators, it is important to understand the histories and strategies of the two companies, as well as the technical aspects of their dispute. Two background factors are also important: the differences between American and Japanese intellectual property laws and the controversy over whether Japanese companies unfairly copy technology from overseas.

THE TWO COMPANIES

IBM

By the late 1980s, IBM had dominated the worldwide computer business for more than two decades. Mainframes had been the core of the computer industry, the third largest industry in the United States after automobiles and oil, and IBM dominated the mainframe business. Its success made IBM the most profitable company in history. During the 1980s, IBM earned 70%–75% of world mainframe revenues, and these provided roughly two-thirds of IBM's profits. (See Exhibit 1 for IBM financial information.)

IBM's leadership was based in part on vast expenditures for manufacturing and R&D. Between 1976 and 1987, it spent more than $30 billion on R&D, and IBM held more than 10,000 patents. It invented the industry's first mass-produced electronic computing device, which it shipped in 1948. It took the lead in developing the floppy disk, one-transistor memory cells, the first all-semiconductor computer memory, and it was the first firm to mass produce several generations of memory chips. In two consecutive years, 1986 and 1987, IBM scientists won the Nobel Prize in physics.

IBM's dominant position had been built on the success of two lines of computers, the System 360 and the System 370. The 360, introduced in 1964, was a "bet-the-company" decision that replaced the company's entire product line. In some respects, the 360 was the first "family" of computers, ranging from small units to large ones, that all used the same programming instructions. In the early 1970s, IBM forged further ahead with its 370 series, which incorporated the then-new technology of integrated circuits.

IBM released its computer products in a multiwave attack. It would first introduce a new mainframe series. Then, it would offer improved hardware or software or both, enabling customers to run their computers faster or take advantage of new features. Finally, just as some competitors threatened to close the gap, IBM would introduce a whole new line of mainframes and start the cycle all over again. IBM's success with the System 370 drove rivals like GE and RCA out of the computer industry. IBM's approach was psychological as well. Its competitors had long complained that it played upon fear, uncertainty, and doubt— FUD in industry jargon—to discourage customers from relying on other mainframe suppliers.

By the early 1970s, IBM's position in the U.S. computer market was so strong that its American competitors were sometimes called "the seven dwarfs." One of its rivals observed that "IBM is not the competition; it's the environment." IBM's sales force, larger than the entire work force of most of its competitors, not only sold hardware but provided service and support after a computer was installed. For years, IBM's most daunting adversary was not a computer firm but the Antitrust Division of the U.S. Justice Department, which fought for 12 years to break up IBM, until the Reagan Administration dropped the suit in 1982.

IBM also defended its business in court. *Business Week* called it "one of the world's most ferocious legal combatants." In 1983, for example, after Hitachi pleaded guilty in federal court to criminal charges that it conspired to transport stolen IBM technical documents to Japan, IBM filed its own civil damages suit against Hitachi for stealing the technology. Hitachi settled the civil suit in 1983, agreed to pay IBM about $300 million, and allowed IBM to inspect future Hitachi products. IBM's case against Hitachi resulted from a complex "sting" operation devised by IBM and the Federal Bureau of Investigation. The climax of the effort was a payment of more than $500,000 made by a senior Hitachi engineer to a Silicon Valley consultant for IBM technology. The consultant was actually working for IBM and the FBI. IBM's efforts led one observer to write that "the scale of the operation and the publicity it drew were more reminiscent of a high-security Soviet counterespionage program than a mere effort to protect trade secrets."[1]

EXHIBIT 1

IBM: TWELVE-YEAR COMPARISON OF SELECTED FINANCIAL DATA[a,b] (dollars in millions)

For the year:	1988	1987	1986	1985	1984	1983	1982	1981	1980	1979	1978	1977	1976
Revenue	$59,681	$55,256	$52,160	$50,718	$46,309	$40,180	$34,364	$29,070	$26,213	$22,863	$21,076	$18,133	$16,304
Net earnings	5,806	5,258	4,789	6,555	6,582	5,485	4,409	3,308	3,562	3,011	30.11	2,719	2,398
Return on stockholders' equity	14.9%	14.5%	14.4%	22.4%	26.5%	25.4%	23.4%	21.1%	21.1%	21.2%	23.8%	21.2%	18.8%
At end of year:													
Total assets	$73,037	$70,029	$63,020	$56,983	$44,989	$37,461	$32,591	$29,586	$26,703	$24,529	$20,771	$18,978	$17,723
Net investment in plant, rental machines, and other property	23,426	22,967	21,310	19,713	16,396	16,142	17,563	16,797	15,017	12,193	9,302	7,889	7,341
Long-term debt	8,518	7,108	6,923	6,368	4,232	2,674	2,851	2,669	2,099	1,589	285	256	275
Stockholders' equity	39,509	38,263	34,374	31,990	26,489	23,219	19,960	17,676	16,453	14,961	13,493	12,618	12,749

[a]IBM financial statement, *Annual Report*, 1989, p. 43.
[b]*Moody's Industrial Manual*, 1989, p. 463.

EXHIBIT 2

FUJITSU: TWELVE-YEAR COMPARISON OF SELECTED FINANCIAL DATA[a] (in millions of U.S. dollars)

For the year:	1988	1987	1986	1985	1984	1983	1982	1981	1980	1979	1978	1977	1976
Net sales	$16,374	$12,256	$9,399	$6,175	$5,401	$3,987	$2,353	$2,769	$2,004	$2,100	$1,761	$1,171	$1,029
Net income	337	148	216	352	298	201	129	88	63	51	37	33	22
Return on stockholders' equity[a]	6.0%	3.6%	7.3%	16.2%	17.5%	15.1%	12.8%	13.1%	12.0%	10.3%	9.5%	10.5%	8.4%
At end of year:													
Total assets	18,533	13,686	10,399	6,801	5,699	4,181	3,482	2,691	2,005	2,107	1,829	1,381	1,138
Net investment in plant, rental machines, and other property	4,735	3,741	3,078	1,996	1,467	1,039	815	646	443	450	398	288	439
Long-term debt	2,413	2,313	1,978	998	915	526	340	317	263	240	190	142	137
Common equity	6,616	4,660	3,535	2,405	1,935	1,465	1,140	825	514	541	442	339	287

[a]All financial data are from Fujitsu's annual reports for current year. The exchange rate used in converting from yen to dollars ranged from ¥125 = US$1 in 1988 to ¥253 = US$1 in 1985, ¥224 = US$1 in 1984, and ¥300 = US$1 in 1975.

During the mid-1980s, IBM's market had begun to change. The computer industry shifted from emphasis on single, large, central processing units, typically mainframes, to networks of computers. Mainframe sales slowed; some forecasts showed them growing only 3% a year between 1986 and 1996. Analysts also predicted that the personal computer market would soon surpass the mainframe market in sales volume. Moreover, hardware revenues were expected to grow at only sightly more than a third of the 20% annual rate of growth predicted for software revenues in the late 1980s and 1990s. IBM was moving into these new areas, but it faced much greater competition there than in mainframes.

Fujitsu

In 1988, Fujitsu was Japan's largest computer maker and the third largest in the world. Fujitsu also sold telecommunications equipment, supercomputers, cellular telephones, and laptop computers. It was also one of the major Japanese semiconductor manufacturers, specializing in advanced logic chips and semiconductors made from advanced materials. *Fortune* described Fujitsu as "a technology-driven company run by engineers."[2]

Like IBM, Fujitsu depended heavily on mainframe sales (which accounted for more than 60% of its profits and 70% of its sales), it built most of the parts it used, and its culture was said to be a Japanese version of IBM's stern, non-nonsense approach. Fujitsu distributed internationally but had limited influence outside Japan. Its overseas sales amounted to only 23% of total revenues (about half of IBM's comparable figures), and its profit margins were less than half of IBM's 9.7%. (See Exhibit 2 for Fujitsu financial information.)

Many factors—including management talent, manufacturing skills, a booming national economy—had contributed to Fujitsu's success. In the early years, government policy also played an important role. For example, during the 1960s, the government raised the tariff on computer imports from 15% to 20%. It also compelled the weaker overseas computer makers that wanted to do business in Japan to create technology licensing agreements with Japanese firms. Hitachi linked up with RCA, Mitsubishi with TRW, NEC with Honeywell, and Toshiba with General Electric. In the early 1960s, the Ministry of International Trade and Industry secured basic patents from IBM in exchange for the right to produce computers in Japan and pressured Japanese firms to buy domestic machines, despite bitter complaints about their quality.

The government itself, which accounted for about a quarter of domestic computer sales during the 1960s and 1970s, bought domestic machines almost exclusively. To expand the market for computers, MITI helped create the Japan Electronic Computer Company. Although JECC was jointly owned by the major Japanese computer makers, the government lent it approximately $2 billion between 1961 and 1981 so it could buy computers from its member firms and then lease them to customers at low rates.

During the 1960s and 1970s, the government provided low-interest loans, tax benefits, loan guarantees, and subsidies for high-risk R&D efforts. In the early 1970s, for example, MITI provided more than $200 million for the "New Series" project, a response to IBM's 370 series. It required the six firms receiving funding to work in three separate, but coordinated groups, each concentrating on a different size of computer. Fujitsu and Hitachi were charged with entering the mainframe business. Fujitsu and Hitachi both chose a plug compatibility strategy. This meant their customers could buy mainframes and then run IBM applications software—programs for payroll, data processing, and other functions—on these machines.

Fujitsu's efforts benefitted from strategic alliance with Amdahl Corporation, a California-based manufacturer of mainframes founded by Gene Amdahl. Even though Amdahl had designed the IBM 360 computer, he had difficulty raising capital in the United States for his new firm, so he accepted a $5 million investment from Fujitsu. By the mid-1970s, Amdahl had built mainframes that outperformed IBM's 370 series. While Fujitsu executives left the day-to-day operation of Amdahl to its American managers, they sent teams of engineers to work at Amdahl and eventually increased Fujitsu's stake in the company to 44%.

Government funds also flowed into computer research through Nippon Telephone & Telegraph, the government monopoly that controlled the telephone system. NTT used these funds to finance research and development at Fujitsu, NEC, Oki and Hitachi, its principal suppliers. To help Japanese firms learn to make very large integrated circuits, MITI provided nearly $200 million in funding to two groups of laboratories, one at Mitsubishi, Fujitsu, and Hitachi and the other at Toshiba and NEC.

In 1981, MITI and the major Japanese computer firms announced their Fifth-Generation computer project. Japanese firms believed they had caught up with IBM, at least in technology, but wanted to set industry standards themselves rather than play follow the leader. The Fifth-Generation project aimed to enable computers to recognize Japanese characters, recognize voices, process images, and even think— through artificial intelligence. These computers would be "knowledge processors," not mere data processors, and like humans, they would learn, associate, and draw inferences from information.

By the early 1980s, Fujitsu was the center of an industrial group. The Fujitsu Group had nearly two hundred subsidiaries and approximately fifty affiliated companies, which competed in the electronics industry, trading, chemicals, and several service industries. Fujitsu was also the principal electronics and communications firm in the large industrial group—or "keiretsu"—centered on the Dai-Ichi Kangyo Bank. DKB was one of the eight major industrial groups in Japan. Its member firms were part of a loose federation overseen by a presidential council, the "Sankin-Kai." This body consisted of the presidents of the leading companies in the DKB group. It met every month so members could exchange views on the general economic and financial situation, promising business opportunities, the maintenance of intragroup trademarks, and labor problems. The presidential council was not a policy-making body and Japanese observers said it was simply a forum to encourage friendship among presidents of group companies. Each company, they stressed, was independent and none was bound by the decisions or recommendations of the council.

By the mid-1980s, some Fujitsu mainframes outperformed comparable IBM products on a price-performance basis. By 1986, Fujitsu and NEC were the second- and third-largest mainframe makers in the world, and Hitachi ranked fifth. Amdahl was also prospering. In 1988, it had begun to sell new Fujitsu-made disc drives and controllers, along with new Fujitsu-supplied large-scale microprocessors that had almost a 50% performance edge over comparable IBM units and were cheaper, smaller and lighter. Traditional IBM customers, such as Monsanto, General Electric, and General Motors' EDS subsidiary, had ordered the Amdahl machine.

Fujitsu was also expanding its overseas efforts through alliances with smaller companies. For example, in 1987 it bought Intellistor, a Colorado-based firm specializing in computer memories. While Intellistor had some impressive advanced technologies, its financial position was marginal. The Fujitsu acquisition brought it stability and the opportunity for engineers from both companies to share their expertise.

Fujitsu's success had taken a toll on IBM Japan. It held less than 30% of the Japanese computer market, by far the lowest market share of any IBM subsidiary around the world. In 1978, Fujitsu's domestic computer revenue had surpassed IBM's, as did NEC's in 1986. In response, "IBM Japan had dramatically changed its way of doing business. It forged alliances with scores of other firms in Japan, ranging from giants like Nippon Steel and the Mitsubishi Bank, to tiny software houses, all in an effort to turn itself into a version of a Japanese industrial group.

Despite its success, Fujitsu viewed itself, as did many outside observers, as an underdog in its contest with IBM. During the early 1980s, the sales of IBM's Japanese subsidiary alone were almost as large as Fujitsu's worldwide sales. In the minds of the Japanese the IBM-Hitachi conflict "symbolized the ever-present threat of an IBM so powerful it could squash its competitors."[3]

While Fujitsu's domestic sales were growing very strongly, its foreign sales had suffered from IBM's allegations about Fujitsu's behavior and their protracted dispute. Fujitsu's European distributor, Siemens-AG, stopped selling Fujitsu equipment in 1986 after IBM alleged copyright infringement. According to one press report, some Siemens customers were embarrassed by surprise visits from auditors sent by IBM to determine the type of software they were using.

THE CENTRAL DISPUTE

The IBM-Fujitsu dispute was the most prominent in a long series of commercial and trade battles over technology. These controversies increasingly focused on protection of intellectual property rights, particularly for software and patents. The costs of developing new products and the increasing ease of copying, cloning, and improvement engineering exacerbated the problem. Disputes between nations were numerous, and many companies were involved in protracted litigation.

Trade negotiation bodies, such as the General Agreement on Tariffs and Trade (GATT), were trying to create minimum standards for protecting intellectual property and mechanisms for resolving disputes. Some countries had enacted new legislation. In 1988, for example, a new U.S. trade law made it easier to limit and penalize imports that infringed upon American patents.

While U.S. trade policy treated intellectual property rights as its most important trade issue—after farm products—not all countries endorsed stronger protection. Developing nations, such as Brazil, believed stronger protection kept them dependent on the technology and creativity of the industrialized world and stopped them from developing local capabilities to invent and create. Believing "knowledge was the heritage of all mankind," these countries viewed protection as "denying them the educational and instructional tools available from copyrighted works and the social and industrial contributions of patented products." Protection, they believed, made these tools and contributions too expensive for developing countries and available only under conditions that "violated the sovereignty of those countries."[4]

Operating system software stood at the center of the dispute between IBM and Fujitsu. IBM's principal charge was that Fujitsu had violated IBM's intellectual property rights in the operating system software it had developed. IBM had dominated the world market for operating system software for mainframe computers. During the 1980s, the price of its software products grew at a compound annual rate of 28%.

An operating system is a collection of software that controls a computer's inner workings. Typically, it coordinates the flow of data between the computer's memory and peripheral devices like disc drives, keyboards, and printers, performs basic housekeeping functions for the computer system, and enables the computer to execute applications programs.

System software is like the phonograph stylus that turns the grooves on a record into music.[5] The better the operating system's design, the more efficiently applications software runs on it. Moreover, the operating system of a mainframe determines whether competitors' products such as disk drives, personal computers, and other software can be used with the mainframe. According to some computer experts, operating systems are the principal products of the industry and are critical to securing hardware orders.

This software was among the most complex programs in existence, with millions of lines of code, and IBM had thousands of programmers working continuously to develop it. Developing alternative products was extremely difficult: Amdahl, for example, spent six years and $10 million in such an effort and then gave up in 1988 because it concluded customers would not want to risk an alternative to IBM system software, especially when they already had millions of dollars of customized software written for IBM mainframes and operating system software.

Operating system software contains two kinds of information. One type tells what a computer does. Customers and others get this information so they can determine what peripheral equipment will be compatible with the computer or so they can write applications programs the computer can run. The second kind of information tells *how* the computer does what it does. Fujitsu had sought the second, more sensitive information because it believed it was necessary for designing IBM-compatible mainframes, and IBM objected strongly to this.

In the 1970s, when Fujitsu developed its first IBM-compatible operating systems, its programmers made substantial use of IBM programming material.[6] Fujitsu's later operating systems, which it developed and introduced in the early 1980s, relied in part on its earlier systems and the IBM material included in them. IBM first sought U.S. copyrights for its operating system software in 1978. At the time, however, it was unclear whether Japanese or American copyright law protected operating system software. (This uncertainty was reduced in 1983 when a U.S. appeals court ruled that copyright protection did extend to operating systems, but the scope of protection for interface information remained unclear.)

Moreover, IBM had not clearly distinguished information about the internal design of its operating systems from interface information that outsiders could use. Interface information is like the specifications for plugs and holes in the back of a stereo amplifier, as opposed to information about the amplifier's internal design. IBM had revealed internal design information to customers, so they could develop their own applications software, and to independent software developers. Nevertheless, IBM and Fujitsu disagreed sharply about whether Fujitsu was right to use this information in developing its early operating systems.

INTELLECTUAL PROPERTY LAWS IN AMERICA AND JAPAN

Legal protection for intellectual property differs between the United States and Japan. (In many respects the Japanese approach is closer to that of Continental Europe.) Copyright, patent, and trade secret laws in the countries differ between the United States and Japan, as do the legal theories justifying the protection. Under these laws, protection for computer software was ambiguous in both countries.

Copyrights

A copyright, in essence, protects the expression of an idea. Both American and Japanese systems protect the particular form in which an idea is expressed but not the underlying idea. Under both systems, the work must be original and fall within the broad realms of literature, science, fine arts, or music to be eligible for protection.

Until 1985, American and Japanese systems' copyright protection differed in duration. Generally, U.S. law gave works created on or after January 1, 1978, copyright protection for life of the author, plus 50 years after the author's death. Japan formerly protected the work for only 20 years from the date of granting of the copyright, but in 1985 it adopted provisions like those in the United States.

Copyright infringement is the violation of any of the copyright owner's exclusive rights. Japan, however, permitted uses of copyrighted material that American law scrutinized more carefully. For example, under Japanese law a user of a copyrighted computer program could debug and upgrade it, and even modify it for the purpose of replacement. Japanese copyright law also left ambiguous the distinction between upgrading and revising a computer program.

Patents

Patents, in essence, protect ownership rights in ways of doing things. American and Japanese patent law systems both required that patentable inventions be novel or contain an inventive step, and be nonobvious or useful. Both covered processes as well as products, and improvements to either.

Japan and most industrialized countries gave priority to the first of competing patent applicants to file an application for the patent on the technology. The United States granted the patent to the first to invent.

In general, a Japanese patent covered a single claim or novel advance. American patents, in contrast, often listed several independently valid claims. This compels Japanese inventors to file more patents to cover a single technology. In 1983, for example, about 100,000 patent applications were filed in the United States, while more than 250,000 were filed in Japan.[7]

Japanese law, unlike U.S. law, permitted the government to grant other parties the right to use an invention if an inventor failed to do so or if working the patent would serve the public interest. This created incentives to make a patent as *narrow* as possible to maintain its exclusivity and, hence, its economic value. Multiple, narrow patents were each more likely to be worked sufficiently, and a narrow patent had more limited economic consequences than one encompassing a class of related inventions.

The application process in the two countries also differed. The U.S. system examined patent applications in the order in which applicants filed them. Japan examined applications only at the patent applicant's request and could defer examination for up to seven years. Confidentiality of the patent application was absolute in the United States; publication followed the grant of the patent, at which time the patentee could take legal action for copying and other infringement. Patent applications in Japan were published or "laid open" after 18 months, often before the patent was granted. Opponents of the grant of a patent could oppose it during the three months after examination was requested and before the patent was granted. In the United States, opponents had to wait until the patent was granted.

Some analysts believed that Japan's "laying open" of patent applications promoted a practice called "patent flooding": competitors would file multiple improvement patents to force the inventor to cross-license its technology rather than defend the patent in litigation. Protection of rights in the technology also depended on the length of time between filing a patent application and the issuing of a patent on the technology. That period in Japan averaged six years, compared to a 20-month average in the United States.

Trade Secrets

Most U.S. states defined trade secrets as any "formula, pattern, device, or compilation of information used in one's business and which gives him an opportunity to obtain an advantage over competitors who do not know or use it."[8] Examples included chemical formulas, manufacturing processes, machine patterns, and customer lists. Japan did not identify any such trade secrets by statute, but it did protect trade secrets covered by contract.

U.S. law provided several ways of protecting trade secrets: trade secret and criminal statutes, explicit contracts such as postemployment noncompetition agreements and nondisclosure agreements, and implied contracts, created by special relationships such as licensor/licensee. Japan relied only on contracts.

In both countries, victims of infringement could seek damages and criminal sanctions. In the United States, however, it was easier to get a court injunction halting the infringement; and unlike Japan, the United States had criminal sanctions covering infringement.

IMITATION IN JAPANESE CULTURE

The many, heated intellectual property disputes between American and Japanese companies led some observers to seek cultural perspectives on the issues. The most controversial of these, and perhaps the most common, was the view that Japanese culture sanctioned imitation to a greater degree than the American.

Proponents of this view emphasized that Japan has borrowed extensively from foreign cultures. Through contacts with China, for example, Japan imitated elements of Chinese culture, adopting a Chinese-style legal code as the basis for the criminal and administrative codes of its legal system. During the nineteenth century, Japan emulated European and American technology. Meiji Japan consciously imitated European and American organizational models in developing its postal and police systems and its newspapers. Japan selected its parliamentary system of government from among American and European models, and Germanic law informed Japan's civil law system, as did Anglo-American influences during the postwar occupation period.

Japanese artists have traditionally studied their crafts in apprenticeships and learned technique by copying that of the master. Between 1750 and 1850, Japanese artists, particularly Hokusai and Hiroshige, learned by imitating: their works and sketches originated in the drawings of seventh-century Buddhist figures. Masters generated schools of artists, whose followers produced works in a particular style. Japanese artists did not begin to sign their works until the sixteenth century. The Zen tradition of repetition of a task or skill to yield mastery or perfection also greatly influenced and informed the arts, as well as other aspects of Japanese culture.

Scholars who have studied the history of Japanese fine arts have acknowledged a tendency toward imitation. One wrote, for example:

> It has been remarked that a pupil's training consists in copying and recopying his master's works and that there are model-books which show the proper method of painting various subjects. So much stress upon tradition, at once a safeguard against radicalism and an obstacle to free development, naturally gave birth to pronounced school mannerisms and to restrictions which extend even to choice of subject and result in inevitable repetition. . . . It is probable, however, that the special references in the "Six Canons"

[a classic guide to Japanese painting] to copying old masters was not intended to mean mere copying; rather it should be interpreted as emphasizing the importance of preserving that part of tradition which ever lies as an eternal principle and of transmitting it to the next generation.[9]

Explanations of Japan's alleged tendency to emulation are diverse. Some suggest it is Japanese openness to other cultures. The Dutch journalist Karel Van Wolferen, a long-time resident of Japan, asserts that Japanese culture is based on "the notion that there is a perfect way of doing things . . . that mastery is reached by the removal of the obstacles between the self and the perfect model, embodied by the teacher, a view which emphasizes great technical skill with a lack of personal expression, there is no room for the idiosyncratic individual."[10] In this view, imitation of aspects of Chinese, European, or American civilizations is part of Japan's "catching-up disposition," emulation deriving not merely from pursuit of perfection, but also from a self-perception of "falling short."

In contrast, other writers attributed cultural emulation to Japanese self-assertion, viewing it as an effort to make Japan respected internationally. Still others argued that Japan was seeking to prevent any one nation from becoming indispensable to its modernization, while some believed Japan sought not only to hold its own but ultimately to grow dominant.

The view of Japan as a peculiarly imitative nation was often criticized for bias. Some historical studies pointed to Japanese creativity. Its postal and police systems and its newspapers had been interpreted as examples of rapid, innovative adaptations of overseas models to Japanese circumstances. Other studies noted that numerous schools of artists existed in Japan, often at the same time and new masters often emerged, establishing new schools and traditions. Even Zen acts of repetition had been interpreted variously. Former Harvard professor and ambassador to Japan Edwin Reischauer saw them as triumphs of individualism and innovation—the application of one's whole being to a task and a reliance on individual will, discovery, and self-discipline to master a practice or an idea.

Emulation was hardly unique to Japan, so the whole copying issue was a question of degree. Many other nations have looked to other nations' cultures and civilizations when developing their own. For example, British industrialists were horrified at the quality of the American guns on display at the Great Exhibition in London in 1851. They believed the Americans had unfairly appropriated British designs. In later decades, the British made similar complaints about German and American efforts in synthetic dyes, metals, armaments, penicillin, radar and computerized tomography. Japan's defenders also pointed out that by 1986 Japan had a higher percentage of its population engaged in R&D than America, and by the mid-1980s it accounted for 20% of new ceramics patents, 26% in communication equipment, and 33% in office-computing and accounting machines.

CONCLUSION

The two arbitrators confronted a wide range of questions. Did Fujitsu violate IBM's intellectual property rights in the early 1970s, before IBM sought a U.S. copyright for its system software? Did Fujitsu violate IBM's rights in subsequent years? What compensation, if any, was IBM owed? On what terms, if any, could Fujitsu inspect and use IBM programming material for system software in the future? To what extent should the arbitrators consider the interests of computer customers in making their decision? What precedent would their decision create for other intellectual property disputes?

The arbitrators' challenge was compounded by the acrimony between the companies. One arbitrator commented: "These two parties have hardly been able to agree what color a stoplight is."

SOURCES

In addition to the documents cited in the notes, the data in this case were drawn from articles in the general business press and more specialized publications covering the computer industry.

The discussion of Japanese culture and emulation draws, in part, upon D. Eleanor Westney, *Imitation and Innovation: The Transfer of Western Organizational Patterns to Meiji Japan* (Cambridge: Harvard University Press, 1987); William Watson, ed., *Artistic Personality and Decorative Style in Japanese Art* (London: University of London Colloquies on Art and Archeology in Asia, no. 6, 1976); and Henry P. Bowie, *On the Laws of Japanese Painting* (New York: Dover Publications, 1951).

The section on intellectual property laws in the United States and Japan is intended for background information only. It is not legal advice. This section draws upon the following sources: Jay

Dratler, Jr., "Trade Secrets in the United States and Japan: A Comparison and Prognosis, 14 *Yale Journal of International Law* 68 (1989); Michael A. Epstein, *Modern Intellectual Property* (New York: Law & Business Inc./Harcourt Brace Jovanovich, 1989); Tohru Nakajima, "Legal Protection of Computer Programs in Japan: The Conflict Between Economic and Artistic Goals," *Columbia Journal of Transnational Law* 143 (1988), p. 27; Robert P. Benko, *Protecting Intellectual Property Rights: Issues and Controversies* (Washington, D.C.: American Enterprise Institute for Public Policy Research, 1987); Mary Ann Glendon, Michael Wallace Gordon, and Christopher Osakwe, *Comparative Legal Traditions: Text, Materials and Cases* (St. Paul, Minn.: West Publishing Co., 1958); Robert W. Russell, compiler, *Patents and Trademarks in Japan (A Handy Book)* (Tokyo, Japan, 1984); Fenwick, Stone, Davis & West, "Legal Protection of Computer Software in Japan," in Miles R. Gilburne, [symposium] chairman, *Intellectual Property Rights in High Technology Products and Sensitive Business Information* (New York: Law and Business, Inc./Harcourt Brace Jovanovich, 1982); Earl W. Kitner and Jack Lahr, *An Intellectual Property Law Primer: A Survey of the Law of Patents, Trade Secrets, Trademarks, Franchises, Copyrights and Personality and Entertainment Rights* (New York: Clark Boardman Company Ltd., 1982); and Tervo Doi, *The Intellectual Property Law of Japan* (Alphen aan den rijn; Germantown, Nd.: Sijhoff and Noordhoff, 1980).

NOTES

1 Marie Anchordoguy, *Computers Incorporated* (Cambridge, MA: Council on East Asian Studies, Harvard University, 1989), p. 1.
2 Brenton R. Schlender, "How Fujitsu Will Tackle the Giants," *Fortune,* July 1, 1991, p. 82.
3 Marie Anchordoguy, *Computers Incorporated,* p. 2.
4 Helena Stalson, *Intellectual Property Rights and U.S. Competitiveness in Trade* (Washington, D.C.: National Planning Association, 1987), p. 48.
5 Michael Miller, "Fujitsu Can Legally Clone IBM Software: The Question Now, Will It Be Able To?" *Wall Street Journal,* December 1, 1988, p. B1.
6 This account of the dispute is based upon *International Business Machines Corporation v. Fujitsu Limited,* American Arbitration Association, Commercial Arbitration Tribunal Opinion, Case No. 13T-117-0636-85, November 29, 1988.

7 Krista McQuade and Professor Gomes-Casseres, "Fusion Systems Corporation," HBS Case No. 390.021, 1990.

8 Restatement of Torts §757, comment (b)(1939) as cited in Michael A. Epstein, *Modern Intellectual Property* (New York: Law & Business, Inc./Harcourt Brace Jovanovich, 1989), p. 3, n.3.

9 Kojiro Tomita, "Art—Far Eastern Methods," in *Japanese Art: A Selection from the Encyclopedia Britannica* (New York: Encyclopedia Britannica, 1933), p. 34.

10 Karel Van Wolferen, *The Enigma of Japanese Power: People and Politics in a Stateless Nation* (Knopf, 1989), pp. 378–379.

Key Ethical Concepts in Business Ethics

The following discussions of key concepts in business ethics were developed for the Committee for Education in Business Ethics of the American Philosophical Association and are useful in the analysis of ethical issues raised in case studies. Professor Kurt Baier wrote the analysis of the following: obligation, autonomy-dependence-paternalism, freedom, justice, self-respect and dignity. Professor Norman Bowie wrote the analysis of rights. Excerpts from Professor Baier's discussion of honesty, fidelity, and loyalty are included in Chapter 9.

OBLIGATION

For Smith to have an obligation or to be obligated to do A means that there is some act, A, by Smith which it would be wrong for him not to perform. Obligations can come into being in various ways. They may be incurred, as when a person causes another harm thus incurring the obligation to repair the harm done; or they may be assumed as when someone promises or undertakes to do something; or they may be imposed on others as when someone with authority to do so, orders someone under his authority to do something within the scope of his authority. If the obligation is *to* someone, Jones, then that person may release Smith from the obligation, thus making it not wrong for him not to perform A, or to set in motion some corrective machinery either punishing Smith or compensating Jones for Smith's failure.

Obligations should be contrasted with permissions. If you are permitted to do A, your not doing A is not wrong. If you are obligated to do A, your not doing A is wrong. Moreover, note that if you are obligated to do S, you are still physically free not to do it even though morality requires that you do it. In other words, obligation must not be confused with compulsion or force. Finally, the content of obligations may vary; obligations may be arbitrarily delimited in time and person as when I promise not to look until you count to ten: I am not obligated not to look, after you have reached ten, nor need anyone else be obligated not to look. Hence, obligations do not necessarily depend on the nature of the conduct in question or on its consequences. In this way obligations can be distinguished from intrinsic wrongs like killing or lying.

AUTONOMY—DEPENDENCE—PATERNALISM

Autonomy is either a psychological condition, reached by all normal adults, of being able to make rational decisions about what to do, or a right to make and act on such decisions. Dependence is the opposite of autonomy. It refers either to a psychological condition in which someone is in the habit of acting in accordance with the decisions made by someone else, usually one person such as his father or teacher on whom he is said to be dependent, or else to a legal or conventional position of dependence, in which a person (say, a minor) is conventionally precluded from making legally effective decisions on certain matters, as when he needs the approval, consent, or permission of a parent or guardian.

Paternalism is the view that in certain conditions people's autonomy should be disregarded, whether by the state (legal paternalism) or by other individuals, that they should not be asked or allowed to make decisions on certain matters, if it is clear to (specified) others that their decisions would gravely, perhaps irreversibly, affect their own good, as when a person decided to commit suicide, to take up heroin, or to embark on an extremely hazardous enterprise. Mill, the most widely respected anti-paternalist, opposed only the strong form of paternalism which insists that a person should not be permitted to harm himself even when he acts of his own free will and in full knowledge of the harm involved in his act. He did not object to interference where the person is not acting voluntarily (as when he is delirious, under hypnosis, or in a state of uncontrollable excitement) or is not adequately informed (as when he does not know the gun is loaded, the bridge is unsafe, or the drug lethal). However, Mill himself would seem to have embraced the strong principle of paternalism when he argued that no one should be allowed to sell himself into slavery, on the grounds that "the principle of freedom cannot require that he should be free not to be free." It is not clear to me why the principle of freedom, i.e., autonomy—that every man has a right to determine the shape of his own life, whatever the effect on his own balance of goods—should not require this. In any case, it is worth noting that the strong form of paternalism is incompatible with Mill's first principle, the so-called "harm principle," which says that the only purpose for which people may be coerced by law is to protect *others* from harm they would, if not coerced, be inflicting on them.

FREEDOM

Freedom, in the important sense, with which we are concerned here, is a certain sort of ideal condition or state of affairs, considered by some to be so central to human lives that they are willing to fight in its defense or promotion. This condition concerns the structure of and relation between political societies. It is either the freedom *of* or *for* such societies, that is, their independence or autonomy or self-government. Or it is the freedom *in* such societies, consisting in the freedom *of* or *for* its citizens, that is, freedom for their major pursuits: freedom of religion, association, movement, economic enterprise, speech and communication, and so on, or the untrammelled functioning of the institutions promoting these activities: freedom of or for the press, the churches, the parties, the universities, the corporations. Societies can be less or more free in either or both of these two ways. A colony may be completely unfree, that is wholly governed by the mother country, but there may be complete freedom in that society. Conversely, after "liberation," the society may be wholly self-governing, but there may be little freedom in the newly sovereign society.

We think of freedom as tending towards a limit, complete freedom, beyond which it is impossible further to reform the society in respect of the extent of freedom. In such a completely free society, everyone is *free to do* what he ought to be free to do. And he ought to be free to do whatever he can do without thereby preventing others from doing what they ought to be free to do. Complete freedom thus prevails in a society if everyone has the greatest *possible extent* of freedom compatible with a like extent of freedom for everyone. That implies (i) that the law forbids no one to do anything he ought to be free to do, (ii) that it forbids people including government officials to interfere with other people's doing what they ought to be free to do, and (iii) that it has institutions designed to ensure that the substantive principles determining what people ought to be free to do are continually clarified and properly applied to individual cases as social conditions change.

Regarding the freedom of citizens in a society, some philosophers have distinguished between positive and negative freedom. Negative freedom is simply the absence of external constraints. For example, the freedom of speech is a negative freedom. We are free to speak our mind because there are no laws prohibiting it. The concept of positive liberty is a little harder to capture. The British philosopher Isaiah Berlin defines it as self-mastery. One lacks positive freedom if one cannot reach some end for reasons such as indecisiveness, compulsive desires or perhaps ignorance. Consider an alcoholic trying to stop drinking. No one forces him to take that drink, so he is, in the negative sense, free to drink or not. But his compulsion to drink is so strong, that he cannot help himself. Berlin would say he lacked freedom in the positive sense. Other philosophers suggest that rather than distinguish between types of freedom, we should define freedom simply as absence of constraints and distinguish between internal and external constraints.

JUSTICE

Justice can be considered as a social ideal. While freedom is concerned essentially with mutual non-interference, with what people must (or need not) refrain from doing in order that others be able to do what they want to do, justice is concerned with determining *what is due from whom to whom.* It is often said that "a society is perfectly just if and only if everyone gets what is his due." I accept this for the present occasion, though I shall add the proviso: "and it has institutions designed to see to it that people get their due." These institutions serve two major tasks: determining *what* is due and distributing what is due either as benefits or sanctions.

Accordingly, we can distinguish various kinds of justice. We can distinguish, "horizontally," so to speak, between various domains of justice, such as distributive, economic, criminal, legal, parental, social, or cosmic justice. And we can distinguish "vertically," so to speak, between the first-order or declarative, and the second-order, or corrective levels of justice. An example may help make this distinction clearer. Thus horizontally, criminal justice covers a certain area, distinguishing it from economic justice. Vertically at first-order level, criminal justice determines what are crimes, that is, modes of behavior deserving the criminal sanctions (punishment). At the second-order or corrective level, criminal justice determines who, if anyone, has engaged in such criminal behavior and precisely what sanctions are to be imposed on him or her. Another example is obtained from the area lawyers call torts. The first-order level determines what sorts of behavior are torts, that is, behavior for which the agent deserves to be made to pay compensation. The second-order level determines who has become liable to pay compensation, to whom, and how much.

No one has so far worked out the proper relationship between these various domains of justice. Even the contemporary philosopher John Rawls speaks only of what he calls social or distributive justice, not the whole of justice. Moreover, Rawls does not make completely clear what exactly is to be included in his treatment. He refers to what he calls the basic structure of society, but he does not clearly identify precisely which institutions in our society are to be considered part of the basic structure. Does it, for instance, include the relation between the members of a family? If not, why is not this part of the basic structure? It surely is a very important factor in determining the character of the lives of those involved. And if it is part of the basic structure, then he does not make clear how his two principles of justice are to apply to it and how the roles of husband, wife, and child, are to be incorporated in the system of roles created by the economic and other institutions of our society.

Nevertheless, it is perhaps worth stating Rawls' two by now famous principles of social justice:

1st principle: each person is to have an equal right to the most extensive total system of equal basic liberties compatible with a similar system of liberty for all.

2nd principle: social and economic inequalities are to be arranged so that they are both (a) to the greatest benefit of the least advantaged and (b) attached to offices and positions open to all under conditions of fair equality of opportunity.

Priority Rule: The principles of justice are to be ranked in lexical order and therefore liberty can be restricted only for the sake of liberty.

SELF-RESPECT AND DIGNITY

Self-respect is normally respect for oneself as a person. A person has respect or is shown respect when his or her interests are taken into account and when his or her rights are honored. What these claims and rights are is contentious, but they include claims concerning life and health, claims to be dealt with honestly, and claims to be dealt with in a manner befitting the dignity of mankind.

To have self-respect, then, is to take seriously the claims and rights one has, simply on the grounds that one is a person. Hence one lacks self-respect if he or she is servile or craven, allows himself or herself to be humiliated or exploited without protest, fails to stand up for his or her rights, or submits to indignities as if he or she did not deserve any better, and so on. Such behavior suggests or implies that he or she does not think he or she has the basic rights of a person.

To lack self-respect in this sense is not a matter of degree: one either has it or one lacks it. However, people can differ from one another in respect of *how strong* their self-respect is, how easily they lose it under pressure, how firmly their readiness to stand up for their rights is entrenched, how sure they are of their basic rights as persons. Jones cannot (in this sense) have greater or a higher degree of self-respect than Smith, but his self-respect can be stronger, firmer, more deeply entrenched than Smith's.

Self-respect as a tendency to behave in certain ways on account of taking seriously the claims or rights one has as a person, should perhaps be distinguished from self-respect as a species of self-esteem, that is, respect for oneself by comparison with others. In this second sense, self-respect is a matter of degree. One may respect oneself more than one respects some other person, and more at one time than another. Self-respect in this sense is the opposite of self-contempt. It is not a tendency to behave in a right- or claim-respecting way, but simply represents a favorable opinion of oneself based on a comparison of one's worth with that of others. But while in cases of self-esteem the basis of the comparison may be any type of excellence, in cases of self-respect the basis is always a suitable character trait. One respects oneself as a consequence of a favorable comparative judgment based on the sorts of character traits, e.g., honesty, truthfulness, fidelity, trustworthiness, justice, rectitude, which one must have if one respects others as persons. Thus, self-respect in this second sense is simply self-esteem based on certain moral characteristics relevant to self-respect in the first sense.

Dignity is ordinarily a characteristic of persons: the self-assurance and poise acquired when one has no doubt about one's own worth and its recognition by others. Dignity is closely related to self-respect. To be subjected to indignities is to be treated in ways which tend to undermine one's self-respect and rob one of one's dignity. Such treatment is incompatible with the dignity of persons. Ordinarily, the rights and claims related to the dignity of persons are concerned primarily with the person's sense of his own worth. Insults, humiliations, degradations, ridicule, public mockery, are typical forms of such behavior. However, some philosophers have used "self-respect" in a much wider sense, involving all those rights and claims which a person respects who respects another as a person, e.g., the right to honesty, fidelity, or fairness.

RIGHTS

What are rights? They are moral entitlements—moral claims we can make against other persons and against institutions. They usually invoke corresponding duties on the part of others—be they persons or institutions. American democracy was born in a time when ethics was dominated by a philosophy of rights:

> We hold these truths to be self-evident: that all men are endowed by their Creator with certain unalienable rights; that among these are life, liberty, and the pursuit of happiness.

Since Great Britain had allegedly denied these rights, the signers of the Declaration of Independence believed they had moral justification for rebelling. During the transition of the United States from a confederation to a federation, many individual states adopted the constitution only if a series of amendments (now called the Bill of Rights) were enacted to protect individuals from the state. The Bill of Rights is a statement of the moral entitlements that individuals have against the state. In political philosophy the vocabulary of rights has long been in use.

But what kinds of rights are there and more specifically what rights do we have? Basically rights have been divided into two classes, those which are created by societal agreement—e.g., rights created by a collective bargaining agreement, and rights persons have independently of any societal agreement.

These latter are called natural rights. The rights referred to in the Declaration of Independence are natural rights. They are the rights that individual persons have against all social institutions. Rather than being created by society, natural rights are entitlements that morally constrain how social institutions ought to develop.

But how does one prove that one has natural rights? Those within the Roman Catholic tradition utilize the language of the Declaration of Independence. Just as God created laws of nature which transcend different cultures and which are available to human reason, so God created laws of morality which transcend different cultures and which are available to human reason. Applied ethics is the application of these universal laws to particular historical circumstances and business ethics is the application of these universal moral norms to business.

With the rise of secularism in intellectual life, Roman Catholic natural law philosophy declined in influence. Certain individualist philosophers, like John Locke, narrowed the natural law tradition to claims of individual natural rights which were taken to be self-evident. As a result of these claims of self-evidence in conjunction with so many competing theories of the natural rights, serious questions have been raised as to whether natural rights could be justified at all. As a result, the natural rights philosophy did not fair well in competition with the ethical philosophy of utilitarianism. One of the chief intellectual spokesmen of utilitarianism, Jeremy Bentham, referred to natural rights as "nonsense on stilts."

Still additional problems were created when defenders of natural rights sought empirical support for the view that natural rights were possessed equally by all men and women. Whatever characteristic one picked out—intelligence, virtue, physical similarity—were all distributed unequally. If such characteristics were distributed unequally, how could they be the basis for an egalitarian theory of individual rights?

In the last few years there has been a tremendous resurgence in the philosophy of natural rights. Now there are a number of new proofs justifying their existence. All the arguments have as their starting point human experience. One then asks what must be presupposed to make sense of (explain) that experience. In every case the answer is *natural* (or as they are now sometimes called *human*) rights.

One of the chief characteristics of human beings is that they engage in moral discourse. Several philosophers (A. Phillips Griffiths, A. I. Melden, Robert Simon, and Richard Wasserstrom) argue that natural rights must be presupposed to account for our use of moral language and moral concepts. The following quotation is illustrative:

> Rights, we are suggesting, are fundamental moral commodities because they enable us to stand up on our own two feet, "to look others in the eye," and to feel in some fundamental way the equal of anyone. To think of oneself as

the holder of rights is not to be unduly but properly proud, to have that minimal self-respect that is necessary to be worthy of the love and esteem of others. Conversely, to lack the concept of oneself as a rights bearer is to be bereft of a significant element of human dignity. Without such a concept, we could not view ourselves as beings entitled to be treated as not simply means but ends as well.

Alan Gewirth starts with the fact that human beings are purposive agents. As purposive agents they must claim natural rights to freedom and well being since freedom and well being are the necessary conditions for purposive action. Each of the arguments is long and complicated and beyond the scope of this analysis. However, serious, able and sophisticated scholars are once again taking rights seriously.

If one successfully justifies the existence of natural rights, then the controversy focuses on the natural rights we have. All natural rights philosophers agree that we have a natural right to liberty although they disagree as to what liberty is. The natural right to liberty is especially central to libertarian political philosophy. The legal philosopher H. L. A. Hart has argued that all other rights have as a necessary condition the natural right to liberty.

Many other philosophers argue that persons also have a natural right to a minimum standard of well being. Libertarian philosophers reject the notion of such a natural right on the grounds that such a right cannot be universal (given the scarcity of material resources in some countries) and that such a right depends on the state. Proponents of the right concede that implementation of the right may depend on material circumstances and may need the support of the state. Such a concession would not show that a right is not universal. Moreover, the same arguments that establish a natural right to liberty establish a natural right to a minimum standard of well being.

Glossary for Business Ethics

Some of the definitions below are derived from the list of "key ethical concepts" developed for the Committee for Education in Business Ethics of the American Philosophical Association. Definitions of those concepts were written by Kurt Baier and Norman Bowie.

abstraction: The act of thinking about something in terms of some but not all of its characteristics. Can also apply to actions that deal with people in a way that fails to acknowledge their full humanity, as when we speak of workers as merely another variable in a production process.

act utilitarianism: That form of utilitarianism in which every action is to be judged by standards of utility rather than by rules which are derived from utilitarian considerations. *See* **rule utilitarianism.**

argument: A series of statements that are related in such a way that some of the statements, called premises, are said to provide proof for another statement, referred to as the conclusion.

autonomy: The term literally means "self-legislated." For Kant, autonomy was a key notion for morality, since an act can have moral significance only if it is willed freely by a rational being and without compulsion.

bad faith: A phrase used by Jean-Paul Sartre for human self-deception in which we blame others for actions that we have freely chosen. The central feature of bad faith is that the deceiver and the deceived are one and the same.

capitalism: An economic system in which the means of production are privately owned and government does not interfere with the free market forces of supply and demand.

casuistry: A view in ethics that right conduct is to be achieved by the application of rules to particular cases. The term has taken on a negative sense because this approach frequently leads to ever more complex and subtle rules for defining right from wrong.

categorical imperative: For Kant, the unconditional moral law that can be expressed as the rule that we should act on that principle that we could make a universal law. If we cannot universalize our principle without contradiction, the action resulting from the principle is immoral.

command economy: An economic system in which decisions about prices and resource allocation are made by a central governmental authority.

communitarian capitalism: Harvard professor George C. Lodge's phrase for German and Japanese forms of capitalism that stress teamwork and social values, as opposed to **individualistic capitalism.**

consequentialist ethics: Ethics that assess actions as right or wrong on the basis of the consequences generated by those actions.

consistency: In logic, a proposition or set of propositions is consistent when there is no interpretation of them that generates a contradiction. When applied to moral actions, consistency is the characteristic of following the same principle, given the same circumstances, at all times.

cultural relativism: The claim that there are no cross-cultural standards of right and wrong and that each culture or society determines its own moral values, which are as correct as those of any other culture even though they differ.

demand economy: An economic system in which prices and resource allocation are determined by market forces rather than by a central governmental authority.

deontological: Derived from the Greek word for obligation and refers to any ethical system in which the morality of an action depends on one's acting out of a sense of duty and not for the sake of consequences.

depersonalization: In contemporary moral philosophy, persons are to be distinguished from things and are to be treated with respect in a way that acknowledges their dignity. To treat persons as things, thereby robbing them of dignity and respect, is to depersonalize them. In the language of Martin Buber, depersonalization would be to treat a *thou* as an *it*.

dialectic: In contemporary usage the term can refer to difficulties one encounters when faced by two opposite views, neither of which is adequate as an explanatory principle. In such cases one can speak of a dialectical tension which prevents the resolution of the issue in terms of either pole of the dialectic. This usage is derivative from Kant, who used the term dialectic to describe the difficulties that human understanding encounters when it tries to extend beyond its proper limitations.

dialectical tension: The interplay between two opposed views when it is unclear which of the two is stronger and whether the two views can be subsumed under a third view which combines both.

difference principle: Rawls's second principle of justice (second in order of priority) which demands that any inequality in the distribution of social goods can be justified only if it contributes to the improvement of everyone in the society, especially the least well-off.

dignity: Dignity is closely related to self-respect, which is respect for oneself as a person. Kant defined respect as "value without price" and thought that this attitude is essential for recognizing the moral worth of persons.

dilemma: The problem that occurs when a theory or belief leads to one of two unacceptable consequences.

distributive justice: The fairest way of dividing the total amount of social goods among all the citizens.

dogmatism: A term used by Immanuel Kant to refer to philosophical views, and especially metaphysical theories, offering principles that are not rationally grounded.

duty: What one is morally required to do. *See* **obligation.**

egalitarian: Advocating equal political, economic, and legal rights for all citizens.

egoism: The ethical view that self-interest is the rule of conduct. There are two types of egoism: psychological egoism, the claim that as a matter of fact people do act only out of self-interest; and ethical egoism, the claim that people ought to act only out of self-interest.

emotivism: The doctrine claiming that moral judgments do not convey information about the world but rather express the emotions of the speaker and perhaps attempt to evoke similar emotions in the hearers. Emotivism is a form of **subjectivism in ethics.**

empirical: Refers to knowledge that is derived from the senses.

epicurean: Refers to followers of Epicurus (341–270 B.C.E.), who set forth a strategy for achieving truly human happiness by emphasizing the delights of the mind (over which a person has control) rather than the delights derived from material things (which are so often beyond one's personal control).

epistemology: The theory of knowledge; an inquiry into the origin, validity, and limits of knowledge.

essence: The defining characteristics of an object. Sartre thought that human beings have no predetermined essence but choose what they will be in total freedom and with total responsibility for those choices.

ethical absolutism: The view that there are absolutes in ethics, that is, moral standards that are independent of the personal preferences of individuals.

ethical problem: An ethical problem occurs when we are faced with a conflict between ethical principles, both of which are values that we accept (for example, telling the truth and avoiding injury to others). An ethical problem can also arise when we are faced with a decision and do not know which ethical principle to use in making a decision.

ethical relativism: The view that there are no objective moral standards, and that the principles for conduct are relative to individuals or societies. *See* **cultural relativism.**

ethics: The philosophical investigation of the principles governing human actions in terms of their goodness, badness, rightness, and wrongness.

ethnocentrism: The belief that the values and practices of one's own culture are superior to those of other cultures.

existence: The mere *thatness* of something as opposed to its essence or *whatness*. Some existential philosophers, notably Sartre, use the term "existence" to characterize human beings as having no predetermined essence but rather choosing what they will be and are therefore totally responsible for those choices. Sartre saw that people flee this responsibility by blaming their decisions and actions on others in acts of **bad faith.**

existentialism: A philosophical view that takes the central question of philosophy to be that of the meaning of human existence and emphasizes individual freedom, choice, and responsibility. Although it has roots in the thought of such nineteenth-century philosophers as Søren Kierkegaard and Friedrich Nietzsche, existentialism emerged as a distinctive philosophical movement in Europe after World War II and is associated with the work of such thinkers as Jean-Paul Sartre and Gabriel Marcel in France and Martin Heidegger in Germany.

fairness: In the philosophy of John Rawls, fairness in society results when the standards of distribution of society's benefits and burdens are such that free and impartial individuals would agree to those standards not knowing how they individually would be affected by them. Derived from Kant's moral philosophy which holds that a moral principle is one that the moral agent is willing to allow everyone else to act on as well.

fidelity: Keeping one's word and doing what one has agreed to do either as a result of making promises or by entering into contracts with others.

formal: In Kantian ethics, the moral acceptability of a principle lies in its formal structure as opposed to its content; that is, its acceptability as a principle of action depends specifically on whether the person acting on the principle could or would will it as universal law.

freedom: The absence of coercion and external constraints which allows one to act in a self-directed manner. The existential philosopher Jean-Paul Sartre argued that freedom is the defining characteristic of being human.

greatest equal liberty principle: Rawls's first principle of justice (first in order of priority); it requires that each person is to have an equal right to the most extensive total system of equal basic liberties compatible with everyone else having an equal right to the same total system.

hedonism: Derived from the Greek word for pleasure, hedonism is the ethical philosophy that holds the view that pleasure is the goal of life. Most philosophical hedonists have held, however, that intellectual pleasures are superior to sensual pleasures.

hedonistic calculus: Bentham's strategy for quantifying the pleasure and/or pain that a given action is likely to generate, using the categories of intensity, duration, certainty, propinquity, fecundity, purity, and extent.

hedonistic utilitarianism: Held by utilitarians who believe that only the quantity of pleasure is relevant to the calculations of the hedonistic calculus.

heteronomy: Term used by Kant to refer to principles of action that are directed toward the ends to be achieved, not on the motives and intentions of the moral agent.

honesty: The characteristic of being straightforward and trustworthy in dealings with others and not misrepresenting one's own feelings or withholding relevant parts of the truth.

hypothetical imperative: Kant's term for a command that is conditional; a command of if-then form would be a hypothetical imperative.

idealism: In philosophy, idealism refers to the view that all reality is mind-dependent and can be accounted for in terms of minds and ideas. For most idealists, such as Bradley, idealism produces a view of the interconnectedness of all things.

individualistic capitalism: A description originated by Harvard professor George C. Lodge and used by Lester Thurow to describe British and American forms of capitalism that stress individualistic values and accomplishments rather than the **communitarian capitalism** that stresses teamwork and social values.

justice: A social ideal concerned with distribution of society's benefits and burdens. In contemporary philosophical writings, such as those by John Rawls, justice is treated as a principle of fairness. Discussions of justice can relate to various spheres of action, hence one can speak of economic justice, distributive justice, criminal justice, even cosmic justice.

liberalism: In its classic statement, liberalism is the view that individuals should be free from governmental restraint, especially in matters that do not harm others—freedom of speech, conscience, association, religion. In more recent usage liberalism has come to be used for an attitude that favors government attempts to provide for the general welfare through legislation and governmental action. Used in this sense, liberalism differs from libertarianism primarily in the libertarian emphasis on the right of an individual to accumulate an unequal share of wealth through native talent and ability, which the liberal opposes as harmful to others.

libertarianism: Political view that each individual should be maximally free from governmental restraint, especially as regards the freedom of the individual to accumulate and dispose of an unequal share of social goods through superior intelligence or other talents and abilities.

loyalty: Closely associated with fidelity; the willingness to promote the interests of someone to whom one has an obligation, such as an employer.

maxim: According to Kant, the principle of action that is presupposed by a deliberate act.

maximin rule: This rule states that when confronted by competing alternative futures, one should choose the alternative that has the best worst outcome.

metaphysics: The philosophical inquiry into the nature of ultimate reality. The term can also refer to the analysis of fundamental principles used in philosophical analysis.

morality: In general usage, morality is synonymous with ethics.

naive relativism: The view that each individual determines what is right or wrong and that these moral standards cannot validly be judged by others.

natural law: The universally valid principles of conduct known by reason alone and therefore accessible to all people, as opposed to the positive law of a state or society. Originating in ancient Greek philosophy, natural law theories were used by philosophers of the Middle Ages as another proof of the existence of God, who was thought to be the author of the natural law.

necessary conditions: Necessary conditions for something are those factors without which that thing cannot exist, as breathing is a necessary condition for human life.

necessity: In contemporary usage, necessity characterizes propositions whose truth is known on purely logical (that is, a priori) grounds. "All bachelors are males" is necessarily true. Necessity also characterizes the relation of the conclusion to the premises in a valid deductive argument. If the statements in a valid deductive argument are true, the conclusion follows of necessity.

normative: That function of philosophy concerned with establishing standards for distinguishing the correct from the incorrect, whether in ways of reasoning, believing, esthetic judgment, or acting.

norms: Standards by which something is measured. In ethics, norms are standards for judging proper conduct.

objectivism: In ethics the view that there are objective principles that are true or false independent of people's feelings about them. Regarding ethical statements, objectivism holds that such statements have a truth value; that is, they can be true or false. The opposite of **subjectivism.**

obligation: A requirement for a person either to do or to refrain from performing an act. Obligations may be *incurred,* as when one causes harm to another and thereby incurs the obligation to remedy the fault; or obligations may be *assumed,* as when one promises to perform a certain act.

Finally, obligations may be *imposed* by someone in authority, as when the government places us under obligation to pay taxes.

paternalism: Disregarding individuals' autonomy by refusing to allow them to make decisions concerning their welfare on the grounds that someone else can better decide for them.

rationalism: The view that appeals to reason, not the senses, as the source of knowledge. In its most extreme form, rationalism insists that *all* knowledge is derived from reason.

relativism: *See* **ethical relativism.**

responsibility: Closely associated with duty and obligation. An individual has a responsibility to do those things which are one's moral duty and for those actions which one freely chooses. In existential philosophy, our total freedom implies total responsibility for our actions.

reversibility: A term used by some contemporary moral philosophers to characterize that aspect of Kant's moral philosophy which found that a principle is a moral one if the persons acting on that principle would also accept its being applied to them. Kant's example is that a person could not adopt the principle of refraining from helping those in need because that same person would want to be helped when in a situation of need. *See* **universalizability.**

rights: In social and political philosophy, rights are legitimate claims which one person has or can make on another, whether those claims are based on innate, universal human characteristics ("unalienable rights"), morality, or social legislation. Rights can be thought of as moral entitlements that invoke corresponding duties on the part of others.

rule utilitarianism: That form of utilitarianism in which general rules are derived from utilitarian principles and are used as guides for action.

second-order activity: A first-order intellectual activity (talking, thinking, describing) is one which is concerned with the things we experience in the ordinary world. A second-order intellectual activity is one which is concerned with a first-order activity: for example, thinking about thinking, talking about talking.

skepticism: The view that it is impossible to obtain certain types of knowledge.

social contract: A theory used to explain the origin and nature of the state; it holds that the obligation which people have to obey the laws and the reciprocal obligations and responsibilities of the state to its citizens is to be understood as though based on a mutually binding contract between citizens and government.

social good: Whatever the members of a given society value positively, including money, power, respect, education, health care, and so on.

socratic method: Philosophical method first used by Socrates in which one examines existing theories to determine their soundness or unsoundness; a method of questioning a person in order to bring about a further examination of the logical implications of the person's views.

soundness: The soundness of an argument requires both that the argument be valid and that all its premises be true.

state of nature: The phrase used by Thomas Hobbes to describe human life where there is no morality or pattern of law. Life in the state of nature, Hobbes thought, would be "solitary, poor, nasty, brutish, and short."

subjectivism: Any view which places primary emphasis on the knowing or acting subject in contrast to principles or standards that are objective, that is, independent of the knowing or acting subject.

subjectivism in ethics: The view that statements involving ethical terms (right, wrong, good, bad) are neither true nor false but rather express the preferences of the person uttering these terms. According to subjectivism, there are no moral standards independent of human feelings or preferences. **Emotivism** is a form of subjectivism.

sufficient conditions: Sufficient conditions for something are those factors which will, by themselves, bring about a certain result. Prolonged absence of food for an individual is a sufficient condition for death.

teleological: The term is derived from the Greek word *telos*, which means "end" or "purpose." Actions can be teleological when they aim at an end to be achieved. Ethical positions that determine the rightness or wrongness of acts on the basis of their consequences are teleological in their emphases, although the term **consequentialist ethics** is the more current term to describe such views.

universality: The property of being at all times and at all places recognized as the case. In logic a predicate is said to be universal if its extension is over all members of a class.

universalizability: In Kant's moral philosophy, universalizability characterizes a principle of action that all persons could follow. Kant recognized two senses in which a principle might not be universalizable: in the first, a principle cannot be universalized if doing so would make the contemplated action impossible. False advertising would fail this test, for if made a universal principle, advertising would cease to be effective. In the second sense, a principle fails the test of universalizability if the moral agent would will a different principle were the circumstances to change. For example, one would not be willing to be the recipient of false advertising; therefore, one cannot morally produce false advertising. This latter sense is sometimes referred to as **reversibility,** though Kant himself did not use this term.

utilitarianism: The ethical theory associated with the work of Jeremy Bentham, James Mill, and John Stuart Mill in the nineteenth century. Utilitarians hold that actions are moral if they aim at the general good, or the greatest good for the greatest number of people.

utility: The property in any object by which it tends to produce benefit, advantage, pleasure, good, or happiness to the party whose interest is considered.

utility principle: The principle of utilitarianism that says that we ought to do what will produce the greatest good for the greatest number of people. Sometimes it is referred to as "the greatest happiness principle."

validity: A feature of deductive arguments in which the relation between premises and conclusion is such that if the premises are true, the conclusion could not be false.

Index